Product innovation management

Third edition

Product innovation management

A workbook for management in industry

Third edition

Knut Holt

BUTTERWORTHS
London — Boston — Singapore — Sydney — Toronto — Wellington

First published 1977
Second edition 1983
Third edition 1988

© Butterworth & Co. (Publishers) Ltd 1988

British Library Cataloguing in Publication Data
Holt, Knut
    Product innovation management.—3rd ed.
    1. New Products. Management
    I. Title
    658.5'75

    ISBN 0-408-00536-X

Library of Congress Cataloging-in-Publication Data
Holt, Knut.
    Product innovation management: a workbook for management in
    industry/Knut Holt.—3rd ed.
    p.   cm.
    Bibliography: p.
    Includes index.
    ISBN 0-408-00536-X:
    1. New products—Management.   I. Title.
    HD69.N4H564 1988
    658.5'75—dc19

Typeset by TecSet Ltd, Wallington, Surrey
Printed and bound in England at the University Press, Cambridge

Preface to the Third Edition

In the third edition of the book chapters have been added on the financing of innovations in Part I, and three related financial tools in Part II. The provision of money for innovation is primarily the responsibility of the financial function. However, all who participate in innovative projects have a contribution to make, and they should therefore have an understanding of the problems related to the financing of innovations.

The references at the end of the book have been updated by adding 42 recent publications.

One of the reviewers of the second edition rightly pointed out that the index is not as extensive as it ought to be. This weakness has been corrected in the third edition.

The author is greatly indebted to Pål Dick-Henriksen who has reviewed the material on finance and contributed with valuable comments. Acknowledgement is also due to Karsten Jakobsen who has provided relevant literature for the tool references in groups 10, 11 and 12 in Part II.

Finally, the author thanks Ann Holt for typing, checking and revising the manuscript, and Stephen Bailey, Nicholas Pinfield and James Gaussen at Butterworths for their cooperation in connection with the planning and production of the book.

Trondheim 1987 Knut Holt

Preface to the previous edition

Product innovation is today a key factor in industrial success and is the concern of management in more and more enterprises. The importance of the topic is reflected in the growing number of publications. Successful innovation depends on a positive attitude towards change. It requires a future-oriented strategy, proper product planning, an efficient organisation, and appropriate tools.

This book is an expansion of a previous book *Product Innovation – a workbook for management in industry*. In addition to several revisions, a substantial amount of new material has been added, covering strategy, product planning and organisation of product innovation activities.

The purpose of the book is to present in a systematic way relevant concepts, models and methods. The book is basically a three stage rocket that can be adopted to specific needs of individual users. Those who are only interested in a broad overview can limit their attention to the first stage (Part I), which gives a concentrated presentation of the topic. Readers who want more information can move to the next stage (Part II) and study those tools that are of particular interest. Finally, if one wants to go further, an in-depth study can be undertaken by selecting one or several of the references listed at the end of each tool description.

The book is originally written for practitioners who are responsible for, or actively participate in, product innovation processes. This includes executives, who should provide the staff with the right tools and encourage their use, and functional heads and employees at the operational level concerned with conception, evaluation, development, manufacturing and marketing of new and improved products. These employees will mainly come from departments such as R & D, manufacturing, marketing, purchasing, finance and personnel. Those concerned should learn to use the various tools and apply them when appropriate. Of course, one individual cannot be expected to master all tools presented in the book. However, those taking part in the product innovation process should, as a group, be able to do so. Like a carpenter, they must have a tool kit, and at each stage in their work they should know which tools to use and how to apply them properly.

Experience shows that the diffusion of new ideas and approaches is a time-consuming process. This may also be the case with the material presented in this book. However, it is up to the management of each company to decide whether to be among the leaders or among the followers. By taking appropriate action in time, one may be among the early users, who normally get the benefits associated with being progressive and adopting new ideas early. This book should be of help in this context.

In addition to being useful as an introduction and handbook for industrial readers, the experience of the author at the University of Trondheim, Norwegian Institute of Technology, has shown that the book can be a useful textbook for engineering students. The author also has gained positive results with the book as a teaching aid at seminars for practitioners in Italy and postgraduate scholars in Austria.

By covering all aspects of product innovation activities both at the strategic and tactical level, the book may be used as a supplementary text for students taking courses in industrial administration, organisation theory, business policy, management of technological innovation, R & D management, marketing management, and similar topics.

In order to increase the value as a teaching aid, at the end of the book have been added three cases (see Appendix 1, 2 and 3) and a checklist for evaluation of new knowledge acquired (see Appendix 4).

The book is based on theoretical input from many sources as well as the practical experience of the author. The aim has been to satisfy the needs of both practitioners and students by combining for practical purposes what is best in the many theories of organisations or management schools. Particular emphasis has been given to theories related to change and renewal. Those who are interested in an overview of the various theories are referred to Appendix 5.

The author wants to express his gratitude to S. Andersen for valuable advice and constructive suggestions, to S. Gulás, J. Novickas, P. Planke, and R. Skaar for useful comments, and to Ann Holt for typing of the manuscript. Finally, he thanks the publisher for flexibility and pleasant co-operation in connection with the planning and production of the book.

Trondheim 1983   Knut Holt

Contents

Part I

SUMMARY   1

1 INTRODUCTION   3

  1.1 Purpose   3
  1.2 Models   3
  1.3 Limitations   7

2 TERMINOLOGY AND MODELS   13

  2.1 Innovation   13
  2.2 Creativity   16
  2.3 Diffusion   17

3 GENERATION OF IDEAS   21

  3.1 Models   21
  3.2 Methods   25

4 UTILISATION OF IDEAS   30

  4.1 Model   31
  4.2 Methods   33

5 PREPARATION FOR IMPLEMENTATION   40

  5.1 Model   40
  5.2 Methods   41

6 MANUFACTURING AND MARKETING   44

  6.1 Model   45
  6.2 Methods   46

7	STRATEGY	50
	7.1 Strategy formulation — models	52
	7.2 Strategy formulation — methods	58
	7.3 Diversification studies — models	59
	7.4 Diversification studies — methods	62

8	PRODUCT PLANNING	64
	8.1 Models	67
	8.2 Methods	77

9	ORGANISATION	79
	9.1 Models	79
	9.2 Methods	87

10	FINANCING OF INNOVATIONS	90
	10.1 Innovation projects	91
	10.2 Capital requirements	94
	10.3 Capital sources	98
	10.4 The financial proposal	105

Part II

1	INTELLIGENCE — NEED RELATED	125
	1.1 Need confrontation	125
	1.2 User observation	126
	1.3 User contacts	127
	1.4 Surveillance of competitors	129
	1.5 Surveillance of government regulations	130
	1.6 Surveillance of market sectors	131

2	INTELLIGENCE — TECHNOLOGY RELATED	133
	2.1 Surveillance of technology	133
	2.2 Development of technological competence	134
	2.3 Surveillance of resources	135
	2.4 Industrial espionage	136

3	FORECASTING	139
	3.1 Scenario technique	139
	3.2 Delphi technique	141
	3.3 Trend extrapolation technique	142
	3.4 Relevance-tree technique	144

3.5 System dynamics 146
3.6 Structural models 148
3.7 Cross-impact analysis 149

4 DEVELOPMENT OF CREATIVITY 152

4.1 Creativity tests 152
4.2 Climate measurements (organisational climate) 153
4.3 Morphological technique 155
4.4 Brainstorming 157
4.5 Forced relationship technique 158
4.6 Synectics 159
4.7 Eclectic approach for creative thinking 161
4.8 Work simplification 162
4.9 Suggestion system 162

5 PRELIMINARY STUDY 163

5.1 Feasibility study 163
5.2 Technology assessment 164
5.3 Patent search 166
5.4 Ecological analysis 167
5.5 Resource analysis 169
5.6 Legal analysis 170

6 PROJECT FORMULATION 172

6.1 Project selection technique 172
6.2 Develop/buy analysis 174
6.3 Acquisition of licences 175
6.4 Legal protection 176

7 PRELIMINARY ANALYSIS 179

7.1 Quality level planning 179
7.2 Scheduling — network models 180
7.3 Scheduling — gantt charts 182

8 MARKET RESEARCH 183

8.1 Use of internal market statistics 183
8.2 Use of external market statistics 184
8.3 Current market studies 186
8.4 Special market studies 187

9 COST ESTIMATES 189

9.1 Risk analysis 189

9.2	Project cost	191
9.3	Product cost	191
9.4	Investment cost and profitability	191

10	**DESIGN**	**193**
10.1	Applied research	193
10.2	Styling (shape and colour)	194
10.3	Catalogue aided design	196
10.4	Alternative design approaches	197
10.5	Computer aided design	198
10.6	Design and testing of models	199
10.7	Standardisation	201
10.8	Design for demanufacturing (recycling)	202

11	**DESIGN EVALUATION**	**204**
11.1	Value analysis	204
11.2	Reliability analysis	205
11.3	Ergonomic analysis	206
11.4	Useful life analysis	208
11.5	Maintenance analysis	209
11.6	Fault analysis by brainstorming	210
11.7	Fault analysis by logical methods	211
11.8	Design review	212

12	**DESIGN CALCULATION**	**214**
12.1	Stress calculation	214
12.2	Mechanical vibration calculation	214
12.3	Flow calculation	214
12.4	Thermal calculation	215
12.5	Cybernetic calculation	215

13	**QUALITY VERIFICATION**	**216**
13.1	Laboratory testing	216
13.2	User testing	217

14	**MANUFACTURING PREPARATION**	**219**
14.1	Make/buy analysis	219

14.2 Equipment and tooling 219
14.3 Process and operation planning 219
14.4 Material planning 220
14.5 Quality control planning 220
14.6 Design for manufacturing 220

15 MARKETING PREPARATION 222

15.1 Distribution 222
15.2 Sale of licences 224
15.3 Advertising 225
15.4 Sales promotion 225
15.5 Sales planning 225
15.6 Trade marks 226

16 TEST MARKETING 227

16.1 Use of test area 227
16.2 Use of trade fairs 228

17 INTRODUCTION 231

17.1 Selection of strategy for introduction 231
17.2 Recording of actual sales 232

18 REGISTRATION OF MANUFACTURING AND MARKETING DATA 233

18.1 Registration of quality parameters 233
18.2 Quantity 234
18.3 Sales 234
18.4 Costs 234

19 METHODS FOR EVALUATION OF PRODUCTS AND PROCESSES 235

19.1 Field reports 235
19.2 Project evaluation 236

20 ELIMINATION ANALYSIS 238

20.1 Product – market matrix 238
20.2 Life cycle analysis 239
20.3 Sales trends 240
20.4 Profit data 242

21 STRATEGY FORMULATION 244

21.1 Gap analysis 244
21.2 Capability analysis 245
21.3 Competitive strengths – market attractiveness matrix 247
21.4 Market share – market growth matrix 250
21.5 Product/market – strategic option matrix 252
21.6 Performance criteria 254

22 DIVERSIFICATION STUDIES 256

22.1 Need–technology–customer matrix 256
22.2 Diversification area – capability matrix 258
22.3 Screening procedures 259

23 PRODUCT PLANNING TOOLS 262

23.1 Product proposal form 262
23.2 Product council 263
23.3 Development order (specifications) 265
23.4 Product calendar 267

24 PRODUCT INNOVATION ORGANISATION 269

24.1 Preparation checklist 269
24.2 Factor checklist 271
24.3 Problem definition checklist 273
24.4 Integration checklist 275
24.5 Structure checklist 277
24.6 Idea generation checklist 279
24.7 Idea realisation checklist 281

25 FINANCIAL TOOLS 284

25.1 The balance sheet 284
25.2 The income statement 285
25.3 Financial ratios 287

APPENDICES 289

1 Scansteel – case study 289
2 Mentronics – case study 306
3 Norsk data – case study 317
4 Acquisition of knowledge – checklist 329
5 Organisation theories/management schools 330

REFERENCES 335
INDEX 343

Part I Summary

In a rapidly changing environment the survival of a company depends to a large extent on its capacity to develop and market new or radically improved products. The purpose of the book is by means of relevant models to present necessary tools for product innovators and demonstrate how and where to apply them.

The term 'product innovators' refers to those who are responsible for or actively participate in the product innovation process. This will be executives, who should provide the staff with the right tools, and functional heads and employees at the operating level concerned with creation, development, manufacturing and marketing of new and improved products.

The product innovation process can be divided into four stages:

Generation of ideas.
Use of ideas.
Preparation.
Implementation.

Creativity, or that thinking which results in novel and worthwhile ideas, is required at all stages. However, it is most important at the first stage, the generation of the basic idea, as this determines the course of the following stages.

Generation of an idea represents a coupling of a perceived need and a technological opportunity that satisfies the need. The appropriate tool groups at this stage are need-related intelligence, technology-related intelligence, forecasting techniques, methods for development of creativity, preliminary studies and project formulation.

Use of ideas is brought about by acquisition of the appropriate technology or by developing it inside the company. The tool groups for this stage are preliminary project analysis, market research, cost estimates, design, design evaluation and design calculation.

Preparation is concerned with planning the manufacturing and marketing operations of the new or improved product. The tool groups at this stage are quality verification, manufacturing preparation, market preparation and test marketing.

1

Implementation starts with market introduction and continues with regular manufacturing and marketing until the product sooner or later reaches the end of its life and is eliminated. The appropriate tool groups are introduction, registration of manufacturing and marketing data, methods for evaluation of products and processes and elimination analysis.

Product innovation activities should be guided by corporate strategy. This can be done in several ways. One extreme is a bottom-up approach where new product ideas are generated in various departments, evaluated and integrated in an over-all corporate plan. The other extreme is a top-down approach based on a realistic business concept, concrete objectives and a systematic diversification procedure.

Product planning is concerned with improvement of existing products, introduction of new products and withdrawal of unprofitable products. Depending on type of market, size of the firm, attitude of management towards planning, etc., one may use formal or informal approaches. In a competitive environment a market-oriented approach is most often required, but the needs of all concerned should be taken into account.

The organisation of innovative activities should ideally be treated as an entity together with current activities. In practice one may benefit by using a modular approach comprising integration devices, basic organisational structure, idea generation activities, and idea realisation activities. Whereas current activities may be performed within a relatively formalised, mechanistic structure, innovative activities require a more informal, organic structure.

The financing of innovative projects involves the determination of capital requirements and the selection of financial sources. The evaluation of a project requires seed capital, the R&D effort requires development capital, the exploitation of the technology requires first stage capital, and later growth requires expansion capital or second stage financing. Necessary money can be provided from within through retained earnings, and from outside sources such as commercial banks, insurance companies, venture capital companies, and public funds. To obtain capital from outside, a well written financial proposal (covering relevant information about the company) and a realistic description of the project (including information about marketing, technical, financial and risk factors) are needed.

1. Introduction

In a dynamic environment with technological advances occurring at an accelerating pace, rapidly changing need patterns, increasing international competition and decreasing life cycle of products, the ability of an industrial firm to survive depends on its innovative power, on its capacity to anticipate new user needs, recognise technological opportunities, and develop, launch and market new or radically improved products.

1.1 PURPOSE

The result of the innovative activities of a company depends on a number of factors such as corporate strategy and organisation, and the application of appropriate tools by the various functions and persons involved in the innovation process. The purpose of this book is to focus attention on concepts, models and tools that are available for product innovators, i.e. those responsible for or actively participating in the innovation process.

1.2 MODELS

Considerable time has been spent in developing a model that would give an overview of the product innovation process comprising all stages from idea conception to market introduction and regular production. This has been a difficult task. It is not easy to make a static, simplified picture of a process which in real life is highly dynamic and of an iterative nature with many feed-back loops. Having considered a number of relatively complicated models, what has finally been decided upon is a system of models based on the black box principle. These models can be referred to various levels with increasing degrees of complexity.

1.2.1 First level

Here a simple one-dimensional model is used, as shown in *Figure 1.1*.

3

The model illustrates that needs are satisfied by the conversion of resources into products.

The products may be new only for the company — this approach is based on imported technology, on the adoption of products developed by other firms. The products may also be new for the market — this requires a pioneering effort of an advanced nature, often resulting in a new or radically improved technology.

Figure 1.1 Product innovation as a one-dimensional model

The resources are of a *human* nature, such as a certain number of employees with various educational and practical backgrounds, of a *physical* nature, such as plant, equipment and materials, and of a *financial* nature, such as money supplied through loans or from own funds. In addition to these internal resources one may use services from external sources, such as consultants, research laboratories, etc. The major input of information is data regarding user needs and technological opportunities. Output of information is data regarding design and application of the products.

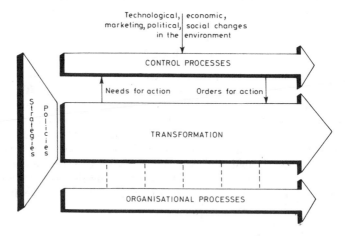

Figure 1.2 Product innovation as a three-dimensional process

1.2.2   Second level

The one-dimensional model can be expanded into a three-dimensional model, as shown in *Figure 1.2*.

Strategies and policies are guidelines for the product innovation activity. They are based on an analysis of strengths and weaknesses of the company and a study of threats and opportunities in the environment. The result may be one of the strategies indicated in *Figure 1.3*.

Improvement of current operations by changing management or increasing the efficiency in one or more of the functional areas.

Divestment by elimination of unprofitable products or departments.

Scale increase by expanding existing facilities or by acquisition or mergers with other firms.

Innovation by developing new or radically improved products.

Diversification by taking up new products that are unrelated or related horizontally or vertically to existing products.

Market segmentation by concentrating the resources upon selected segments (niches) of the market.

Combination of two or more of the strategies listed above.

Figure 1.3 Alternative strategies

If a diversification strategy is chosen the following steps are required:

Diversification studies, i.e. search and selection of diversification areas.
Product selection, i.e., search and selection of products within the area selected for diversification.
Product development, i.e. the processing of individual projects.

Transformation processes are the core of individual innovation projects. By utilisation of available resources, information about needs and technological opportunities are transformed into marketable products. *Control processes* consist of activities which guide the transformations. Inputs are information about changes in the environment and progress reports from the various stages of the transformation processes about results obtained. Based on this and information about company strategies and policies, decisions are made and information produced in terms of orders and instructions for action to those who actively participate in the transformations. The need for control usually increases as one moves from the front end of the transformation process, where ideas are generated, to the back end where manufacturing and marketing take place.

Organisational processes are concerned with integration of the activities of all who take part in the transformation and control processes. One of the most important problems is to decide to what extent innovative functions should be separated from routine functions. Other decisions concerned with the development and modification of the basic organisation structure include the degree of formalisation and centralisation, the use of permanent committees and temporary project groups, and the development of procedures for processing and control of individual projects.

In order to give a clear and systematic presentation, the book first introduces the tools that are available for transformation and control processes at the operating level, i.e. in connection with the handling of individual projects. Then follow the most important models and tools for formulation of strategy, product planning and organisation of product innovation activities.

1.2.3   Third level

A simple model illustrating the basic stages of the transformation and control processes is shown in *Figure 1.4.* The iterative character of a trial and error process with many feedback loops is indicated with dotted lines.

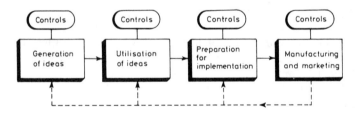

Figure 1.4 A four-stage model of the product innovation process

Generation of ideas is the first stage of the innovation process. It is in itself a process consisting of the fusion of a perceived need with a technological opportunity. This stage ends with an idea that is evaluated and accepted for further processing.

Utilisation of ideas is basically a problem-solving process aiming at an optimal technical solution for the problem specified or implied by the accepted idea. The solution may be brought in from outside or developed within the company. Output of this stage is a prototype or a product specification depicted by drawings showing shape and major dimensions of the product.

Preparation for implementation is concerned with the practical application of the results from the preceding stages. It involves a number of tasks in connection with finalising the design of the product, planning of plant, equipment and manufacturing operations, as well as planning of the introduction and marketing operations.

Manufacturing and marketing is the last stage of the innovation process. It is concerned with the implementation of the manufacturing and marketing plans and involves the break-in and debugging of the manufacturing operations, the introduction at the market place and regular manufacturing and marketing.

Control of the innovation process involving time, cost and results, is done both during and at the end of each transformation stage.

1.2.4 Fourth level

A detailed breakdown showing the major transformation and control operations of each of the four stages of the innovation process is given in *Figure 1.5 (a)* and *(b)*.

Information is the nerve system which links all operations in the model together. At each stage information is obtained from the preceding stage. Information is forwarded to and received from the control operations, and information is provided as input to the next transformation operation. For the sake of simplicity the information flow is not indicated in *Figure 1.5*.

Tools of various kinds are available for the provision of information. The most important ones are listed in *Figure 1.5*. Some of them are well known and used by most companies. These tools are indicated with (x) in the figure. Other tools are relatively new and have not been applied by all who can benefit from them. Many can be used throughout the whole innovation process; others are limited to a specific stage. Most of this book will be devoted to a presentation of these tools and their applicability.

1.3 LIMITATIONS

The development of models that are applicable to all firms is a complex and difficult task. There are great differences between various companies with regard to the degree of change and novelty in their product innovations. Companies also differ in size, technology, organisation, type of manufacturing, etc. These and other factors will have an influence on the way the product innovation process is organised and implemented

8

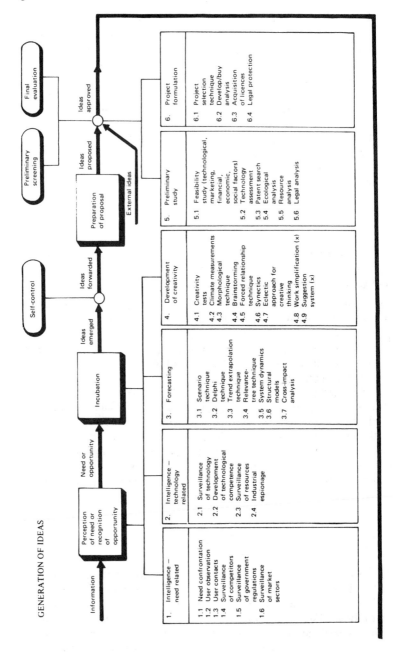

GENERATION OF IDEAS

| Information → | Perception of need or recognition of opportunity | Need or opportunity → | Incubation | Ideas emerged → | Self-control | Ideas forwarded → | Preparation of proposal | Ideas proposed → | Preliminary screening | Ideas approved → | Final evaluation |

External ideas

1. Intelligence – need related	2. Intelligence – technology related	3. Forecasting	4. Development of creativity	5. Preliminary study	6. Project formulation
1.1 Need confrontation	2.1 Surveillance of technology	3.1 Scenario technique	4.1 Creativity tests	5.1 Feasibility study (technological, marketing, financial, economic, social factors)	6.1 Project selection technique
1.2 User observation	2.2 Development of technological competence	3.2 Delphi technique	4.2 Climate measurements		6.2 Develop/buy analysis
1.3 User contacts	2.3 Surveillance of resources	3.3 Trend extrapolation technique	4.3 Morphological technique	5.2 Technology assessment	6.3 Acquisition of licences
1.4 Surveillance of competitors	2.4 Industrial espionage	3.4 Relevance-tree technique	4.4 Brainstorming	5.3 Patent search	6.4 Legal protection
1.5 Surveillance of government regulations		3.5 System dynamics	4.5 Forced relationship technique	5.4 Ecological analysis	
1.6 Surveillance of market sectors		3.6 Structural models	4.6 Synectics	5.5 Resource analysis	
		3.7 Cross-impact analysis	4.7 Eclectic approach for creative thinking	5.6 Legal analysis	
			4.8 Work simplification (x)		
			4.9 Suggestion system (x)		

9

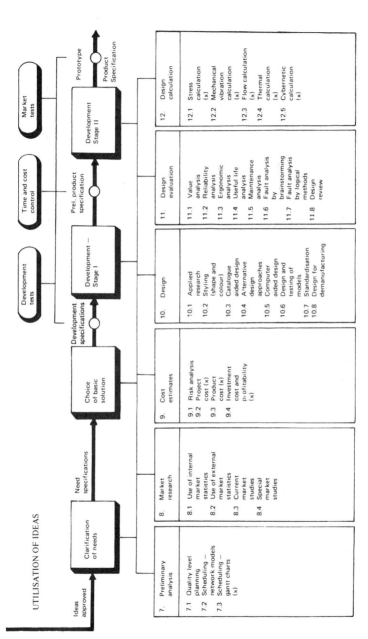

Figure 1.5 (a) Model of the first and second stage of the product innovation process

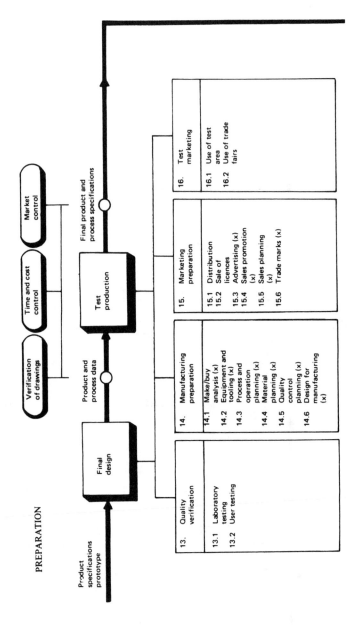

PREPARATION

Product specifications prototype

Verification of drawings | Time and cost control | Market control

Final design

Product and process data

Test production

Final product and process specifications

13. Quality verification

13.1 Laboratory testing
13.2 User testing

14. Manufacturing preparation

14.1 Make/buy analysis (x)
14.2 Equipment and tooling (x)
14.3 Process and operation planning (x)
14.4 Material planning (x)
14.5 Quality control planning (x)
14.6 Design for manufacturing (x)

15. Marketing preparation

15.1 Distribution
15.2 Sale of licences
15.3 Advertising (x)
15.4 Sales promotion (x)
15.5 Sales planning (x)
15.6 Trade marks (x)

16. Test marketing

16.1 Use of test area
16.2 Use of trade fairs

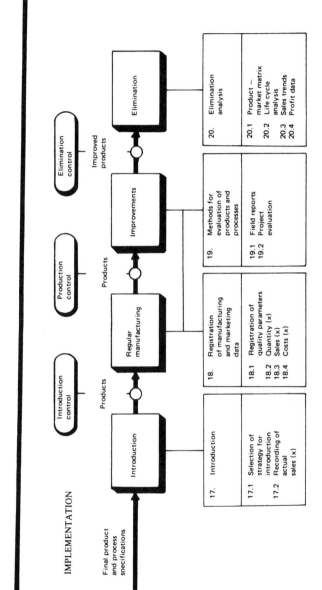

Figure 1.5 (b) Model of the third and fourth stage of the product innovation process

in actual practice. However, an attempt has been made to present in *Figure 1.5* a model so general that it could be applied to any organisation, be it a small job lot firm or a large mass producing company. Each will have to select those items in the model that are relevant to their particular situation.

2. Terminology and Models

During recent years the words *innovation* and *creativity* have gained great publicity. Like many other popular words they are misused and often have different meanings for different people. In addition to these key concepts there is also, as indicated in *Figure 2.1*, a third word, *diffusion*, which should be mentioned in the same context.

| (1) Innovation |
| (2) Creativity |
| (3) Diffusion |

Figure 2.1 Key concept relevant to the innovation process

In order to reduce the semantic aspects of the problem as much as possible it is necessary to clarify what is meant by these terms.

2.1 INNOVATION

'Innovation' can be defined and classified in different ways; it can also be studied as a process both from a societal and company point of view.

2.1.1 Definition

There are numerous definitions of innovation. Tinnesand[1] has made a study of one hundred and eight of them which resulted in six different groups: (1) new idea, (2) introduction of a new idea, (3) invention, (4) introduction of an invention, (5) an idea different from existing forms, (6) introduction of an idea disrupting prevailing behaviour.

Here the word innovation will be used in a broad sense, defined as follows:

'Innovation is a process which covers the use of knowledge or relevant information for creation and introduction of something that is new and useful.'

Depending on the object, various types of innovation can be distinguished. *Technological innovations* are concerned with the use of knowledge for creation and implementation of new technologies. A technological innovation can be either a *product innovation*, which is the topic of this book, or a *process innovation*.

Administrative innovations deal with application of new administrative methods and systems, *social* or *organisational innovations* with new patterns of human interaction, *financial innovations* with new ways of securing and using capital, and *marketing innovations* with new approaches to the marketing of products and services.

2.1.2 The innovation process

Innovation is a complex process, requiring the use of knowledge in order to create and apply something that is new.

From a societal point of view the innovation process can be described as suggested by Globe et al.[2]. A graphical presentation is given in *Figure 2.2*. The various stages seldom take place at the same location, and different persons and organisations usually take part.

Preconception period	Innovative period		Postinnovative period
Discovery Technological advances	Invention	Application (first realisation)	Diffusion New applications Improvements

Figure 2.2 Model of the innovation process in a societal context

In the preconception period the scientific and technological foundation for the innovation is laid; it is not possible to indicate the start of this period. The postinnovative period ends with the extinction of the innovation.

The innovation process takes a long time, but there are great differences both between industries and within the same industry. Based on a number of empirical studies, Gregory[3] states that in order to make a major innovation, more than 20 years is required if basic research is involved, more than 10 years if applied research is involved, and on average five years if development can be based on available technological knowledge.

A study by Globe et al.[2] of ten major innovations (the heart pace-maker, hybrid grains, electrophotography, oral contraception, video tape recorder, etc.) showed that the period from conception to the first realisation varied from 6 to 32 years, with an average of 19 years.

From a company point of view the innovation process can be illustrated with various models as shown in Chapter 1. The various stages of this process with relevant tools will be dealt with in subsequent chapters.

2.1.3 Classification of innovations

Innovations are concerned with change. Depending on the degree of change and novelty, seen from the point of view of the individual company, a project can be classified as shown in *Figure 2.3*.

```
Original product innovations
(1)   Basic (technical break-throughs)
(2)   Incremental (improvement innovations)

Adopted product innovations
(1)   Adapted adoptions (improvements)
(2)   Pure adoptions (copying)

Product improvements
(1)   Major improvements
(2)   Minor improvements
```

Figure 2.3 Classes of product innovations

```
(1)   Products new for the market

(2)   Products new for the company

(3)   Improved company products
```

Figure 2.4 Simplified classification of product innovations

There is, however, no sharp distinction between the various classes. If, for example, a company makes a radical improvement of a product which has been developed and introduced by another company, it may be difficult to decide whether the result should be classified as an original or adopted innovation.

Another way of classifying product innovations is shown in *Figure 2.4*. Here, also, the various classes are ranked according to the degree of novelty and change involved.

An innovation is a sort of game involving risk. The amount of risk will depend on how radical and unfamiliar the changes are for the company concerned. The risk is particularly great when working with basic innovations, which also require great resources for creation and implementation.

2.1.4 Promotion of innovation

Very few companies are able to spend a major part of their resources on basic innovations. Most have to work at a lower level. However, there are great opportunities for promotion of innovation by improving own products or products made by others. Known elements can be combined in many different ways. Substantial improvements often can be made by developing innovative elements in one or more of the functional characteristics of old as well as new products. For many companies the best solution may therefore be to focus upon a broad improvement effort of an innovative character. If a company succeeds in this, the innovative level will increase and perhaps make it possible occasionally to make a major advance of a more fundamental character.

2.2 CREATIVITY

Perhaps the most important aspect of the innovation process is creativity. However, it is also the most difficult to handle; the field is new and immature as a scientific discipline.

2.2.1 Definition

Although millions of words have been written about creativity, a commonly recognised, all-purpose definition is lacking. For practical purposes the following one, presented by Taylor[4], appears to be most appropriate:

'Creativity is that thinking which results in the production of ideas that are both novel and worthwhile.'

This definition does not require that the idea is developed into a successful product. In order to be recognised as a creative contribution, it is enough that the idea is accepted as worthy of further investigation by the person or group who does the first evaluation.

One weakness of the definition is that it depends entirely on a subjective assessment of what is worthwhile. On the other hand, it is dynamic and action oriented. It is not enough that an idea demonstrates imagination. Industry needs practical ideas — creative thinking must be converted into innovative action.

2.2.2 Innovation and creativity

Creativity and good ideas are needed at all stages of the innovation process. Morton[5] has emphasised it in this way: 'Innovation is not just a new understanding or the discovery of a new phenomenon, not just a flash of creative invention, not just the development of a new product or manufacturing process; nor is it simply the creation of new capital and consumer markets. Rather innovation involves related creative activity in all these areas. It is a connected process in which many and sufficient creative acts, from research through service, are coupled together in an integrated way for a common goal.'

The impact of creative behaviour is strongest at the first stage, generation of ideas. This is a crucial point, as it gives the direction of the whole process. It will determine the type of product, the nature of the manufacturing processes, the kind of suppliers and customers, and the organisation needed for utilisation of the idea and application of the result.

2.2.3 The need for creativity

Creative behaviour is needed in all departments and at all levels. The higher up in the hierarchy, the more important it is. Far-reaching strategic decisions are taken at the highest level.

Although creative behaviour is of particular importance for radical innovations, it is also required in connection with improvements of existing products, processes and systems. In many companies this is perhaps the area where the great majority of employees have an opportunity to utilise their creative potential.

2.3 DIFFUSION

The last part of the innovation process — diffusion into the market — takes place in the postinnovative period.

Diffusion is a time consuming process, even in those cases where the economic benefits are obvious. The time from the first user application of an innovation to adoption by all those who can benefit is long. It may often be 15–20 years or more. Thus for a long period of time there will be a gap between what is known and what is put effectively into use. This phenomenon also applies for the techniques presented in this book. Hopefully information about their application will help to reduce the time that is needed to bridge the gap.

2.3.1 Definition

The concept of diffusion can be defined in the following way:

'Diffusion is the process of communication and use by which an innovation is spread from the source to potential users.'

From a societal point of view the diffusion process is perhaps more important than the innovation itself. Now the social and economic impacts are fully realised by all who adopt the innovation. In addition to this comes an important stimulus to new innovations.

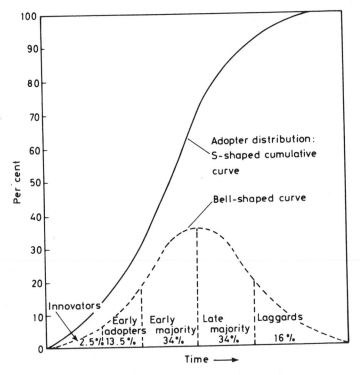

Figure 2.5 Theoretical diffusion curve and user distribution

2.3.2   The diffusion process

The way an innovation is spread follows a typical pattern as shown in *Figure 2.5*. The more the curve is S-shaped the closer it comes to the theoretical curve, the so-called *logistical growth curve*. This is the curve one obtains when somebody with an idea communicates it with constant frequency to everybody within the population who does not know of it.

The *rate of diffusion* is the relative speed with which an innovation is spread to members of a population. It is measured by the length of time that has passed before a certain percentage of the population (e.g. 75%) has started to use the innovation.

2.3.3   Adoption

Closely related to diffusion is the concept of adoption, which is concerned with the use of new advances in individual companies. It can be defined in the following manner:

'Adoption is the decision to acquire and to utilise an innovation as the best course of action available.'

Few firms are in such a position that they can be first and break new ground, and no company can be number one in all areas all the time. Most have to follow after the pioneers and use what is available.

So far, most attention has been devoted to the stimulation of innovation in companies through own effort in creation, development, manufacturing and marketing of new or improved products. However, there are often great possibilities in the efficient use of innovations made by others. In many cases it may be cheaper to buy an invention than to make it. Many companies have their strength in this approach. Instead of focusing on the front end of the innovation process — research and development — they concentrate effort on the back end — manufacturing and marketing. They have organised the work in such a way that they are able quickly to adopt and use new advances, often by at the same time improving them or adapting them to the special needs of their customers.

Companies vary considerably in their behaviour with regard to adopting innovations. As shown in *Figure 2.5*, one can distinguish between the innovators (pioneers), the early adopters, the early majority, the late majority and the laggards.

Although it is important to be alert and use new developments, adoption should not be a goal in itself. There is a danger of going too far or moving too quickly. There are both companies and persons who have a tendency to *overadopt*, i.e. to use new advances which cannot be justified from an analysis based on rational criteria.

According to Rogers and Shoemaker[6], the decision to adopt is a process that can be divided into four steps, as shown in *Figure 2.6*. It depends both on the type of information received and the attitude which this information creates.

---

(1) *Knowledge* — the individual is exposed to the innovation's existence and gains some understanding of how it functions.

(2) *Persuasion* — the individual forms a favourable or unfavourable attitude towards the innovation.

(3) *Decision* — the individual engages in activities which lead to a choice to adopt or reject the innovation.

(4) *Confirmation* — the individual seeks reinforcement for the innovation decision he has made, but he may reverse his previous decision if exposed to conflicting reactions about the innovation.

Figure 2.6 The adoption decision process

The benefits of new advances go to the early adopters. The late majority and the laggards usually do not have much to gain, but may be forced to adopt in order to survive. It is therefore important to get the right type of information about new advances early in the diffusion process.

REFERENCES

1. Tinnesand, B., *Toward a General Theory of Innovation*, PhD Thesis, University of Wisconsin, Madison, 258 (1973)
2. Globe, S., *et al.*, 'Innovation — the Creation and Implementation of New Technology', *Tappi*, 54–59, Feb. (1974)
3. Gregory, S.A. (ed.), *Creativity and Innovation in Engineering*, 313, London (1972)
4. Taylor, D.W., 'Thinking and Creativity', *Annals of the New York Academy of Sciences*, 91, 108–127 (1960)
5. Morton, J.A., *Organizing for Innovation*, 171, New York (1976)
6. Rogers, M., and Shoemaker, F.F., *Communication of Innovations*, 476, New York (1971)

3. Generation of Ideas

The starting point of an innovation is the generation of an idea that is new and appears to be worth while for further use. This is a creative act of fundamental importance for the final result of the innovation effort.

3.1 MODELS

The generation of an idea is in itself a complex psychological process. The theoretical foundations of this process are weak; there is no generally accepted theory or model available.

To increase understanding of the complexity of the problem, a perception model based on research in psychotronics is first presented, followed by two simplified models that are more suitable for practical purposes.

3.1.1 The perception model

This model, developed by Guláš[1], involves both sensory and extra-sensory perception, as shown in *Figure 3.1*. A problem is recognised through consciously received information (1) and forwarded into the subconscious (2) and the superego (3). The subconscious mind is important. The nucleus of creativity, intuitive thinking, takes place here. Intuition is the ability to conceive the whole without knowing all of its parts. This is typical for the creative individual who is able to substitute lacking conscious information by subconscious information or by unconsciously received information (4) through extrasensory perception. The superego, which also receives external information unconsciously (5), has a controlling function on the thinking processes; it acts as a moral or preventive filter derived from acknowledged authorities, accepted norms, etc. The 'filtered' intuitive idea for solution (7) appears in the conscious mind (illumination) where it is verified by logical thinking involving interaction between the problem and the idea (8) and (9). Output of the process (10) is the verified intuitive idea.

21

The practical lesson to be drawn from the model is that the creative process cannot be managed as a physical phenomenon. With existing knowledge it is not possible to determine the time required for the conscious and unconscious thinking processes. The output of creative

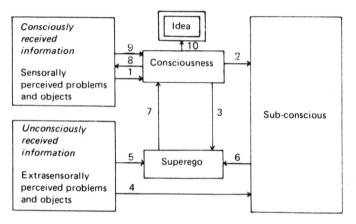

Figure 3.1 Model for idea generation involving sensory and extrasensory perception

thinking therefore cannot be scheduled in advance. Psychotronic research may in the future unfold new laws that will make predictions possible and allow for a better control of creative processes.

3.1.2 The fusion model

A model of the idea generation process, where information is a key concept, is shown in *Figure 3.2*. This model is based on the assumption that an innovative idea emerges as a fusion of a perceived need with the recognition of a technical opportunity or 'solution concept'.

Definition of the problem will depend on the perceived need, which again depends on the kind of information which the problem solver is exposed to. The need may have existed for a long time, it may be rather new or it may be only latent. The need may be unfulfilled or it may be inadequately or inefficiently fulfilled.

Solution of the problem will emerge as a technological opportunity, the character of which is dependent on the kind of information received. It may be stored information in terms of knowledge received earlier through studies, practical experience, etc., or direct information acquired

in connection with a specific problem through printed material or by
talking to people.
    The capability of the company will influence the generation of the
idea. Thus a company with a strong marketing capability may choose
a more radical solution than a company weak in this area.

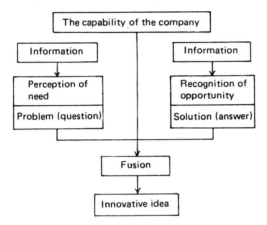

Figure 3.2 Model of idea generation as a fusion of
needs and opportunities

    Initiation of the idea may be done by perceiving a need or by
recognising a solution, as indicated in *Figure 3.2*. Regarding the
relative importance of these approaches the Italian inventor Marconi
once said: 'Necessity is the cause of most innovations, but the best
come out of desire'[2]. His statement can be related to two of the many
theories that have been developed to explain creative behaviour.
According to the 'need theory' creative behaviour is motivated by
information from outside about a need which is not covered satisfactorily. An opposite explanation is given by the 'achievement theory',
which assumes that creative behaviour is born out of a desire to
accomplish something[3, 4].
    A quantitative indication of the relative importance of the 'need
pull' and the 'technology push' is given in empirical studies by Globe
et al.[5], Langrish *et al.*[6], Myers and Marquis[7] and TNO[8]. It appears
that most basic innovations, which represent major technological
breakthroughs, are initiated by the discovery of an opportunity. On the
other hand, most incremental or improvement innovations, which
represent most innovations in industrial companies, start by receiving
information that leads to the perception of a need, which then triggers
off a technological solution.

3.1.3   The flow model

In *Figure 3.3* a simple model of idea generation designed around a horizontal flow line is shown. The information input to the process may in some cases be a technical opportunity. However, most often the process starts with the perception of an existing or latent user

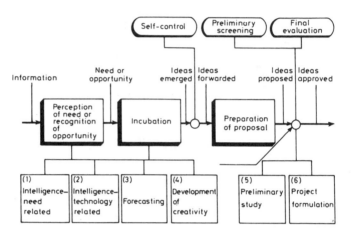

Figure 3.3 Model of idea generation with related groups of tools

need. This information may be received or collected more or less systematically. At this stage some kind of problem clarification takes place. This triggers off several subconscious processes which take place during the next step, the incubation period. The problem is here dropped for some time from the conscious level. Sooner or later a solution is found, resulting in the creation of an idea that emerges from the subconscious to the conscious level. This idea represents a synthesis of the need and the solution. In some cases a number of solutions may be found. The application of various techniques for creative thinking will stimulate the creation of many solutions.

Among the ideas that emerge, some are forwarded to the appropriate body for further consideration. A certain self-control regulates the flow. The number forwarded will therefore be smaller than the number that have emerged. An idea may be presented to the person or group concerned quite informally or through a written proposal. The next step is a preliminary screening where ideas which are not consistent with the objectives and policies of the company are dropped. The remaining ideas are investigated through a preliminary study in order to get a better base for final evaluation. The outcome of this evaluation determines whether the idea will be dropped, postponed or further utilised.

The information output of the idea generation stage is a more or less complete description of the ideas approved for further use.

3.2   METHODS

A number of tools are available for those who are participating in the idea generation process. These tools can broadly be classified in six groups, as shown in *Figure 3.3.*

3.2.1   Intelligence – need related

Several tools developed for this purpose are listed in *Figure 3.4* and described in Part II.

1.1 Need confrontation	1.4 Surveillance of competitors
1.2 User observation	
	1.5 Surveillance of government regulations
1.3 User contacts (panels, employment, cooperation, sales force, dealers, customers)	
	1.6 Surveillance of market sectors

Figure 3.4 Tools for need-related intelligence

Uncovering latent and future needs is a challenging, difficult task. Most firms are experiencing a highly dynamic situation. A number of factors such as growing urbanisation, increasing purchasing power and a much higher educational level are causing rapid changes in need patterns and user preferences. As many of the new needs will emerge to the conscious level only when new products are presented, it is difficult to assess them before the products are developed. Under such conditions it appears that need assessment requires a good understanding of the user environment, his preferences and anticipated changes in them. The importance of this aspect of the innovation process is clearly demonstrated by the British *Sappho* project, which included a study of innovations in the chemical industry and the scientific instrument industry. The result clearly showed that the most important measure discriminating between failure and success was the degree to which one tried to satisfy the needs or requirements of potential users[9].

3.2.2 Intelligence – technology related

The importance of information about needs can hardly be overestimated. However, an innovative idea also requires recognition of technological opportunities. A number of methods for this purpose are shown in *Figure 3.5* and described in Part II.

2.1 Surveillance of technology	2.3 Surveillance of resources
2.2 Development of technological competence	2.4 Industrial espionage

Figure 3.5 Tools for technology-related intelligence

3.2.3 Forecasting

The creation of new products is based on certain assumptions about future development. Various techniques, listed in *Figure 3.6* and described in Part II, are available for the forecasting of economic,

3.1 Scenario technique	3.4 Relevance-tree technique
3.2 Delphi technique	3.5 System dynamics
3.3 Trend extrapolation technique	3.6 Structural models
	3.7 Cross-impact analysis

Figure 3.6 Tools for forecasting

technological, social and political changes in the environment. These tools are of particular relevance for strategic planning, but may also help to uncover needs and possibilities that will lead directly to the creation of ideas for new products.

Most of these tools are of an exploratory nature. However, there are also normative methods such as the relevance-tree technique. Here one starts by clarifying what is wanted from the future and converts this into desirable objectives. From these one works backwards in order to find out the alternative paths by which the objectives can be achieved.

3.2.4 Development of creativity

Creativity is one of the most important aspects of the innovation process, but also one of the most difficult to handle. There are a number

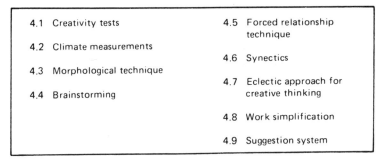

4.1 Creativity tests	4.5 Forced relationship technique
4.2 Climate measurements	
	4.6 Synectics
4.3 Morphological technique	
	4.7 Eclectic approach for
4.4 Brainstorming	creative thinking
	4.8 Work simplification
	4.9 Suggestion system

Figure 3.7 Tools for development of creativity

of techniques available for the stimulation of creativity, as listed in Figure 3.7 and described in Part II. However, even with proper application of the most sophisticated tools, the result may be bad if the organisational climate is such that it does not promote creative behaviour. Empirical studies have shown that one of the most important dimensions of the organisational climate is the type of leadership that is applied[10, 11].

5.1 Feasibility study (technological, marketing, financial, economic, social factors)	5.4 Ecological analysis
	5.5 Resource analysis
5.2 Technology assessment	5.6 Legal analysis
5.3 Patent search (novelty)	

Figure 3.8 Tools for preliminary study

3.2.5 Preliminary study

After a first screening of proposed ideas, they are scrutinised through a preliminary study. The most important tools for this purpose are listed in *Figure 3.8* and described in Part II.

A new technique that deserves special attention is technology assessment. This technique was originally developed in order to assist political bodies in evaluating the impact on society of new technological developments. However, the technique should also be of value to industrial firms.

3.2.6 Project formulation

Based on the material from the preliminary study it is decided whether the idea should be dropped, postponed or approved for further

6.1	Project selection technique	6.3	Acquisition of licences
6.2	Develop/buy analysis	6.4	Legal protection

Figure 3.9 Tools for project formulation

processing. For approved ideas it must be decided whether the technological solution will have to be developed inside the firm or bought from outside.

Some tools applicable to project formulation are listed in *Figure 3.9* and described in Part II. For other aspects of project formulation see 23.1 and 23.3.

REFERENCES

1. Guláš, S., *Possibilities of taking advantage of psychotronics in creative activity with substituting the factor of casualness by the factor of information*, paper presented at first international conference on psychotronic/parapsychological research, 7, Prague, 19 June (1973)
2. Marconi, G., *Every Man his own Inventor*, 70, 5–6, Collins (1922)
3. Lattman, C., 'Die psychosozialen Grundlagen und Auswirkungen der Neuerung in der Unternehmung', *Führung und Organization der Unternehmung*, 7, 217–243 Verlag Paul Haupt, Bern and Stuttgart (1969)
4. Rossman, J., *Industrial Creativity. The Psychology of the Inventor*, 252, University books, New York (1964)
5. Globe, S., Levy, G.W., and Schwartz, C.M., 'Key Factors in the Innovation Process, *Research Management*, 8–15, July (1973)
6. Langrish, J., *et al.*, *Wealth from Knowledge*, 477, MacMillan, Edinburgh (1972)

7. Myers, S., and Marquis, D.,*Successful Industrial Innovations*, Superintendent of Documents, 117, Washington D.C. (1969)
8. *Innovatieprocessen in de Nederlandse industri*, 158, TNO, Apeldoorn (1974)
9. *Success and Failure in Industrial Innovation*, Report on the project *Sappho* by the Science Policy Research Unit of the University of Sussex Centre for the Study of Industrial Innovation, 36, London (1972).
10. Holt, K., *Creativity and Organizational Climate*, 576–583, Work Study & Management Services, Sept. (1971)
11. Holt, K., *The Scanship Case. A Programme for Promotion of Innovation*, 76, The International Institute for the Management of Technology, Milan (1972)

4. Utilisation of Ideas

After an idea is approved for further processing, it must be converted into a working reality. The objective is to find the best possible solution to the problem as it is defined explicitly or implicitly by the approved idea.

In principle, the solution may appear in four different forms and result in approaches as indicated in *Figure 4.1*. Whether the technology is developed by the firm itself or brought in from outside is not a

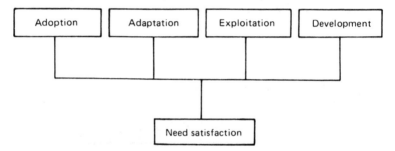

Figure 4.1 Approaches for satisfying a perceived need

principal question. In many cases the best solution may be to adopt and use an existing technology directly, e.g. by obtaining necessary information through licensing or other forms of commercial agreements. In other cases one has to adapt the new technology to meet the specific requirements following from the needs that have to be satisfied. In both approaches the emphasis is on the back end of the innovation process — on the acquisition and use of an existing technology. A third option may be to acquire knowledge by buying an invention and exploiting it commercially.

Many companies are reluctant to use available technologies. However, normally it will not pay to rediscover what others already have done. An active policy for buying licences may therefore be worth while considering. This view is supported by the study of Myers and Marquis[1] which covered nearly 600 innovations in American companies. The findings clearly indicate that both original and adopted technology contribute to commercial success. The study was mainly concerned with 'bread and butter' innovations, but the authors conclude that adoptions may be even more important for major innovations. There is often no ready solution available. An important part of the work will then be to develop a solution that will cover the perceived needs; the emphasis is then on the front end of the innovation process.

If the degree of novelty is rather low, it may be a question of development through engineering and design. However, if the solution requires a new technology in terms of an invention, one may have to spend a considerable amount of resources on applied research and exploratory development before engineering design can take place. Most cases are likely to fall between these extremes.

In the model of the first stage of the innovation process, generation of ideas, shown in *Figure 3.3*, it is assumed that the decision whether the technological solution should be bought from outside or developed within the company is made by the use of a *develop/buy analysis* as referred to in *Figure 3.9*. The following presentation is based on a decision in favour of development.

4.1   MODEL

A simple model of the second stage of the innovation process is shown in *Figure 4.2*. The information input to this stage is ideas approved

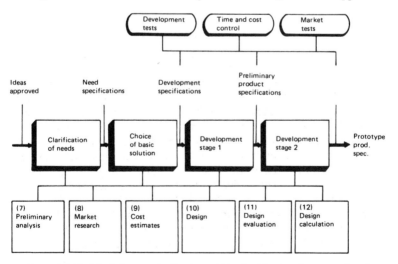

Figure 4.2 Model of the stage 'utilisation of ideas' with related groups of tools

for processing. These ideas may be more or less clearly described in terms of user needs. The first step is to clarify this point. Several of the tools referred to in Chapter 3 may be relevant in this context. Based on need specifications covering both rational and non-rational needs, various approaches are considered and a choice of basic solution is made.

In the model the actual development is visualised in two stages. The first development stage is concerned with the application of research findings or general technological knowledge with the aim of developing, testing and evaluating the technical feasibility and practicability of the proposed solution and determining the key parameters. In this context a rough experimental model (mock-up) may be made without regard to the overall design or final form. The output of this stage is preliminary product specifications.

The second development stage is concerned with the development of hardware for experimental or operational tests. The aim is to demonstrate the actual feasibility and raise confidence in a combination of components that have proved to be technically feasible. The stage also includes the preparation of detailed specifications for products, sub-assemblies and components, regarding materials, shape, dimensions and colour. It may include various types of design and performance calculations, the production of engineering drawings with tolerances and instructions for assembly and testing. In order to verify the calculations, test the result from a technical and commercial point of view, and make the necessary design adjustments, a prototype is often made showing the final mechanical and electrical form.

For products where appearance is of great importance for user acceptance, one often uses internal or external specialists in industrial design. Although this function is primarily concerned with the aesthetic aspects of the product, modern industrial designers also take into consideration functional and social aspects.

In connection with the development of a product, proper attention must be given to the packaging of it. In some cases this may be a rather simple task. However, often the package will have to satisfy a number of requirements such as protection of the product against physical and chemical stress, facilitation of transport, storage, display and handling, information about name, content, characteristics and use, sales appeal and advertising. In such cases, the design of the package may be a complex process requiring the same basic approach and the same tools as for the creation and development of a new product. As a consequence of this, packaging is not treated as a special topic in this book.

The information output of the second stage of the innovation process is final product specifications, which may be in the form of drawings, bills of materials, part lists, etc.

4.2   METHODS

The various tools that are available for the second stage of the innovation process can be grouped in six classes as shown in *Figure 4.2*. They are elaborated upon in Part II and briefly referred to below.

4.2.1   Preliminary analysis

A study of the requirements of potential users and of the formulation of need specifications is done at the beginning of the second stage. In addition to tools mentioned in Chapter 3 come tools shown in *Figure 4.3*.

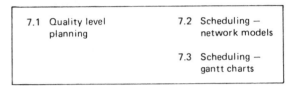

7.1 Quality level planning	7.2 Scheduling — network models
	7.3 Scheduling — gantt charts

Figure 4.3 Tools for preliminary analysis

Of particular importance at this stage is the quality level planning, the effort of which is directed towards meeting the requirements of potential users as far as possible within the existing technical, economical, legal and social constraints.

The term 'quality' according to Jersin[2] can be broken into three elements:

Intended quality, which is the degree of conformity between the need specifications and the development specifications. It decides the 'quality level' of the product. Since there will always be certain technological and price limitations when developing a new product, the producer is usually forced deliberately to plan a user satisfaction less than 100%. When developing a new car engine, for example, the user will want many horsepowers, but a minimum of price and fuel consumption. The producer thus has to decide to which extent he intends to fulfil each need specified.

Quality of design, which is the degree to which the design, i.e. the product specifications, fulfil the requirements stipulated by the development specifications. It is determined by the development team. If the functional specifications stipulated a certain amount of effective power and a maximum amount of fuel consumption of an engine to be developed, the design will decide to which extent these requirements will be fulfilled. The quality of design also determines a major part of manufacturing and inspection costs, service needs and maintainability. Thus, the quality of design cannot be completely evaluated until the product has been produced and made use of under actual working conditions by the user.

Quality of manufacturing, which is the degree of conformity between the manufactured product and the product specifications, i.e. the product drawings. It is determined by the manufacturing department. If the engine designed does not yield the amount of power stipulated in the development specifications, the reason may be lack of conformance to the product specifications. If so, the quality of manufacturing is insufficient.

Quite early also development work is planned. The scheduling may be done by means of network models or gantt charts. An important part of the planning is to divide the whole problem into separate subproblems, to set specific goals for each subproblem, and to assign priorities to the goals. This may be a difficult task as the problem often consists of a hierarchy of subproblems, each having a number of possible solutions.

The solution chosen at one level will determine the available alternatives at next level. This makes the planning very complex if one is seeking not only minor improvements in existing designs, but really new solutions. In such cases one must use a functional approach, treat the product as a system and develop a functional model corresponding to the various hierarchical levels of the problem. However, this has to be done during the development stages rather than at the start of them. Each level is actually an idea generation process, which both requires and offers opportunities for creative behaviour. The problem must be defined with due consideration to the solution decided upon at higher levels, and a number of alternatives must be developed before a choice is made. The role of the designer (the development team) in this context is elaborated upon by Jakobsen[3]. It is not the final product, but a white sheet of paper which is the starting point. The only input is a set of functional requirements which the product as a total should meet, together with aesthetic requirements concerned with shape and colour, manufacturing requirements determined by available manufacturing methods, and technical requirements stemming from the basic solution that has been chosen for the product.

The functional requirements should be stated in functional terms, and as far as possible independent of possible solutions. An example is given in *Figure 4.4*, where the functional requirements, F, can be met by three different product solutions, A_1, A_2 and A_3. A simplified example could be as follows:

Functional requirements (F): to transmit a specified torque at different, but specified speed ratios between two shafts (input and output shaft).

Possible solutions: multistage gear box, hydraulic transmission and mechanical variator (A_1, A_2 and A_3), which all have properties satisfying F.

Some alternatives could be rejected due to boundary conditions such as non-available electric or pneumatic power, space restrictions, presence of oxygen preventing use of oil, purity requirements in food

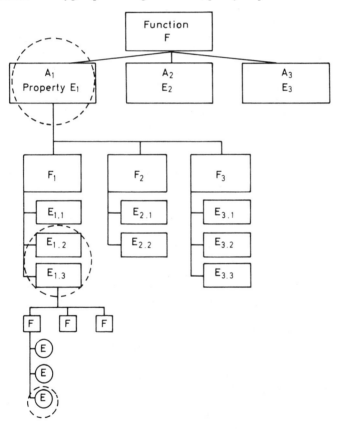

Figure 4.4 The problem facing the designer (the development team)

and medical industries, etc. From the remaining the best alternative is chosen, the choice being based on quality criteria. Suppose A_1 is best – that defines another, and new, set of functions on the next level (level 1), i.e. F_1, F_2 and F_3. This set of functions could have been completely different if another alternative had been chosen. It is therefore impossible to specify functions for level 1 before a solution with acceptable properties is chosen on level 0. Thus, the functional tree is gradually being developed during the design process, rather than being the starting point of it.

4.2.2 Market research

In connection with the clarification of user needs it is often useful to make some kind of market research in order to study the reactions of potential customers to the proposed product. The importance of this approach is emphasised by Robertson[4], who states that it is misleading to assume, as too many innovators have done, that there is a market waiting for new and ingenious products.

Based on a study of 34 failure cases, he found that four had made no enquiries to potential users, six had made too few enquiries, two had ignored the results of the enquiries, two misinterpreted the answers they received, six were committed to preconceived designs and three failed to understand the working environment to which their product would be subjected.

All the errors listed are avoidable, and his conclusion is that in order to get an understanding of the user's needs, the innovative firm should make few assumptions about the wants of potential customers. At every major decision point during the development period, the reality and practicability of harmonising potential user's demands with the capability of the firm should be checked. One should also study the probability of getting a wider market beyond the selected sample, which may not be fully representative however carefully it has been chosen.

8.1 Use of internal market statistics	8.3 Current market studies
8.2 Use of external market statistics	8.4 Special market studies

Figure 4.5 Tools for market research

The various tools available at this stage are shown in *Figure 4.5*. In addition to information about needs of potential users, the methods listed may contribute to the collection of information about existing and potential markets, location of users, where and how they buy, the price they are willing to pay, opinions regarding existing products, etc.

4.2.3   Cost estimates

Rather early in the second stage – and at appropriate intervals later in the innovation process – various types of cost estimates are undertaken. An overview of the methods is given in *Figure 4.6*.

9.1 Risk analysis	9.3 Product cost
9.2 Project cost	9.4 Investment cost and profitability

Figure 4.6 Cost estimates

With the exception of project risk, the other types of cost estimates are considered rather well known. They are therefore referred to only briefly in Part II.

4.2.4   Design

Under this heading a variety of methods is covered that can be applied in the process of transforming the idea from the conceptual stage into hardware. An overview of available methods is given in *Figure 4.7*.

10.1 Applied research	10.5 Computer aided design
10.2 Styling (shape and colour)	10.6 Design and testing of models
10.3 Catalogue aided design	10.7 Standardisation
10.4 Alternative design approaches	10.8 Design for demanufacturing

Figure 4.7 Design methods

In recent years computers have come more and more into use in the design process.

4.2.5 *Design evaluation*

During the design process the project will have to be evaluated from various points of view, such as economy, impact on people, reliability, etc. Tools available for this purpose are shown in *Figure 4.8*. One interesting development is the application of brainstorming for fault analysis.

11.1 Value analysis	11.5 Maintenance analysis
11.2 Reliability analysis	11.6 Fault analysis by brainstorming
11.3 Ergonomic analysis	
11.4 Useful life analysis	11.7 Fault analysis by logical methods
	11.8 Design review

Figure 4.8 Tools for design evaluation

Amundsen[5] explains the philosophy behind the method as follows. Experience shows that faults often have a stochastic way of appearing, and they occur where and when they are not expected. Most people have a rather conventional view, not only concerning the make and properties of a product, but also as to which faults are associated with it. A method is therefore needed to dig out the more improbable faults, and eventually take steps to prevent them.

By using brainstorming ideas will be created of faults which are not only connected with the product itself, but also with the environmental conditions like moisture, temperature changes, transport, etc. Which persons will be using the product and what kind of maltreatment it may suffer are factors to be especially aware of. A fault analysis may easily come up with 30–50 possible proposals of possible faults. In this list there will be faults which would not have been thought of during a normal procedure of development, design and manufacturing. There will also be recorded faults which cannot be considered 'conventional faults' for the product in question. If the fault analysis could reveal only one of the faults which would not otherwise have been thought of, then fault analysis by brainstorming has certainly been useful.

4.2.6   *Design calculation*

In order to determine the functional properties of a given product, it may be necessary to carry out extensive and complex design calculations, of a degree related to the complexity of the product itself. In each case it is necessary to establish a mathematical model which represents the physical properties of the problem. The model must include both the external conditions under which the product will work, and how the product will behave and respond to these conditions. The calculations thus carried out may be based on a wide range of engineering sciences

12.1	Stress calculation	12.3	Flow calculation
12.2	Mechanical vibration calculation	12.4	Thermal calculation
		12.5	Cybernetic calculation

Figure 4.9 Major types of design calculation

and applied physics. An overview of the most important types is given in *Figure 4.9*. Each type represents in fact an applied science of its own. They are assumed to be well known to those involved in development work. If not, information must be collected from other sources, briefly referred to in Part II.

REFERENCES

1. Myers, S., and Marquis, D., *Successful Industrial Innovations*, Superintendent of Documents, 117, Washington D.C. (1969)
2. Jersin, E., *Quality Control in the Innovation Process*, Paper presented at the First International Expert Meeting on Product Innovation Research and Practice, Trondheim, 20–21 June, 1974.
3. Jakobsen, K., *Functional Design in the Innovation Process*, Paper presented at the First International Expert Meeting on Product Innovation Research and Practice, Trondheim 20–21 June, 1974.
4. Robertson, A., 'The Marketing Factor in Successful Industrial Innovation', *Industrial Marketing Management*, 2, 369–374 (1973)
5. Amundsen, A.R., *Fault Analysis by Brainstorming*, Paper presented at the First International Expert Meeting on Product Innovation Research and Practice, Trondheim, 20–21 June, 1974.

5. Preparation for Implementation

Having bought or developed the best possible technical solution, the next stage comprises planning for its practical application. A number of company functions such as purchasing, manufacturing, marketing, finance and personnel may be involved. The key tasks are usually related to the preparation for manufacturing and marketing.

In some cases a product innovation is the result of a straight forward process consisting of a number of consecutive steps starting with the generation of an idea and ending with the introduction and diffusion in the market. The manufacturing and marketing staff may enter the process at the completion of the stage 'Utilisation of ideas', i.e. when starting the preparation for implementation. However, it is now getting more and more common to involve these people in the whole innovation process. They can contribute at the first stage by generating valuable ideas for new products and processes, and they can provide relevant information and take part in the evaluation of the project at various points throughout the process.

5.1 MODEL

A simple model of the third stage is shown in *Figure 5.1*. The information input at this stage is product specifications in the form of drawings, bills of materials, etc. It is indicated that the stage starts with final design, i.e. the production of detailed drawings and other written descriptions and instructions, which will serve as a base for the planning of the manufacturing operations. For products to be manufactured in large quantities, one also should include the planning of test production early in Stage 3. In this case the preparation for implementation ends with the testing of market acceptance by bringing products from one or several test runs to potential users.

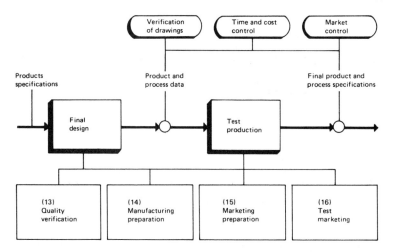

Figure 5.1 Model of the stage 'preparation for implementation' with related groups of tools

The information output of Stage 3 of the innovation process is final product and process specifications in the form of detailed drawings, descriptions, instructions, etc., of components, process equipment, tools, etc.

5.2   METHODS

As shown in *Figure 5.1*, the various tools applicable for the third stage can be divided into four classes.

5.2.1   Quality verification

As indicated in *Figure 5.2*, two techniques are available for assessing the quality of products made during the test runs. These techniques are described in Part II.

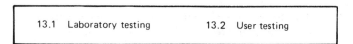

Figure 5.2 Methods for quality verification

5.2.2 Manufacturing preparation

The basic tools for the planning of the manufacturing operations are shown in *Figure 5.3*. All the methods listed are considered to be well known. They are therefore referred to only briefly in Part II.

14.1 Make/buy analysis	14.4 Material planning
14.2 Equipment and tooling	14.5 Quality control planning
14.3 Process and operation planning	14.6 Design for manufacturing

Figure 5.3 Methods for manufacturing planning

5.2.3 Marketing preparation

Marketing is a keystone in successful innovations. A technically perfect product will be of no value if it cannot be brought to the market and sold.

The task of the marketing function first of all is to provide a link to the outside world. In a competitive environment this is a complicated process which has to be managed in such a way that it satisfies the need of the customers and at the same time meets the objectives of the company.

Some major activities in connection with the launching of a new product, handled by marketing alone or in cooperation with other departments, are:

Distribution (including establishment and development of distribution channels, physical distribution and related activities).
Pricing (considering factors like cost, competition, trading practices, etc.).
Selling (including both direct sales through selection, training and supervision of salesmen, and indirect sales through sales promotion, advertising, etc.).
Service (including advice and training in the use and maintenance of the product, etc.).

Some of the major tools that can be used in connection with marketing preparation are shown in *Figure 5.4*.

Companies who have an offensive R & D policy and develop new and radically improved products with innovative elements should study the possibility of selling licences, as it is difficult to keep new knowledge and developments for oneself over a long period of time. However, it is hard to formulate a general policy in this area. Each case should therefore be evaluated separately before a decision is made, considering both positive and negative effects. Methods concerned with the sales of

15.1	Distribution	15.4	Sales promotion
15.2	Sale of licences	15.5	Sales planning
15.3	Advertising	15.6	Trade marks

Figure 5.4 Tools for marketing preparation

licences are given a detailed description in Part II. So are methods for distribution. The other tools referred to in *Figure 5.4* are considered to be well known and are therefore referred to only briefly.

5.2.4   Test marketing

In order to test the marketing operation in connection with new products, it may be useful to introduce the product to a limited number of potential users. Possible approaches are shown in *Figure 5.5*. By

16.1 Use of test area	16.2 Use of trade fairs

Figure 5.5 Methods for test marketing

selecting a test area representative of the population of potential users, it is possible not only to test user acceptance, but also to check the efficiency of the whole marketing operation. This approach is described in Part II. A less sophisticated method also is listed in *Figure 5.5*; here one demonstrates and sells the product at one or more trade fairs.

6. Manufacturing and Marketing

The last stage of the innovation process comprises *implementation*, i.e. the introduction of the new product in the market, and regular manufacturing and marketing.

At this stage one can verify if the effort spent in the previous stages has resulted in a successful innovation or not. The chances for a good

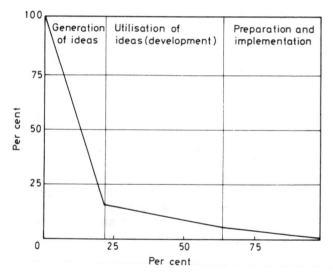

Figure 6.1 Mortality rate through the innovation process

result are not very high, as indicated in *Figure 6.1*, which is based on data from 51 American firms reported by Pedraglio[1]. The data indicate that about 13% of the ideas proposed are accepted for development after preliminary screening, and that only 2% result in a successful product. The data refer to products that are new to the company. The risk is less for improvements in existing well established products.

6.1   MODEL

A simple representation of the last stage of the innovation process is given in *Figure 6.2*. The information input is product and process specifications. The process starts with the introduction of the new product. Here one is concerned with break-in and debugging of the

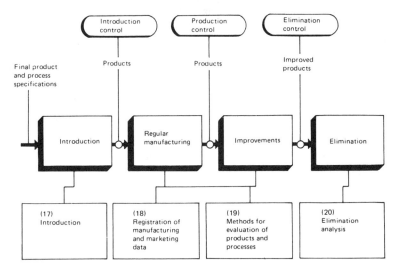

Figure 6.2 Model of the stage 'manufacturing and marketing' with related groups of tools

manufacturing operation and the first selling of the product. Usually, sale is carried on by the sales force of the company, supported by various kinds of advertising and sales promotion. Some companies are using consulting firms for market introduction of products that are new to the company. Such firms use their own sales force and do all the promotional work. After all problems and difficulties have been solved and the marketing operation is running smoothly, the sales force of the manufacturing firm is given a thorough training. They then gradually take over the responsibilities for the marketing of the product.

New products can be introduced with full strength in the market. However, many companies, particularly the smaller ones, are reluctant in taking the great risks involved in a full scale introduction. They therefore start by introducing the product on a more moderate scale and then increase the manufacturing and marketing efforts as the product gains acceptance. Such an approach may be based on two different principles. One is to start the introduction in a limited area with full marketing strength. After this market is conquered, one moves to the next area, until the whole market is covered. The other principle is based on simultaneous introduction to the whole market, but with a limited effort. Gradually the effort is increased until the whole area has been satisfactorily covered.

Special attention should be given to products that are completely new to the market. As the users have no previous knowledge about the product, special precautions should be taken to convince them about its advantages. Various types of demonstrations may prove useful in this context.

Those products which succeed in the market by reaching the sales objectives established for the introduction period usually have not exploited their full potential at the end of the introduction period. They are seldom perfect at this stage. Therefore, a number of incremental innovations and improvements are made during the regular manufacturing period. The length of this period will depend on factors such as the development of the purchasing power of the users, and the pace of change in technology and need patterns.

Changes will be undertaken until the possibilities of the original innovation are fully realised and the technology stabilised. Further growth during regular production may still be possible by increasing the volume through measures aiming at improvement of the efficiency of the manufacturing and marketing operations. However, at this stage competition also gets stronger. This results in a growing need for a new technology, and sooner or later the product will be eliminated and replaced by a new product that brings the technology a step forward. The innovation process is brought to an end and is ready to start over again.

6.2 METHODS

The various tools applicable at the last stage of the innovation process can broadly be divided in four classes, as shown in *Figure 6.2*.

6.2.1 Introduction

Tools that can be used in connection with the introduction period are shown in *Figure 6.3*. Methods for registration of actual sales are well known, and are therefore referred to only briefly in Part II. However, the importance of recording sales data at rather short time intervals during the introduction period in order to achieve good control of the market acceptance of the new or improved product should be emphasised. This can be done by registering for example every two weeks' orders at the start of the period, orders received during the period, and orders shipped during the period. A more detailed control

```
17.1  Selection of strategy for introduction

17.2  Recording of actual sales
```

Figure 6.3 Tools for the introduction period

can be obtained by registering each day quantities shipped. Changes in customer inventories may cause distortions of the true picture. In order to overcome this a mobile counting team can be used which visits regularly, e.g. every second week, all stores in the area selected for introduction in order to acquire the relevant data.

6.2.2 Manufacturing and marketing data

After the successful introduction of the product, regular production should be controlled from both a technical, marketing and economic

```
18.1  Registration of          18.3  Sales
      quality parameters

                                18.4  Costs
18.2  Quantity
```

Figure 6.4 Tools for registration of marketing and manufacturing data

point of view. This control can be obtained by registration of relevant data at regular intervals or when needed. The most appropriate tools for this purpose are shown in *Figure 6.4*. All are well known and are therefore referred to only briefly in Part II.

6.2.3 Evaluation of products and processes

In addition to the control obtained through registration and reporting of manufacturing and marketing data, one may also use the tools listed in *Figure 6.5*.

As far as the efficiency of the marketing operation is concerned, the whole picture may not be revealed through sales data, field reports and customer complaints. This material may therefore be supplemented with special field studies (see *Figure 4.5*).

It is also worthwhile emphasising that there is much to gain by a systematic evaluation of the history of the completed project, also

19.1	Field reports
19.2	Project evaluation

Figure 6.5 Methods for evaluation of products and processes

of those which failed. Such an evaluation is basically a comparison of the results with the assumptions, expectations and objectives at the start of the project. It may include target dates as well as the technical, economical and financial aspects of the project.

6.2.4 Elimination analysis

The life cycle of most products is becoming shorter and shorter. Sooner or later the question of elimination will arise. Some tools that can be used for this analysis are listed in *Figure 6.6*. This is an important, but

20.1	Product–market matrix
20.2	Life cycle analysis
20.3	Sales trends
20.4	Profit data

Figure 6.6 Tools for elimination analysis

frequently overlooked step. Many unprofitable products are allowed to continue, thereby reducing overall profit and the ability to take advantage of new opportunities. However, one of the most difficult decisions to take is to eliminate a product. Many people have usually participated in the development, manufacturing and marketing of it; they therefore feel closely attached and resist parting with it.

Although elimination decisions in most companies are considered to be so important that they require top management action, the methods used to provide the necessary information are often poor. This is not satisfactory. An innovative organisation should not be concerned only with the creation and introduction of new or improved products, but also with the systematic discontinuation of existing products. According to Kotler[2] arguments favouring such an approach are:

Products whose discontinuation has been unnecessarily delayed represent uncovered overheads.

Such products tend to consume a disproportionate amount of management's time.

They often require frequent price and inventory adjustments.

They generally involve short production runs in spite of expensive set-up times.

They require both advertising and sales force attention that might better be diverted to making 'healthy' products more profitable.

They can, by their very unsuitability, give customers misgivings and cast a shadow on the company's image.

They may delay the search for replacement products.

They depress present profitability and weaken the company's foot-hold on the future.

To avoid such shortcomings a system for periodic product review, with the following features, is recommended:

A review team of high-level executives covering major company functions.

Well defined objectives and procedures.

Operational steps. These can take many forms. As an example a six-step approach is indicated, comprising 1. Compilation of product sheets with data for determination if the product is considered to be weak; 2. Determination of dubious products by means of a computer program with decision rules and data from the product sheets; 3. Application of rating forms for dubious products by the management review team; 4. Determination of a product retention index for each dubious product by means of a computer program; 5. Review of the product indices by the management team who decide on products to drop; 6. Development of policies and plans for phasing out products to be eliminated by the management review team. The selection of tools for the operational step will depend on the attitude and competence of those responsible for the elimination decisions and the data that can be provided at reasonable cost. In order to build a good base for more important decisions it may prove valuable to use several tools.

REFERENCES

1. Pedraglio, G., 'Getting into Shape to Manage New Products', *European Business*, 38–47, Summer (1971)
2. Kotler, P., 'Phasing out Weak Products', *Harvard Business Review*, 107–118, Mar.–Apr. (1965)

7. Strategy

Industrial firms exist in an environment characterised by rapid and often unexpected changes. Technology is advancing at an unprecedented pace, often of an exponential nature. This is illustrated by the *J-curve* which reflects successive technological advances covering the same function. One example of such a curve is given in *Figure 7.1*, which

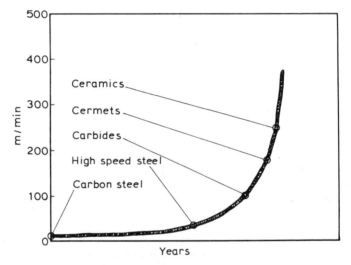

Figure 7.1 Cutting speed of machine tools

shows how new materials have increased the speed of the cutting function in machine tools. An example from the office is given in *Figure 7.2*. Here is shown how the time for calculating has been drastically improved by rapid technological advances. Changes in marketing, economic, political and social factors also greatly contribute to a dynamic environment. Many firms respond to such a situation by product innovation.

In the preceding chapters models and methods for the processing of individual product innovation projects have been presented. Such projects are usually stimulated by perception of user needs or by

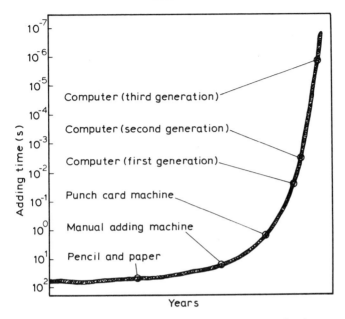

Figure 7.2 Office machines (adding ten four-digit numbers)

recognition of technological possibilities.

In many firms the decision to go ahead with a project is made in an improvised or unsystematic manner unrelated to an overall strategy. A manager, for example, gets an idea for a new product through a chance occurrence and decides to go ahead because he thinks it will sell. Such an approach does not necessarily lead to poor results. In many instances, gifted managers with intuition and courage to make decisions have been able to perceive and utilise opportunities and successfully move their companies in new directions. However, there are also numerous cases where the results have been failures. It appears therefore that intuition should be supplemented by a systematic approach based on a well-defined corporate strategy. By making the strategy known to all concerned, the company will be able to integrate and better utilise the talents of its staff as well as its physical and financial resources.

In principle there are two ways to go. At one extreme is a decentralised, bottom-up approach where ideas are generated in various departments, evaluated and integrated in an over-all corporate plan. The other extreme is a centralised, top-down approach comprising a formalised strategy formulation based on a realistic business concept, concrete objectives and a systematical diversification procedure. The purpose of this chapter is to present a framework for the latter approach with relevant models and tools.

7.1   STRATEGY FORMULATION – MODELS

The strategy of a firm may be based on a formalised approach as shown
in *Figure 7.3.*   Here the starting point is the *business concept* or the

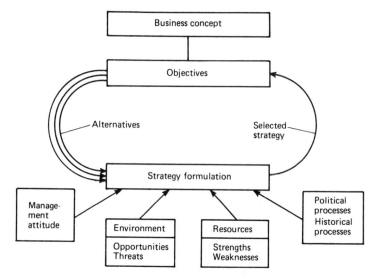

Figure 7.3 Flow model of strategy formulation

basic idea underlying the activities of the firm. It may be analysed and
discussed by formulating questions such as:

what is the purpose of the firm? what business are we in?

what can we do? what do we want to do? what does the market
want?

what should we do?

The business concept should, according to Normann[1], reflect some
kind of superiority or *'distinctive competence'*; a description of it
should include:

the market segment or niche in the environment dominated by the
company (its 'territory')

the products supplied to the market

the resources and the internal conditions by means of which domi-
nence is acquired.

Webster[2] states that the *distinctive competence* may be found in any
area such as R & D, engineering, production, marketing, distribution, or

from a synergy of several elements. In defining the distinctive competence he suggests that one should focus on the users served, the nature of their needs and the role of the firm's products and services in satisfying these needs over the long run. In this context it may be helpful to answer the question 'what business are we in?' in terms of user-need satisfaction.

By clarifying and defining the business concept along the lines indicated one should avoid the pitfalls in making the business concept too broad and general, and thereby reducing its value as a planning aid.

At the time a firm is founded, it has a strong and future-oriented concept. As time passes, external and internal conditions as well as underlying assumptions will change. The original concept will gradually become more and more irrelevant. In some firms it may keep its strength over a long period of time. However, most firms now find themselves in a situation where the business concept will become obsolete relatively fast; rapid changes in technologies and markets as well as social and political trends contribute to such a development. However, in order to cope effectively with change, the environment must be continuously surveyed. When required, action should be taken to review the business concept by redefining where the company should go. The business concept will direct and control the whole effort of the firm. A sound need oriented concept will stimulate the whole organisation to think in terms of markets and needs. It will provide a powerful base for formulation of strategies and criteria that will guide product innovation activities.

In old and well established firms it is often difficult to define, or even find, a meaningful business concept. Many of them have grown by diversifying into new fields on the initiative of strong managers who have acted in an improvised manner and utilised opportunities without guidance of a strategic concept. The result has often been a company with highly varied products with regard to materials, technology, users and distribution methods. A typical example is a firm making industrial robots, bicycles, medical equipment, and working clothes. In addition it has a wholesale division for fertilisers and a retail chain for garments. In such a case it is necessary to analyse and formulate business concepts for each division or major product group. In addition to providing a basis for strategic thinking and operational decisions on product innovation activities, such an approach will give a good foundation for development of the organisational structure.

Closely related to the business concept, but somewhat wider in scope, are the concepts of organisational culture and management philosophy.

The *organisational culture* stands for the underlying attitudes, values and beliefs that govern the behaviour of the firm. Several firms have analysed its culture and documented it in writing; it is then often referred to as *management philosophy*. Included in such a statement may be the purpose of the firm, major long-term objectives, relationship to the various interests involved, products or services to be offered, the way of doing business, etc.

Whereas the focus of the business concept is upon product, product technology, and market needs, the employees of the firm have a central position in the management philosophy. At least this is the lesson that can be drawn from a study by Ouchi[3] of several successful organisations in Japan and USA with the aim of detecting what western firms can learn from Japanese business practices. Although the American and Japanese firms that were studied represented different cultures, some of the American firms demonstrated remarkable similarities with the Japanese firms. Thus, they were characterised by

a long-term view in planning and decision making;
life-long job rotation;
heavy investment in employee training;
great attention to the needs of all interests such as owners, employees, suppliers, the community, the society, etc.

So far only a few western firms have tried to apply them. In the West most firms are characterised by the short-term view of performance, individualism, highly specialised professions, fragmented operations, explicit control, many conflicts and high turnover.

It appears that theory Z can be of help in adopting and adapting the best from *Japanese organisation theory* and management methods in western firms. A well understood and accepted management philosophy will provide a general background for co-operation and united effort. It may be a powerful guide for consistent thinking in formulation of objectives, development of plans, and making decisions that will suit changing conditions.

The benefits that appear to be associated with the type Z organisation are not easily acquired. To change the culture of an organisation is an ambitious task. It is a complex process that will take time. It will require a high degree of motivation as well as a determined effort of those involved. A failure may be disastrous. Before attempting to apply theory Z one should carefully study not only benefits to be obtained, but also the problems that have to be solved and the risks that are involved. In some cases one may find it more realistic to start with analysing and formulating a future-oriented business concept. At least this appears to be a realistic alternative in firms where the key problem is to create an effective product innovation organisation.

Having clarified the business concept, the next step is an evaluation and possible reformulation of *major objectives (corporate objectives)*.

The type of objectives depends on the situation of the firm and attitudes and preferences among key decision makers. Selection and proper formulation is a vital but difficult task. It is also difficult to distinguish between business concept and objectives as both are of the 'what should we do' type of question. Often both are of a qualitative nature. Ideally, objectives should reflect a conscious choice of business areas, and within these quantified economical, social and technological success indicators.

In actual practice one finds a variety of approaches. This is reflected in the literature. Thus, Burns[4] indicates that possible objectives may be type of products, geographical areas to be served, type of customers, quality—price level, corporate image desired, share of total market to be captured, rate, dimension and method of growth, risk level, and return on investment.

Steele[4] focuses upon large firms that adapt to change by means of technological innovation, and suggests that the objectives should include the role of technology and major technological areas of interest.

Having determined objectives, the next step according to the model in *Figure 7.3* is to formulate alternative strategies and select the most promising among them. Key elements in this process are analysis of the environment and of the resources of the firm. As indicated, the decision will also be influenced by the attitude of management as well as by political and historical processes.

---

(1) Quantified economical, social and other relevant objectives

(2) Formulation of divisional plans based on analysis of
     opportunities and threats in the environment and analysis
     of strengths and weaknesses of each division

(3) Gap analysis based on quantified objectives and sales forecasts
     for existing products and new products that are planned for
     introduction

(4) Search for alternative ways of realising the objectives
     ('filling the gap')

(5) Formulation of strategy (selection of solution)

(6) Implementation of strategy, measurement of results,
     comparison with objectives, and corrective action

Figure 7.4 Procedural model of strategy formulation and implementation

A procedural model for *strategy formulation* and implementation based on the top-down approach is shown in *Figure 7.4.* The model is rather elaborate and suited to fit the needs of companies organised in product divisions. A modified version may be used in smaller and functionally organised firms.

The result of the planning process is often a combination of several of the strategies shown in *Figure 1.3.* The strategy may vary for different groups. In many firms one may find a combination of an evolutionary strategy, focusing upon cost reduction and improvement of existing products and processes as well as upon introduction of existing products into new markets, and a diversification strategy with periodical introduction of new products into existing or new markets. These products may be developed by the firm or bought from outside through a commercial agreement. It is a difficult, but important task to find a proper balance between the allocation of resources to improvements and innovative activities.

If the strategy adopted involves frequent introduction of new products, one may develop a special *product strategy* based on the degree of novelty as shown in *Figure 7.5.*

---

(1) *Product leadership*; developing and introducing products which are new to the market

(2) *Early adoption*; quick adoption, and if possible, improving products with a high degree of novelty developed outside the firm

(3) *Segment adaptation*; adopting products developed outside and adapting them to the needs of special market segments ('niches')

(4) *Late adoption*; adopting (copying) well-established products ('me-too products') and competing on strength in administration or functional areas such as manufacturing, marketing, purchasing, etc.

(5) *Combination*; two or more of the strategies listed above are combined, e.g. product leadership and segment adaptation

---

Figure 7.5 Product strategies

A strategy of 'product leadership', or being first, offers great possibilities, but it involves severe risks. It requires good ideas, a considerable market potential and large investments of human and financial resources in research and development. Following the leader by 'early adoption' requires a strong marketing capability and a flexible development and manufacturing organisation which can react quickly. As an alternative to developing the product, one may make a licensing arrangement or buy the company that did the pioneering work. In medium-sized and smaller firms 'segment adaptation' is often found to be a good solution. Great attention should be given to finding the proper segment or niche. 'Late adoption' requires high, overall efficiency of the firm and a very strong market effort; often benefits can be obtained by finding a new area of application.

The models presented in *Figures 7.3* and *7.4* are based on the *traditional problem solving* approach which presupposes a stable situation with complete knowledge regarding external and internal factors. One can then analyse the situation, formulate well-defined objectives, develop alternatives, and make a rational choice. However, such an ideal situation does not exist when one has to tackle fundamental problems such as changes in business concept or objectives. One is then faced with a complex, uncertain and rapidly changing situation with incomplete information. In such situations strategies can not be derived logically from well-defined objectives. The focus must be upon *'knowledge development'* as emphasised by Normann[1]. The planning will have character of a step-by-step learning process. After each step the whole situation has to be reconsidered before taking further steps. One starts with a vision, i.e. an intuitive idea of a wanted future state. Having determined consequences of the vision and evaluated the conclusions arrived at, more information is acquired and analysed, the vision is adjusted and so on.

The human interests involved will make the process even more complex and uncertain. The planning is done by people and the result arrived at will have an influence upon the needs of many people. There will be different views of what is desirable. This situation is discussed by Checkland[6] who claims that the ranking of different needs is a value judgement subject to changing criteria. As an example he refers to the increased emphasis that is now given to needs related to quality of working life as well as to environmental and ecological problems. In such situations one is faced with a continuous process of making different views explicit, working out implications, and testing them against other views which may be equally valid within other frames of reference.

In actual practice the process will have an iterative character and be some place between the extremes described above. One may start and define the problem by formulating a tentative objective, select and analyse relevant facts regarding the situation, move back and redefine the problem, develop alternatives, collect and analyse facts regarding the alternatives, select and implement a solution, if necessary, redefine the problem, collect new facts, etc. Thus, one may actually have to go through a rather elaborate process before arriving at a satisfactory formulation of objectives.

Another alternative is to start the process by making a thorough analysis of the situation before formulating objectives. This is recommended by Lorange[7] who defines corporate objectives as statements where the firm should go without specific time targets. He suggests that this stage should include assessment of environmental opportunities and threats, comparison of own performance criteria with available outside criteria for comparable organisations, delineation of assumptions and constraints including general economic factors, and personal aspiration and style of the chief executive and his key men.

Whatever approach is used, proper attention should be given to the marketing aspects of the problem. This view is supported by Gee and Tylor[8] who focus upon matching the technological capability of the firm with opportunities and needs in the market, and upon establishing realistic priorities among them.

7.2   STRATEGY FORMULATION – METHODS

Several tools are available for a systematic approach to strategy formulation. Some of the most important ones are listed in *Figure 7.6* and described in Part II. In addition reference is made to tool groups 1, 2, 3, 5 and 8, which may help to reveal opportunities and threats in the environment, to tool group 4, which may be used for generation of ideas concerning new markets, product lines or products, and to tool groups 18 and 20, which may indicate the need for divestment by elimination of unprofitable products or processes.

21.1	Gap analysis
21.2	Capability analysis
21.3	Competitive strengths – market attractiveness matrix
21.4	Market share – market growth matrix
21.5	Product/market – option matrix
21.6	Performance criteria

Figure 7.6 Tools for strategy formulation

With an increasingly changing and unpredictable environment, it is becoming more and more difficult to visualise future developments. This is demonstrated by Wallander[9] who has compared five-year production forecasts with real developments in industries such as textile, shipbuilding, paper and metal working. Based on detailed data for the period 1960–78, he concludes that the forecasts have been very unreliable. In addition to being unable to make good predictions, forecasters have difficulties in spotting new developments that have already started. They also appear to be very conservative — they avoid strong deviations from previous trends and experiences. Often they use extrapolations ('same weather as yesterday'). In periods with rapid change, they, at a certain point, use the flattening out approach ('it can't go on like this any longer').

When making a forecast, it is important to have a good starting point. However, Wallander claims that many firms do not know where they stand. When making forecasts, long-term plans and budgets, they are often badly informed about the current situation due to incomplete and late reporting of key data.

Firms cannot avoid the problems of the future by neglecting them. Many decisions have long-range implications and should be based on some assumptions about the future. With the speed, scale and unpredictability of the changes that are now taking place in the environment, the reliability of forecasts based on traditional methods are, in most cases, not satisfactory. More and more firms are therefore using the *scenario technique* (method 3.1). Here consequences of various futures are studied and evaluated, taking into account technological, marketing, economical, political and social factors.

Another tool that has gained increasing acceptance in connection with formulation of strategy is *portfolio analysis* (methods 21.3 and 21.4). This approach provides an analytical basis for decisions concerning support to existing product lines, withdrawal of unprofitable products and diversification into new areas.

7.3   DIVERSIFICATION STUDIES – MODELS

As indicated in *Figure 1.3* (page 5), one of the strategies that may be selected for meeting the objectives of the firm is product diversification, which is concerned with the search for and selection of new products (one may also talk about diversification in connection with new markets for existing products). The product diversification may be 'horizontal', i.e., the introduction of new products related to existing products in terms of technological or marketing characteristics, be 'vertical', i.e., the introduction of new products similar or related to products made by suppliers or customers or, be 'lateral' (diagonal), i.e., the introduction of new products unrelated to existing products. The last category, which is often found in the conglomerate holding company, represents the ultimate degree of diversification. It is usually accomplished by buying up individual companies, eliminating unprofitable activities in them, reorganising their management, and installing modern business principles and procedures.

Diversification has been in vogue especially in large and growing companies. However, in one way it is a negative strategy as one leaves well-known ground and moves into new fields with great risks where one has little know-how. One should therefore be careful and avoid 'over-diversification' which may result in dispersion of strength and in inefficient operations. Now there are indications of a more critical attitude ('firms are more profitable when they stick to what they know how to do'). Several firms have concentrated their efforts upon business areas where they are really competent by divesting themselves of those areas in which they do not have enough competitive strength.

Product diversification may be based on intuition or more or less systematical studies. An approach, consisting of two stages, for finding new products is shown in *Figure 7.7*. As an example of the model, a

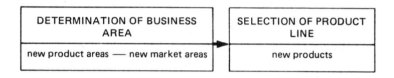

Figure 7.7 Model of a two-stage diversification process

producer of equipment for the paper and pulp industry can be used. The first stage is concerned with finding a new business area. This may be related to products, e.g., pumps, or to markets, e.g., hospitals. The second stage involves the search for and selection of product lines and/or products in the new area, e.g., pumps for unloading of vessels or furniture for hospital nursing units.

A procedural model of the diversification process is shown in *Figure 7.8*. Great attention should be given to the definition of the problem by assessing the needs for diversification which may include inability to survive with existing products, inadequate growth, profit improvement, risk reduction by getting more 'legs' as support, utilisation of special competence within the staff, better utilisation of facilities and equipment, entrance into 'status areas', avoidance of market dominance, get out of cyclical business, enter a growth market, generate cash more quickly, among others. In addition to the needs of the firm the needs of other interested parties such as society, employees, potential users, etc. should be assessed. Finally, internal and external rules and regulations should be clarified, as well as the time available for planning and imple-

(1)	Problem definition through clarification of needs and restrictions
(2)	Quantification of economical, social and other relevant objectives
(3)	Search for new business areas
(4)	Selection of business area
(5)	Search for new products
(6)	Selection of new products

Figure 7.8 Procedural model of the diversification process

mentation of the diversification study. By means of such an analysis, one can formulate concrete objectives for the study and establish a framework for the systematical search for new business areas.

By following a procedure as indicated in *Figure 7.8* one first selects a new business area. In the search for this area, all possible areas may be considered during the idea generation stage. However, in many cases it may be practical to concentrate the search for diversification ideas to a limited number of search areas. These areas may be determined by means of search criteria derived from the business concept of the firm, its objectives and its competitive strengths and weaknesses. In this context a user-oriented business concept will be a valuable aid. However, even if an alternative is not consistent with the firm's user orientation, Webster[2] states that it is not necessary to reject a promising opportunity. The distinctive competence may still be relevant. However, if neither the firm's knowledge about user needs nor its distinctive competence are relevant, it is highly unlikely that present management will be able to manage the new venture successfully. Even in such cases one may find it worthwhile to respond to the new opportunity. However, by moving beyond existing product and market competence, one should evaluate the need to acquire new management capability as part of the move into the new area.

Within the business area selected, e.g. the road sector, a list is made with proposals for new products, e.g. bridges, highway ramps, noise protection walls, etc.

The products selected should be listed according to priority and described by preliminary product specifications. The transformation of the proposals into concrete products may be done as indicated in Chapter 4.

7.4   DIVERSIFICATION STUDIES — METHODS

22.1	Need—technology—customer matrix
22.2	Diversification area—capability matrix
22.3	Screening procedures

Figure 7.9 Tools for diversification studies

Several methods are available for diversification studies. Three of them are listed in *Figure 7.9* and are described in Part II. In addition reference can be made to the following methods for the generation and evaluation of ideas:

Creative techniques; (see tools 4.3 — 4.9)
Delphi technique; (see tool 3.2)
Diversification conference; staff from various departments and levels generate ideas by means of group work — these ideas are then discussed in a plenary session
Systematical collection of ideas; by means of letters and/or oral communications, ideas are collected from knowledgeable persons inside and outside the firm, organisations, institutions and other firms
Literature studies; ideas are collected from relevant books and journals
Feasibility study; (see tool 5.1).

Whatever methods are used for idea generation, one usually gets a large number of ideas for new business areas. By means of a multistage screening procedure these ideas are gradually reduced to one *diversification area* by means of proper search criteria and relevant feasibility studies for the most promising projects. The next stage is concerned with the search for and the selection of products within the new area. Here tools similar to those referred to for diversification studies can be used.

Firms with a high growth objective may have to undertake frequent or even *continuous diversification* studies. Under such circumstances one may use a permanent *project portfolio* where approved ideas are added, possibly after they have been investigated by a preliminary study. In this way one will have at all times several projects ready for further processing.

REFERENCES

1. Normann, R., *Management for Growth*, 210, John Wiley, Chichester (1977)
2. Webster, F.E., *Industrial Marketing Strategy*, 279, John Wiley, New York (1979)
3. Ouchi, W.G., *Theory Z*, 244, Avon, New York (1982)
4. Burns, R.O., *Innovation, the Management Connection*, 157, Lexington Books, Lexington (1975)
5. Steele, L.V., *Innovation in Big Business*, 245, Elsevier, New York (1975)
6. Checkland, P.B., *'The problem of problem formulation in the application of a system approach'*, in: *Education in System Science*, B.A. Bayraktar, (ed.), Nato Conference Series, Taylor & Francis, London (1979)
7. Lorange, P., *Corporate Planning*, 294, Prentice-Hall, Englewood Cliffs (1980)
8. Gee, A.A., and Taylor, C., *Managing Innovation*, 267, John Wiley, London (1976)
9. Wallander, J., 'Om prognoser, budgetar och långtidsplaner', *Jernindustri*, 262–268, No. 10, (1979)

8. Product Planning

Product planning is concerned with development and renewal of the product spectrum. This activity includes improvement of existing products, systematic search, selection and introduction of new products, and withdrawal of unprofitable products.

The way new products are initiated and planned varies greatly, ranging from chance occurrences and informal approaches to highly sophisticated procedures with detailed manuals for every step of the planning process.

Several factors will be decisive of the approach that is used. One of the most important is *type of market*. One can here distinguish between the consumer market, the industrial market, and the government market.

On the *consumer market* are sold standardised products that are made in large quantities and kept in stock for later distribution. The number of customers is large. The sale is controlled by standardised procedures and most often done through wholesalers and retailers. In each purchase only one or a few persons is involved. Many purchases are of an emotional and impulsive nature. The customer has no or only minor influence on product specifications.

A considerable effort is required in order to assess user needs. Some firms have established their own sales organisation, at least for part of their production, in order to get direct user contact. Other firms use special methods for need assessment, such as complaint analysis, surveillance of journals with consumer tests, analysis of competitor's products, dealer questioning, multivariate methods, value analysis and user observation techniques including simulation. Some firms use psychological approaches such as projective test interviews, in-depth psychological interviews, group discussions with potential users, and creativity techniques. The needs of users may also be assessed by means of concept tests, prototype tests and test marketing.

On the *institutional market*, which comprises industrial firms and institutions such as private hospitals and schools, the number of users is relatively small. Often the products are complex with service as an integrated part. In many cases the products are made to order, and in some cases they are even specifically developed to satisfy special user requirements. The sales effort calls for technical competence, and in many cases the buyer has more competence than the salesman. The sale requires few links, and often there is direct personal contact between the firm and the user in connection with acquisition, installation and operation of the product. Mutual trust plays an important role. In the buying process several persons usually participate from the user organisation, each with different needs and requirements. Several of them work outside the purchasing department. Specifications, delivery terms, etc. are often the result of a timeconsuming bargaining process. When making the decision, functional and operational requirements as well as economical considerations count heavily.

User needs are often assessed through open discussions with existing or potential users. One may also work directly with a user as a partner in a pilot project. Cooperation with manufacturers of components and raw materials may also be useful. Upon entering an institutional market that is new to the producer, one may have to acquire information regarding user needs by contacting experts such as consultants and researchers.

On the *government market*, which includes agencies and public institutions at national and regional levels, products tend to be sold in large quantities. According to Webster[1], this market has many similarities to industrial markets. However, there are some differences. Holt et al[2] indicate that many purchases are characterised by public tenders, time-consuming administrative procedures, and legal restrictions. The need for new and improved products often stems from special studies, expert discussions and political debates. In order to compete on the government market the producer should be alert and watch such activities closely and have proper solutions ready at the right moment. This process will be facilitated by employing persons who understand the bureaucratic system with its power relations, and who are able to develop contacts with those responsible for specifying tenders and projects.

Another important factor is the product's *life-cycle*. As indicated in *Figure 8.1* one can distinguish between development, improvement and maturity.

The *development stage* is of an innovative nature. The volume is low and manufacturing processes are characterised by great flexibility. The product has a high degree of novelty, and competitive emphasis is upon functional performance. Through application of new technology one is often able to develop products with unique characteristics. Numerous examples are found in electronic industries.

In order to benefit from technological advances in fields with rapid change, the firm must have sufficient capacity to quickly adopt, adapt

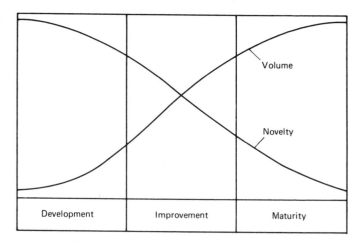

Figure 8.1 Novelty, volume and product life-cycle

and improve the new technology to the needs of its markets. This requires not only know-how regarding technology, but also of what the needs of the market will be when the product is ready for introduction.

The *improvement stage* is characterised by strong competition. The products no longer have unique characteristics. The activities of the firm must be adapted to the new situation. In addition to increasing manufacturing efficiency, great attention should be given to product improvement by close user contact and by application of proper need assessment methods. Top competence in marketing is required in order to inform and reach the users in an efficient manner. Organisational changes are often required during this stage.

The *maturity stage* is characterised by high volume and a low degree of novelty. This is particularly true for consumer products. Here functional characteristics often show small differences between competing products. A product design which satisfies emotional needs such as status and aesthetics can be a strong competitive weapon. Often large-scale production is required in order to obtain the cost benefits reflected by the learning curve. Necessary volume may be obtained through internal growth, or through acquisition of competing firms and restructuring and specialisation of manufacturing units.

Many other factors will have an influence on the product planning process. Thus, increasing size of the firm, increasing number of product lines, increasing frequency of changes in the product spectrum, and increasing size of projects tend to increase complexity and the need for formalisation of the product planning process. Last, but not least, the attitude of the chief executive and his key managers towards planning must be mentioned. Without wholehearted support from the top it is almost impossible to introduce a modern product planning system.

In many firms the composition of the product spectrum is a key determinant of competitive strength and economic success. Changes may have a tremendous effect for good or ill in the future. In order to survive and grow under such circumstances, it is of great importance to develop an efficient system for product planning by selecting proper models and tools.

8.1   MODELS

For analytical purposes one can distinguish between informal and formal approaches or models. In both cases one can have a more or less market-oriented approach. Increasingly will be required a multi-interest approach.

8.1.1   Informal approaches

In most firms an informal approach is used. The initiative to changes in the product spectrum comes from various places throughout the organisation (the 'bottom-up' approach). The most important sources are marketing and R & D. Ideas from marketing are usually concerned with minor improvements in existing products, whereas ideas from R & D often are of an innovative nature, e.g. new products or major improvements in existing products.

The informal approach often results in new products through chance occurrences. In many cases influential managers push pet products based more on intuition and guess work than on facts and rational reasoning.

One example of a chance occurrence is found in a firm making a variety of metal products. One of the most important product lines is fishing hooks. After several years of declining sales, top management decided to find a new product which could help to improve profit. A retired sales manager was hired for this purpose. During a conference on fisheries he happened to meet the owner of a fishing boat who had invented equipment which represented a certain degree of automation of line fishing. Top management got interested and the matter was investigated by representatives of the firm. As none of them had experience from professional fishing, they had to rely on the information provided by the inventor. Based on this an agreement was made giving the firm the right to further develop and exploit the invention.

Another example of chance occurrences is found in a shipbuilding company. Here top management recognised the opportunities created by gas and oil found in the North Sea. In order to enter the oil business, several engineers were sent to USA to study offshore technology. The first practical result was a contract for a drilling rig made after American specifications. At that time the firm had no plans for development of its own rigs. However, shortly after the delivery, the firm hired a marine engineer with several years of offshore experience. This turned out to be an event of significant importance. The engineer suggested that the firm should develop a rig that could better satisfy the needs in the North Sea where there is an extremely hostile environment. The proposal was turned down by top management who felt that the firm did not have the necessary resources for developing and finding a market for a rig of its own design. However, the engineer did not give up. His immediate supervisor gave him support, and thus he was able to develop his idea further, in part during working hours, and in part during his spare time. He finally succeeded in developing a new design that appeared to meet the strict requirements for North Sea operations.

When a shipowner declared interest in the project, top management changed attitude and took responsibility for further development. The result was very satisfactory, and the rig has been the most sold of its kind in the world. This success appears to be more a matter of good luck than the application of purposeful product planning. Thus, the firm happened to hire a very able engineer, who happened to have not only know-how, but also enough drive to go ahead and break through administrative barriers. It was a matter of good luck that the firm was approached by a shipowner who wanted to enter the drilling business at the time when the project had reached such a stage that it could be properly evaluated.

In firms characterised by the informal approach, ideas and proposals are often evaluated by overall judgement. Specific evaluation criteria may also be used. Some strategic thinking may be involved, particularly in cases where one or several members of top management participate in the process. However, in such cases the strategic evaluation is usually of an inactive nature, i.e. one does not accept proposals which are considered to be in conflict with corporate objectives and strategies.

An advantage of the bottom-up model is the stimulating effect it has upon initiative and creative behaviour. A disadvantage is the difficulties involved in utilising new business opportunities.

Most informal approaches are of a decentralised nature. However, there are exceptions. Most of them are found in small firms where the chief executive, usually the owner, makes all decisions. An interesting example is a producer of sophisticated electronic equipment for medical purposes. The firm has no formal planning procedure, but the highly inventive owner actively searches for new market opportunities through extensive contacts with present and potential users. He spends more than 100 days per year travelling around the world visiting hospitals and medical exhibitions. He has established a reputation as a competent problem solver, and those having problems know that they can discuss them openly with him. Being head of the firm gives him a big advantage, as this opens the doors to chief decision makers in hospitals and gives him easy access to the medical staff. In this way he gets useful information about problems and needs that helps him initiate new projects.

8.1.2 Formal approaches

A formal approach is usually characterised by a high degree of centralisation (the 'top-down' approach). An example of a rather elaborate model, developed for a high technology company which pays great attention to R & D is shown in *Figure 8.2*. Here product planning is part of an integrated planning system. The first part of the model is of a similar nature as the models for formulation of strategy as depicted in *Figures 7.3* and *7.4*.

The R & D strategy will largely be derived from corporate strategy related to improvements, innovations, expansions, and diversifications. Thereby areas of major interest will be indicated. Great attention should also be given to societal needs when formulating R & D strategy. It appears that one has now reached a stage where product innovation activities will be influenced as much if not more by societal as by technological considerations. Increasingly one will have to study social trends, identify societal needs, and adapt the activities of the firm to them. There is a large number of unfulfilled needs at the local, national and global level related to areas such as transportation, communication, occupational health and safety, quality of working life, medical care, education, leisure time, resource depletion, energy conservation, environmental protection, etc. Greater sensitivity to such needs may open up new opportunities of an innovative nature.

In addition to relevant product areas, R & D strategy will be influenced by the degree of innovativeness. To a certain extent this will be indicated through corporate strategy. However, one may go somewhat deeper into the matter by analysing various product groups in terms of the alternatives indicated in *Figure 7.5*,

Corporate strategy and the strategy selected for R & D will give a solid basis for product planning. This may result in withdrawal of existing products, and research programmes related to new and improved products. Each programme is confined to one or several user groups. Within each programme projects are initiated through internal and

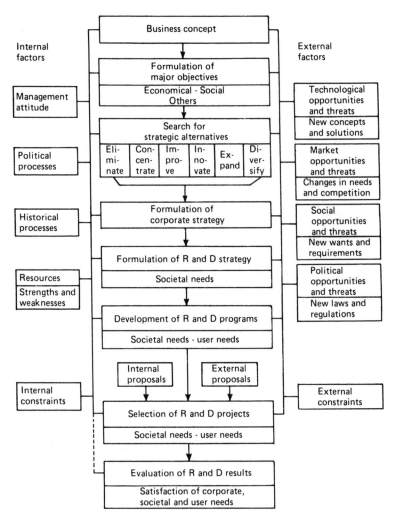

Figure 8.2. Integrated product planning model for descriptive and prescriptive analysis of activities at strategic and tactic levels

external proposals.

As indicated in *Figure 8.2*, attention should be given throughout the entire planning process to external factors such as technological, market, social, and political opportunities and threats, as well as to external constraints, e.g. difficulties in providing energy, key materials, etc.

Internal factors such as strengths and weaknesses of the firm as well as constraints in terms of rules and regulations, etc. will play an important role during the various stages. Further, management attitude, political processes, and historical process, will influence the procedure as indicated.

A somewhat different approach is found at a large producer of wire products. Originally new product lines were initiated through a rather informal approach; somebody happened to discover an opportunity or to get an idea which was evaluated and eventually realised. As the need for new products became stronger, a formalised approach was adopted by organising a special department for new product planning. The first task was to undertake an elaborate study and develop a list of possible business areas, each with an expected annual growth of at least 10%. These areas were then evaluated by work groups using criteria derived from business concept, corporate strategy, and capability in R & D, manufacturing, marketing, and finance. After two years of intensive studies 10 business areas have been identified as promising. An example of such an area is ocean technology comprising sea bottom mining, offshore oil and gas production, aqua-cultures, and coastal protection. The ten business areas are continuously surveyed in order to find new product opportunities. So far three product areas have been selected and given top priority; one is aqua-cultures. The further stages vary from case to case, but basically the planning procedure involves:

problem definition by identification of problems and needs

need research through literature studies, visits to trade fairs and contact with experts

need assessment by interviewing of users and producers of equipment

R & D by central R & D department

prototype testing in cooperation with users.

Based on information from the five stages, top management decides whether the project shall be continued, postponed or stopped. The remaining stages are:

engineering, including detailed design of products and processes

market testing, in cooperation with a group of users

market introduction, in one or several key markets.

An advantage of the formal approach is the possibility it offers for harmonising the R & D effort with corporate objectives and strategies. In a rapidly changing and highly competitive environment this is a strong argument for formalisation of the planning process. In itself the process has a value by developing attitudes and behaviour that will facilitate change.

8.1.3   Combined approaches

Both the informal and the formal approach have advantages and disadvantages. In many cases the optimal solution will be a combination
where local staff is stimulated to generate ideas and make proposals
within a formal planning system that reflects corporate strategy. The
value of such an approach can be increased by giving marketers, technologists and other interested persons opportunity to be trained in idea
generation methods, and by developing an organisational climate that
promotes creativity. Particular attention should be given to highly
creative engineers who may be hampered in their creative behaviour
through the formal approach with its bureaucratic procedures. However,
such engineers are an important resource and can make substantial
contributions of an innovative nature if they are given freedom and
stimulated to use their talents. This requires that one accepts their lack
of capability to follow rules and procedures and shows understanding
for the eccentric form of behaviour that many of them demonstrate.
If one is willing to support them, there are several ways of doing this.

One approach, suggested by Rabinov[3], is to apply the concept of
'illegal' or 'smuggled' research (also called 'moonlighting'), i.e. projects
which do not follow the formal approval procedure. This approach may
put the R & D supervisor in a rather delicate situation. However, as
long as the intention is sound, he should learn to know when to look
the other way and allow for 'sanctioned' but not approved projects
(see also pages 67–68).

A legal approach for supporting gifted engineers, used by Buzy[4], is
to allocate a certain amount of money for individual projects. In small
and medium-sized companies the president himself or a key manager
may distribute the money. In large organisations the president appoints
specific contactmen for the same purpose. When an engineer comes up
with a new idea he has only to convince the local contactman of its
value. He will then get money to carry out a feasibility study within an
agreed time. An arrangement is made with his boss so he can continue
his regular job while working on the idea. If he needs assistance from
other departments, he may get funds from a special source. He may also
be temporarily transferred to another unit, e.g. the central R & D
department, in order to work on his idea. When he has completed the
task, he returns to his old job.

A third approach is to give the engineer opportunity to spend a
certain time working on projects selected by himself. Some firms have
obtained good results in this way. Others have negative experiences,
perhaps because the engineer often gets time for his own project only
after he has finished other tasks.

8.1.4 Market-oriented approaches

The product planning approaches presented above have focused upon the degree of formalisation. Another important dimension, as indicated in *Figure 8.3*, is the orientation of key participants in the product innovation processes. In many firms there is a strong technology

Figure 8.3. Orientation to product innovation

orientation. In such situations the focus is upon technology — do we have enough technological know-how to develop the product? Can we get the necessary materials and components? Are we able to manufacture the product in an efficient manner? Such an attitude is not necessarily bad. As indicated earlier (page 23), many basic innovations have been initiated by the 'technology push'. However, as reported by Holt[5] several empirical studies have demonstrated that most successful product innovations are initiated by the 'need pull', and that a market orientated attitude is important for good results. In such situations it is a practical and economical question whether the technology should be developed inside the firm or acquired from the outside. The key problem is related to the users and their needs. This is actually the essence of the *market concept*. According to Kelly and Lazer[6], it means that the firm focuses its attention upon the market and actively searches for new opportunities and translates them into profitable products, that market potential rather than technological resources guide corporate planning and action, that the system for product planning and marketing is designed to satisfy user needs, and that there is continous evaluation and reshaping of the product in order to meet changing needs more effectively.

In a market-oriented approach an effective product planning procedure should match user needs with corporate capabilities. An example of such a procedure is indicated by Ward[7]. He suggests a market-oriented approach where the first stages include:

planning; determination of strengths and weaknesses; definition of selection criteria consistent with the company's resources and experience; definition of search areas; identification of potential product classes and markets

exploration; identification of emerging or unsatisfied needs, checking of probable demand, recording of parallel developments by competitors, and analysis of attractive product-market sectors

product search; searching systematically for product opportunities which might be introduced under license, by joint venture, by continous subcontracting, by creative imitation, or by independent development

evaluation of product opportunities; screening and ranking of opportunities with reference to competitive activity, standard codes, and potential hazards, through a procedure ranging from coarse screening to in-depth research.

The remaining stages are concerned with planning and implementation of manufacturing and marketing operations.

The importance of user needs in product planning activities is illustrated in *Figure 8.4* which represents a simple integrated planning model of a general nature.

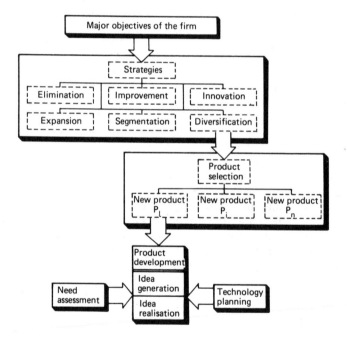

Figure 8.4. From objectives to new products

The key elements related to new products are (see also *Figures 7.7* and *7.8*):

diversification; systematic search for market opportunities and selection of new business area

product selection; systematic search and selection of products priorities within the new business area

product development; assessment of user needs and technology planning including product and manufacturing technologies.

The model shows how marketing and technological activities in product innovation processes can be integrated with corporate objectives and strategies. Successful application requires support and active participation of the chief executive. It also requires well-defined concepts at strategic and tactical levels, application of modern planning techniques, and efficient procedures.

A model illustrating the importance of assessing user needs early in the product innovation process is shown for consumer markets in *Figure 8.5*. Based on a study of the existing situation with respect to

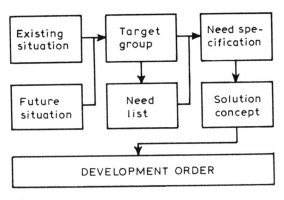

Figure 8.5 User-oriented model of idea generation (consumer products)

competing products, need satisfaction, markets, technologies, etc., and future developments in the environment and in the business area concerned, are determined *target groups*, i.e. those groups that are expected to be key users. For these groups are determined requirements, wants and wishes by means of relevant need assessment methods. The need list thus created is transformed into a need specification by proper methods and criteria. This specification is an important part of the development order.

The consumer market may be segmented into target groups by different criteria. So far *demographic data*, in some cases combined with *geographic data*, have been most commonly used. The market is then divided according to socio-economic income groups. As target groups, two-children families in the high income bracket may be selected.

For many products it appears that their purchases have more relationship to interests and attitudes than to socio-economic status. Therefore *lifestyle* has become increasingly important as a basis for market segmentation.

According to Drucker[8], it appears that the traditional segmentation criteria will now be complemented by *population dynamics*. There are growing groups of older people, of highly educated, two-income families, of part-time employees, etc., who have special needs. As population changes may have a profound impact on buying behaviour, this should be taken into account when determining target groups.

When considering segmentation for institutional markets one can, as suggested by Webster[1], distinguish between three different situations

undifferentiated: no purposeful effort is made to segment the market;
differentiated: distinctive marketing approaches are used for two or more segments;
concentrated: the whole marketing effort is focused upon one carefully defined segment, usually associated with high quality and high price.

For the segmentation, Webster indicates a two-stage approach. First is undertaken a macrosegmentation of the market, for example according to company size, rate of product usage, geographic location, industrial classification (type of product), organisation structure (centralised/decentralised), or new versus repeat purchase. If the segments thus defined do not satisfactorily explain differences in buying behaviour, a microsegmentation may be undertaken. As a basis the behavioural characteristics of the buying centre and its members are used. As examples, position in authority of the firm (e.g. opinion leader), personality (orientation) of those involved, buyer's perceived importance of purchase, attitudes towards venders, decision rules, etc. can be mentioned.

By determining target groups by means of market segmentation one is able to apply a selective marketing approach. This should provide the best match between company capabilities and market opportunities in terms of problems and needs of users.

8.1.5   The multi-interest concept

Proper application of the market concept can be a powerful guide to product innovation planning. However, uncritical use of the concept may have negative side effects such as pollution of the environment, unsafe working conditions, etc. In principle, the need of all stakeholders should be taken into consideration as indicated in *Figure 8.6*.

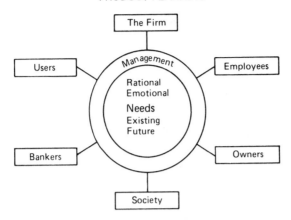

Figure 8.6 The multi-interest concept.

The weight that should be given to the needs of the various groups will depend on the situation, the power of the groups concerned, and the attitudes of those involved in planning and decision making. Political and social trends indicate that more attention should be given to human beings and their needs, whether they are users, employees or citizens. A value concept should be used where not only product functions and costs are considered; one should also take into account societal benefits such as better quality of life, and negative consequences such as unemployment, work frustrations, etc. This is a great challenge to all participants in product innovation processes. As indicated in *Figure 8.7*, it is not enough to focus upon technical and economical aspects. Profitable products are still key objectives, but they must be developed in such a way that they also are socially acceptable.

> TECHNOLOGICALLY FEASIBLE
>
> ECONOMICAL PROFITABLE
>
> SOCIALLY ACCEPTABLE

Figure 8.7. Key criteria for planning and decision making

8.2 METHODS

Successful product planning requires that those involved are provided with and master proper tools. Four of these are shown in *Figure 8.8*. In addition attention is drawn to several tools already presented:

23.1	Product proposal form
23.2	Product council
23.3	Development specification
23.4	Product calender

Figure 8.8. Tools for product planning

analysis of current product lines; portfolio analysis and performance criteria (see tools 21.3, 21.4 and 21.6)

search for new product lines; diversification study (see tools 22.1 – 22.3)

selection of product line; project selection techniques (see tool 6.1)

generation and selection of product ideas; creativity and project selection techniques (see tools 4.3–4.9, 6.1 and 11.6)

need assessment; intelligence-need related (see tools 1.1–1.6)

technological planning; intelligence-technology related (see tools 2.1–2.4 and 5.2–5.3)

evaluation of ideas and project formulation; preliminary study (see tools 5.1, 5.4, 5.5 and 6.1–6.4)

withdrawal of products; elimination analysis (see tools 20.1–20.4).

REFERENCES

1. Webster, F.E., *Industrial Marketing Strategy*, 279, John Wiley, New York (1979)
2. Holt, K., Geschka, H. and Peterlongo, G., *Need Assessment — a Key to User Oriented Product Innovation*, John Wiley, Chichester (1984).
3. Rabinow, J., in Wolff, M.F., 'Managing the creative engineer', *IEEE Spectrum*, 2–57, August (1977)
4. 'Fred Bucy of TE Speech of managing innovation', *Electronic Design*, 108–110, September (1977)
5. Holt, K., 'Generating creativity, ideas and inventions — information and needs analysis in idea generation', *Research Management*, 24–27, May (1975)
6. Kelly, E. and Lazer, W., *Managerial Marketing, Perspectives and Viewpoints*, 508, Irwin, Homewood (1973)
7. Ward, E.P., 'Planning for technological innovation — developing the necessary nerve', *Long Range Planning*, **14**, April, 59–71 (1981)
8. Drucker, P.F., *Managing in Turbulent Times*, 239, Heineman, London (1980)

9. Organisation

A new product represents a coupling between a user need and a technology. In the ideal situation one person has sufficient capacity and knowledge in both areas to make the coupling. This situation is seldom found in practice. Usually several people with different backgrounds from various departments participate in the process. This creates an organisational problem. The matter is further complicated because usually many of those who participate in the product innovation process are, at the same time, engaged in projects or activities related to the improvement, manufacturing and marketing of existing products.

The development of an efficient organisation for product innovation activities requires great effort; the task is not less than when developing a new product. Actually, the work involved is so demanding that it should be given strong top management support and planned and organised as a project. This requires knowledge about relevant models and methods.

9.1   MODELS

The development of an organisation for product innovation activities should, according to Holt[1], be based on participation and on a flexible modular system which can be changed easily and developed further when new needs and requirements occur.

9.1.1   Basic approach

The basic approach recommended consists of seven steps as indicated in *Figure 9.1*. However, in actual practice a project can seldom be planned and implemented by following step-by-step such an orderly procedure. Particularly during the first steps, one has to jump back and forth, collect and analyse more facts, make new conclusions, etc.

Step 1. Preparation. Evaluation of the need for product innovations and their importance. Timing of changes. Determination of those to be involved in the study and their roles. Provision of resources. Planning and organisation of the project. Provision of theoretical support in terms of relevant models and methods.

Step 2. Situational analysis. Determination and analysis of the factors which have an influence upon the organisation of the product innovation process.

Step 3. Problem definition. Clarification of strategic and operational requirements. Division of the project into subsystems. Determination of priorities.

Step 4. Integration. Development of a flexible core module for coordination of those who participate in product innovation activities.

Step 5. Structural design. Evaluation and implementation of possible changes in the basic organisation structure of the firm as well as considerations related to the use of a separate subsidiary for product innovation activities.

Step 6. Generation of ideas. Identification and evaluation of possible alternatives for organisation of need assessment, idea conception, idea evaluation, and project formulation. Study of consequences, and selection of solution.

Step 7. Realisation of ideas. Identification and evaluation of alternative models for the organisation of product innovation projects. Study of consequences and selection of solutions.

Figure 9.1 Model of the basic approach for analysis and design of an organisation for product innovation activities

9.1.2   Organisational modules

Ideally, the organisation of the firm should be analysed and developed as an entity. However, this is a time-consuming process which requires a considerable amount of resources. One may therefore have to limit the study to a part of the whole system. For this purpose it can be divided into four subsystems or modules as shown in *Figure 9.2*.

The sequence of the modules should be adapted to the needs of the specific situation. However, if there are no strong preferences, it is recommended that one starts with the integration module, as an effective integration of product innovation activities is of utmost importance for the final result. When one has found a satisfactory solution for the integration module by studying relevant alternatives based on various combinations of integration devices, one has a good basis for the

(1) *Integration*; in addition to activities for stimulation of self-coordination, one should consider establishing a separate unit for coordination purposes. When needed, this unit may be expanded with more staff or supplemented with other coordination devices such as formal procedures for processing of projects, transfer of personnel between various stages of the innovation process, and the use of permanent or *ad-hoc* committees

(2) **Structural design**; the structural module should be designed with the aim of obtaining an optimal solution with regard to requirements from current and innovative activities. In addition to the development of appropriate departments, one must determine the degree of centralisation and formalisation. One should also investigate advantages and disadvantages of allocating product innovation activities to a separate subsidiary

(3) **Idea generation**; this module should be based on appropriate methods for need assessment, idea conception, idea evaluation, and project formulation. The major responsibility for these activities may be delegated to marketing, R & D or a special unit for coordination of product innovation activities. Special attention must be given to provision of an organisational climate that stimulates the creative behaviour

(4) **Idea realisation**; the module for realisation of ideas includes policies concerning choice between internal and external resources for development and exploitation of the technology, and activities related to internal projects. An important task is to clarify to what extent the basic structure, the matrix organisation and the independent project organisation should be used for processing of projects

Figure 9.2 Model of organisational modules

analysis of the other modules. If practicable, one should investigate the possibility of organising and staffing the integration unit before proceeding with the other modules. This unit will thereby be able to participate actively in the remaining stages.

9.1.3   Structural alternatives

Product innovation activities can be performed within a permanent or temporary structure. A model showing the major structural alternatives and their subdivisions into activities, within permanent structures, is shown in *Figure 9.3*. At one extreme, innovative activities are performed within the functional departments, whereas at the other, they are performed by a separate innovation firm. In general, the degree of

Function-oriented	Pure functional organisation
	Functional organisation with subdivision of major departments according to products
	Functional organisation with integration of two major functions, e.g., marketing and development
Product-oriented	Partly autonomous product divisions supported by functional staff-departments
	Autonomous product divisions
	Autonomous product divisions with central R & D
	Holding company with operating subsidiaries
Innovation-oriented	Autonomous product divisions with divisional innovation units
	New unit (division, group, 'green-house') for new product line
	Autonomous product divisions supported by a corporate innovation department
	Bimodal structure based on separate branches for current and innovative activities
	Innovation firm organised as subsidiary of the mother firm

Figure 9.3 Model of product innovation activities in the basic structure

formalisation of innovative activities decreases as one moves from the one extreme to the other.

There are strong arguments in favour of separating innovative and current activities. They not only represent different organisational cultures with regard to orientation towards time and risk, but they also require a different organisational climate. Radosevick[2] characterises these cultures in terms of several attributes listed in *Figure 9.4*. Although one may not agree 100% with all the statements, the figure indicates that a climate, conducive to efficiency in current operations, will have a negative effect on innovative activities.

In firms with a product-oriented structure, product innovation activities may be more or less decentralised by being performed at corporate, divisional or plant levels. The highest degree of *decentralisation* is represented by the holding company, which has great flexibility in adapting to change by delegating initiative and independent

Attribute	Innovative units	Operating units
(1) Management problem-solving orientation	External, oriented to the environment, long-range time horizons	Internal, short-range time horizons
(2) Activity characteristics	Unique, creative, self-described and self-directed	Repetitive programmable, described by formal job descriptions
(3) Resource inputs	Highly-trained professionals, brain-intensive	Lower-skill personnel, capital-intensive, automation of processes
(4) Reward system basis	Self-actualisation, intellectual curiosity, role autonomy	Economic, status associated with position and title
(5) Management styles	Participative, information-controlled, joint decisions	Reliance upon formal and position-based authority
(6) Decision processes	Primarily intuitive modes with some *ad hoc* analytical studies	Analysable decisions with some explicit quantitative models
(7) Risk attitudes	Take chances, tolerate failures	Control uncertainties at low levels
(8) Evaluation basis	Self and peer (professional) evaluation	Formal system with predetermined criteria
(9) Technology used	Complex, near state-of-the art, often advanced internally	Relatively simple, borrowed or converted from innovative group or from outside the firm
(10) Coordination basis	Face-to-face, two-way communication	Plans, memoranda, one-way directives

Figure 9.4 Attributes characterizing innovative units vis-à-vis operating units

action to each subsidiary. On the other hand, this model requires a large managerial staff and makes it difficult to allow for an optimal allocation of the resources of the firm.

In general, there are strong arguments in favour of a centralisation of innovative activities at a high level, but alternatives based on various degrees of decentralisation should be evaluated.

The degree of *formalisation* is an important aspect of the basic structure. The more innovative the activities of the unit, the more unpredictable, and the more organic the system should be. This means that highly innovative units should have a rather *organic* structure, whereas routine activities may be performed within a relatively *mechanistic* system.

Some characteristics of the organic management system, which was first introduced by Burns and Stalker[3], is indicated in *Figure 9.5*. The system is characterised by few management levels, competence-oriented authority, self-control, participation, joint determination of objectives, and lateral communication (see also *Figure 9.4*).

The *various stages of the product innovation process* have different requirements with regard to the organisation of the activities involved. The idea generation stage, which requires an environment that stimulates creative behaviour, should have a low degree of formalisation. The

---

The *organic system* is characterised by:

few levels and wide spans of control

little specification of authority and tasks

authority is shared between those most qualified for doing a certain task

jobs are designed according to the resources of each individual

initiative and creativity are stimulated, and independent thinking and action are valued

self-control and self-coordination are central concepts

good informal contacts within and between various groups

autocratic orders are replaced by information, advice and encouragement

recognition that knowledge is located throughout the whole organisation

objectives are jointly determined by those involved

detailed planning is largely done at lower levels

communication lines are open for all and run vertically, horizontally and laterally

---

Figure 9.5 Some attributes of the organic management system

following stages, which are concerned with realisation of accepted ideas, are usually organised as projects with schedules and budgets. The closer one comes to the completion of a project, the more predictable the activities are and the more mechanistic the organisation should be.

The *type of innovation* will also have an effect. One can distinguish between improvements of existing products and the development of new products. In firms which undertake both categories, Normann[4] recommends an organisational separation of these activities. Minor improvements of existing products can be undertaken within a relatively mechanistic structure. Major improvements have much in common with new products; they can be developed within a relatively organic structure (systematic reorientation) or within a relatively mechanistic structure (idiosyncratic reorientation). The latter alternative requires strong leadership.

By means of a thorough analysis of relevant alternatives with respect to the type of organisation, degree of centralisation, and degree of formalisation, one should be able to develop a basic structure capable of handling both current operations and innovative activities.

9.1.4   Idea generation alternatives

Some alternatives for organising idea generation activities are shown in *Figure 9.6*.

---

(1)   Idea generation unit

(2)   Centralised problem solving groups

(3)   Decentralised problem solving groups

Figure 9.6 Participants in idea generation activities

A special idea generation unit is a somewhat unusual solution. However, in firms which are highly influenced in their behaviour by the change processes, this alternative may be considered.

Centralised problem solving groups denote one or several 'innovation groups' which from time to time, e.g., once or twice per month, come together to solve problems for clients within the firm by means of creative techniques.

Decentralised problem solving groups are based on key-men in the various departments which are thoroughly trained in the use of creative techniques. When required, they organise and lead problem solving groups.

In addition to the arrangement indicated, creative behaviour may be stimulated in engineers and other employees through special approaches such as allowing a certain amount of illegal research, providing money through special procedures for individual projects, or allowing the employee to work a certain time on projects selected by himself (see page 72).

9.1.5   Idea realisation alternatives

Acceptance of a new product proposal for development represents a key point in the product innovation process. The idea generation stage is brought to an end; the idea has been converted into a project. The following stages aim at realisation of the idea, which now must be converted into a working reality. This represents a drastic change in the process with regard to activities, personnel, behaviour, resources, control and organisational requirements.

Generation of ideas is concerned with software; it is characterised by a loose, informal organisation with a minimum of control. Realisation of ideas is concerned with hardware. It requires a more structured organisation and an orderly programmed procedure with an increasing amount of control as the project approaches completion.

The size and organisation of a project will be greatly influenced by whether the technology is developed inside or outside the firm. The

---

(1) *The basic organisation;* the project is planned and implemented by moving from department to department in a prearranged sequence like the baton in a relay race

(2) *The matrix organisation;* a special group is organised under a project manager with responsibility for the project. He makes agreements with heads of functional departments, who provide the necessary resources in terms of manpower and equipment. The group is composed of part-time and full-time members who are temporarily assigned to the project

(3) *The independent project organisation;* a self-contained group is organised, consisting of full-time members with skills in marketing, development, manufacturing, finance, etc. The group is headed by an appointed project manager with full responsibility for the project, which is exposed to a minimum of control from the management of the basic organisation. The project manager is given all necessary resources for the planning and implementation of the project

---

Figure 9.7 Model of the organisation of product innovation projects

most elaborate task will occur when everything is performed within the firm. In such a situation functional departments like marketing, development, and manufacturing will be strongly involved in the product innovation process. As shown in *Figure 9.7*, there are three major alternatives for organising the activities involved.

In actual practice a combination is often used. An example of this would be a firm where most of the innovation effort, which is focused upon the improvement of existing products, is done in the basic organisation. However, the firm occasionally brings out a new product of a rather innovative nature; this is done in an independent project organisation that reports directly to the chief executive of the firm.

9.2   METHODS

Several approaches are available for those who are faced with the task of improving an existing or creating a new organisation for product innovation activities. As the theoretical foundation for these approaches is rather weak and fragmented, it is not possible to present a complete and detailed recipe. Instead, the most relevant methods are presented as checklists.

9.2.1   Planning the study

The development of a product innovation organisation is of such complexity and magnitude that it should be organised and planned as a project. The most important tools in this context are shown in *Figure 9.8* and are described in Part II.

24.1	Preparation checklist
24.2	Factor checklist
24.3	Problem definition checklist

Figure 9.8 Tools for planning of the study

9.2.2   Implementing the study

The implementation of the study concerns the development of modules for integration, structural design, idea generation, and idea realisation.

The most relevant tools are shown in *Figure 9.9* and are described in Part II.

24.4	Integration checklist
24.5	Structure checklist
24.6	Idea generation checklist
24.7	Idea realisation checklist

Figure 9.9 Tools for implementation of the study

9.2.3 Limitations

In the models and methods presented there are certain limitations. This is due to the fact that the scientific foundation of the field is rather limited. One encounters conceptual difficulties, lacks operational definitions, and is faced with methodological problems. People with technical, economic, social and practical administrative backgrounds have made contributions. Some have based their views on their own practical experience, while others have used sophisticated scientific methods. The result has been the formation of a large number of concepts, principles and theories. Some of them have attained lasting value, while others have proved to be only passing fashions. Strutz[5] gives a blunt characterisation of the situation in the following manner. 'The literature on business and organisation has as good as no works of a theoretical or practical nature that can form a basis for organisational innovations. To be sure, a comprehensive literature is found concerning the social consequences of technological innovations, but up until now there has been surprisingly little done with respect to innovations in connection with the structure of the organisation and related problems.'

This situation will not improve in the near future according to Lorsch[6]. In a discussion of the current state of research in the field of organisational design, he states 'Whatever theoretical approach is used, it is unrealistic to believe that in the life-time of any of the present researchers it will be possible to develop anything like a comprehensive theory of organisational design'.

With this situation prevailing, the various methods should be used with great care. The final result will, to a large extent, depend on the judgement of those involved.

REFERENCES

1. Holt, K., *Organization for Product Innovation*, 207, University of Trondheim, Norwegian Institute of Technology, Trondheim (1977)
2. Radosevick, H.R., 'Strategic implications for organizational design'. In Ansoff, H.I. (ed.), *From Strategic Planning to Strategic Management*, 258, Wiley, London (1976).
3. Burns, T. and Stalker, G.M., *The Management of Innovation*, 269, Tavistock, London (1961)
4. Normann, R., *Management for Growth*, 210, Wiley, Chichester (1977)
5. Strutz, H., *Wandel Industriebetrieblicher Organisationsformen*, 170, Enke, Stuttgard (1976)
6. Lorsch, J.W., 'Contingency theory and organization design: a personal odyssey'. In Kilman, R.H. *et al* (eds.), *The Management of Organizational Design, Volume I*, 296, North Holland, New York (1976)

10. Financing of Innovations

Several factors influence the result of the innovation process. Many claim that the human factor is the most important, and it is hard to argue against this view. The way people are trained and motivated, and the way the work is organised, have a tremendous impact on innovative activities. However, the human resources cannot be utilised without financial resources. Sufficient money must be allocated to the planning and implementation of the innovative projects. It is often difficult to finance such activities. This stems in part from the risk involved, and in part from lack of balance between the demand and supply of risk capital.

The determination of capital requirements and selection of financial sources is the responsibility of the financial function. As the requirements are constantly changing, financial planning and control is a continuous process. By translating long-term and short-term company plans and projects into monetary terms, and by studying the flow of cash in and out of the company, it is possible to make a forecast of the fluctuating demand. Having decided how these demands should be met, one can develop short- and long-term financial budgets. These budgets give a base for financial control which is obtained by comparing at regular intervals budgeted figures with performance as reported through accounting data. Depending on the circumstances, corrective action may take the form of issuing stocks, borrowing money, reduction of inventories, buying bonds, etc.

In a small firm the financial task is handled by the head of the firm personally; large firms have a separate financial staff for this purpose. However, this does not mean that the task can be handled by the financial people alone. Good teamwork is necessary in order to give full consideration to the technical, marketing and financial aspects of the projects.

10.1 INNOVATION PROJECTS

The most important factors that influence the financing of innovative activities are the type of project and the accompanying risk.

Table 10.1   Types of technology strategy

Strategy	Market entrance	Driving force	Technology	Focus of effort
Leadership	First	Technology	Cutting edge	R & D
Follow the leader	Second	Market	State of the art	R & D/Marketing
Me too	Late	Market	State of the art	Marketing/ manufacturing

10.1.1   Type of projects

An innovation project can be characterised by the degree of change and the newness to the company. *Table 10.1* indicates three different technological strategies. In actual practice we have a spectrum, ranging from products new to the market, based on new technology of a pioneering nature, to improvements in products based on state-of-the-art technology. For the study of financial problems it is practical to distinguish between 'Leadership', 'Follow-the-leader' and 'Me-too' strategies.

A *leadership strategy*, also referred to as 'Number one' and 'First-to-the-market' strategy, starts with the development of the technology. If successful, the result will be an incremental, or even a basic, innovation characterised by a high degree of change and newness. Often the new product represents a quantum leap in performance. One is here faced with a learning process where the start is a dream, a vision, or an intuitive sense of what must be done to reach a desired future state. The solution concept emerges through a complex, iterative and interactive process where intuition, creative thinking, research, experiments, literature studies, discussions with knowledgeable persons, etc., enter into the picture. It requires a high degree of technical effort with focus on R & D. The development specifications are loose, the development costs are high, and the development time is long. If successful, the result is usually a product based on a cutting edge technology. The competitive strength is functional performance. If accepted by the market, the product will create new needs, and even new industries.

A *follow-the-leader strategy*, also called 'Number two' and 'Second-to-the-market' strategy, is usually the result of iterative problem solving. At the start of the project one has to make assumptions that may range from pure guesses to well founded forecasts. The competitive strength is based on product differentiation, which requires assessment of rational and non-rational user needs. Small firms often concentrate their resources on a small segment of the market, called a *niche*. The product is based on state-of-the-art technology. It is improved or modified in order to better fulfil the needs of the user. A substantial part of the available resources is allocated to R & D and marketing. Great attention is given to service in connection with ordering, installation, use and maintenance of the product. Follow-the-leader products are usually market driven. The competitive strength is based on features. Such projects start by defining the problem in terms of the needs of the target group.

A *me-too strategy*, also called 'late-to-the-market', is characterised by imitation or minor improvements of existing products. It represents a low degree of change and newness. The development of the product is based on analytic problem solving. Specifications are tight, the development costs are low, and the development time is short. The major competitive strength is cost leadership. Great attention is given to cost control and cost-effective marketing and manufacturing operations, sometimes of an innovative nature. The products are based on state-of-the-art technology. Often great attention is paid to the fulfilment of emotional needs through the application of modern industrial design.

Few companies are based on leadership strategies, and in such cases entirely new products are seldom developed. Most often new products and generated, or incremental improvements in existing products made — 'product development with innovative elements'.

Many companies concentrate their resources on follow-the-leader or me-too products. Others combine two or more strategies: the majority of projects are, for example, based on state-of-the-art technology, but occasionally a 'star' is born.

10.1.2   Risk

An innovation project is associated with uncertainty — 'it takes longer than you think, and it will cost more than you estimate'. The risk, i.e. the probability of failure, depends on the type of project.

In order to assess the risk one has to analyse the project and the nature of the risk, which may be technical, commercial, financial, timing or human risk.

The *technical risk* is concerned with the functioning of the product. It stems from lack of ability to choose the right concept, to develop it with available human, physical and financial resources, and to estimate the cost and time required for completion of the project. For example, the Concorde project was estimated at the start at £175 million, but ended up costing £1200 million. During the ten-year project period, five new estimates were made, all far below actual cost. This case may be extreme, but there is a great difference between estimating the cost of a pioneering innovation and calculating the cost of a minor improvement to a traditional product. A similar situation exists for development time. The managing director of an electronics company describes the situation in this way: 'The engineer is too optimistic when he makes a proposal. I always have to multiply his time estimate by π (3.14)'.

The *commercial risk* concerns resistance from the market. It comes from lack of knowledge about the reactions of people to the product. The price may be wrong, or there may be resistance to change among users, or reactions from competitors. Negative reactions from unions and consumer groups may also influence the market acceptance of the product.

The *financial risk* comes from changes in foreign exchange rates and interest rates. A negative development may have a disastrous effect on the economy of the project.

The *timing risk* is concerned with introduction of the product in the market: too early may be bad, too late may be a disaster. It is not always possible to go as far as the engineer will in developing the technology. Production must be started as soon as the product is good enough for the market. If one attempts to remove all bugs before market introduction, a competitor may already be there. Particularly for radical innovations it is important that they are well timed and fitted to the market situation.

The *human risk* refers to the way the project is planned, evaluated and implemented. This is often done in a bad manner, particularly in small technology-driven firms aiming at basic or incremental innovations. Drucker[1] states that most of the high-tech companies are being mismanaged: 'The leaders are rather 19th-century inventors than 20th-century innovators. They tend to be infatuated with their own technology, believing that quality means what is technically sophisticated rather than what is value to the user'. This situation gives the company with a follow-the-leader strategy an opportunity; it may even take over the market. In evaluating the human risk one should take into consideration initiative and entrepreneurial drive as well as financial, technological, marketing and managerial competence. The importance of good management is demonstrated in studies by Booz, Allen and Hamilton. They show that one in 15 ideas now leads to successful new products, whereas the ratio some years ago was one in 50. This reflects how better product innovation management has reduced the risk of failure.

One must be careful in making broad generalisations about risk. The degree of risk varies greatly with the situation. A small, poorly timed improvement may be very risky, whereas the well planned introduction of a new product may be relatively safe.

The more radical and unfamiliar an innovation, the greater the uncertainty about the outcome, and the greater the risk of losing what is invested in the project. The technical risk increases with the degree of change and newness. On the other hand, if one succeeds, one may create new markets, and even new industries. For commercial risk the situation is almost the opposite: here the greatest risk is with me-too products, whereas a pioneering innovation has a relatively small commercial risk. Above all, one should not forget that it may often be even more risky not to innovate at all.

10.2 CAPITAL REQUIREMENTS

Capital is the life blood of the company — 'it takes money to make money'. There must be sufficient money to provide land, buildings, machines, tools and equipment. Such objects, also referred to as *production capital*, are used over and over again. The corresponding money value is called *fixed capital*. Money is also required for current operations. It is called *working capital* and includes payment of wages, purchase and storage of materials, maintenance of equipment, shipping and transportation of the products, advertising, etc.

Last, but not least, one needs money for innovative activities. This is often called *venture capital*. The need for such capital varies greatly. Well established firms often have a negative attitude toward innovation and are reluctant to move into new fields. As long as they achieve their major objectives, and do not feel threatened by technological or market changes, they concentrate their effort on the manufacturing, marketing and improvement of current products. On the other hand, individual inventors, entrepreneurs and managers in small firms often demonstrate a considerable amount of innovative behaviour. They are open to new ideas and are willing to take the risks involved in transforming them into new products and processes. In some cases they carry the project the whole way throughout the innovation process; in other cases they leave the exploitation to larger firms who have the financial resources and the technological and commercial capability for manufacturing and marketing industrial products in large quantities. This is demonstrated in a study by Langrish et al[3], which revealed that 102 of 158 major technological advances in British firms originated outside the exploiting company. Similar results were obtained by Mueller[4] who studied 25 major innovations in the Du Pont company.

Small and medium-sized companies often have difficulties in reaching the capital market, and many of them are hampered in their innovative attempts by lack of capital for utilisation of their ideas and inventions. Larger firms are usually in a better position, and among them there is an increasing number who work with innovative projects requiring a considerable amount of capital.

It takes several years before money invested in an innovation project is recovered, if ever. The amount of capital required at the various stages of the innovation process varies from industry to industry. It is progressively increasing as the project moves from the idea stage toward completion. The last stage, which comprises production engineering, tooling, acquisition of equipment, planning of market introduction, etc., usually represents more than 50% of the total cost of the project. Based on data from Mansfield[5] and Schoch[6] a rough yardstick can be indicated:

generation of ideas	5–20%
development of the technology	20–30%
preparation for manufacturing and marketing	50–75%

It appears that 'soft' investments, i.e. investments in competence development, R & D and new markets, are increasing. According to Falck[7], they are estimated to be about 6% of annual turnover; the same as in buildings and equipment.

In order to determine the financial requirements one can distinguish between seed capital, development capital, first stage capital, and expansion capital.

10.2.1 Seed capital

To cover expenses in connection with the evaluation of the product concept seed capital is required. This may include a feasibility study of technical, market, economic, financial and social factors. The study may also include ecological and resource factors as well as legal matters, as indicated under Method 5.1.

To demonstrate the technical feasibility, one may contact experts inside and outside the organisation. A certain amount of research, experiments and tests may also be required. The study should conclude with an estimate of the probability of technical success.

The marketing aspects refer to the problems and needs of potential users, their service requirements and what they are willing to pay. One must also study the most important competitors, their products and prices, market trends, marketing potential, expected annual sales, distribution channels, marketing costs and the probability of commercial success.

The economic aspects cover income, and costs related to R & D, equipment and tooling, market introduction, and marketing and manufacturing. Based on the flow of cash in and out of the company the profitability of the project may be estimated.

The financial aspects cover capital requirements and ways of obtaining the necessary capital.

The social aspects refer to the impact of the project on people inside and outside the company (see also Method 5.2). Closely related are studies of ecological and resource factors (see Methods 5.4 and 5.5).

The legal aspects may involve a study of patents recently issued, patents still in force and patents that have expired (see Method 5.3). Old patents that turned out not to be practical when originally granted may later have become feasible because of technological and market changes. The legal studies may also include existing and anticipated legal requirements (see Method 5.6), and studies of legal aspects in connection with the acquisition of licenses (see Method 6.3).

The need for seed capital is relatively small, usually 2-5% of total project cost, but it is often difficult to obtain such money from outside. If the project is initiated by an independent inventor, he may have to spend his own money or money borrowed from friends and acquaintances.

10.2.2 Development capital

If the result of the feasibility study is positive, the project moves into the development stage. It will often involve a considerable amount of R & D. The capital requirements vary from industry to industry, and from project to project. *Table 10.2* gives a rough guide based on data from Wilson[8] and Brauling[9].

Within industries there may also be great variations, depending on the type of project. The more complex and unknown the technology, the higher the cost will be.

10.2.3 First stage capital

The remaining part of the investment, amounting to about two-thirds of total cost, is spent on the exploitation of the invention, often called

Table 10.2 *R & D expenditure as percentage of annual sales*

Industry	Great Britain (Wilson[8])	Germany (Bräuling[9])
aerospace	21.6	30.7
electrical engineering	6.1	4.0
vehicles	1.7	2.6
metal goods	1.5	–
mechanical engineering	0.5	1.7
shipbuilding	0.5	–
chemical industry		3.9
mineral oil	–	0.1
precision and optical goods	–	2.7
textile, leather and clothing	–	0.1
all manufacturing (average)	1.8	1.5

the 'first stage'. This includes planning and acquisition of manufacturing facilities, marketing planning and launching of the product at the marketplace. The expenditures for this stage can roughly be estimated from *Table 10.3*.

Published data must be treated with care and modified according to the type of project one is faced with. The estimate depends on the accuracy of the figures used. In a first-to-the-market project with a vision-based technology, it is often hard to make an estimate at all. Here one may have to leave it with an educated guess. In some cases the best approach will be to ask what will happen if the project is not realised at all. The situation is quite different with a follow-the-leader project, and even more so with a me-too project. The more concrete the plan is, the better the precision of the estimate will be. A safety margin should be included. It is easy to underestimate not only time and cost, but also the capital required for exploitation of the project.

Table 10.3 *Exploitation expenditures as a percentage of total product cost (based on data from Grasley[10])*

Stages	Percentage of total product cost
engineering and design	10–20
preparation for manufacturing	40–60
manufacturing startup	5–15
marketing	10–15

10.2.4   Expansion capital

A successful market introduction of the product is not the same as
instant profit. It may give a much better basis for judging the profit
potential, but this may take several years to materialise. The provision
of money for this period is often called 'second stage' financing. Particularly in fast-growing companies this is a critical problem that must be
solved in a satisfactory manner in order to avoid liquidity problems.

After the product has passed the second stage, it may still be faced
with financial problems. In order to fully exploit its potential one may
have to move into new markets, expand production facilities, etc.
Provision of the necessary capital at this stage is often called 'third stage'
financing or 'bridge' financing.

10.3   CAPITAL SOURCES

There are several sources for the financing of innovations, but many
factors limit their utilisation. An investment in innovation is risky. One
does not know whether the R & D effort will result in a marketable
product or not. Nor is it possible to make a reliable prediction about
the time it will take to complete the research and market the product
successfully. In general, large well known firms are in a better bargaining position when attempting to obtain capital. They can get better
terms than small and unknown companies, which have to take what is
offered to them.

It is easier to get capital from outside in the last stages of the innovation process. Many investors expect the firm itself to provide capital for
idea generation and prototype development. Other investors are not
willing to commit themselves before the product has been introduced
and accepted in the market. It is easiest to obtain money when the
project has begun to earn a profit.

It is difficult to generalise, but Mueller[11] has attempted to make a
model of the financing of technological inventions:

research and development: money is provided by the inventor and
his friends, supplied through internal financing, or furnished by a
government fund;

market introduction: this is usually the time when venture capital
firms move in; one is here faced with the risky startup and growth
period;

growth: money is supplied by companies specialising in such financing, by commercial banks, or by investment banking firms; at this stage

a performance record has been established and the product has reached the business development stage;

consolidation: as growth continues, financing is obtained through the public by issuing shares at the stock market, through mergers or long-term loans.

In evaluating possible alternatives one should consider both the cost of capital, e.g. the interest or the dividend expected and terms of payment, and the degree of control over the company required by the suppliers of capital. In general, the more risky the investment, the more strict is the investor. Furthermore, in a tight money market it is more difficult to finance a new venture than in a period with ample supply of money.

Another factor is the willingness of the investor to wait for a return on the investment. Holland[12] claims that 'staying power' is an important characteristic to look for. Most investors hope to get a high return soon, but one should be careful with such people. Another characteristic is the ability to provide auxiliary services. Some investors can help with temporary personnel, such as accountants and real estate experts. Banks and insurance companies often use their operating staff to assist with new ventures. Other investors seek such help elsewhere, e.g. from the staff of other companies in which they have invested. An investor with good experience in the specific industry of the venture is desirable. This can speed up the evaluation of the project. In some instances the investor will want to control the board of directors. An interested, hard working and competent board can be helpful to the management of the new venture, and some investors can be useful in obtaining competent people to serve on the board.

There are two principal ways of financing innovation projects — internal financing, where money is provided from within the firm through retained earnings, and external financing, where money is provided from outside as loan or equity capital by selling stock. When using external financing, one can distinguish between traditional sources and venture capital.

10.3.1 Internal financing

By this approach money is provided from within the company. This is the most appropriate basis for financing innovations. The larger the number of uncertainties, and the more substantial they are, the more the innovation should be internally financed. This is only possible when the company makes enough profit, i.e. when the equity capital at the end of the year is larger than at the beginning. After taxes are deducted, the remaining surplus can be paid out to shareholders as dividend, or retained to cover capital requirements, for example in connection with innovations.

Large companies often have sufficient financial strength to finance innovations internally. They can take a risk on a promising project and bear the consequences if it fails. On the other hand, a number of innovative companies, many of them small, cannot afford to engage in such ventures without the provision of capital from outside. Their challenge is to find sources that are willing to provide capital for long-term investments that have high risk, but also show high profit potential.

10.3.2   Traditional sources

Here come firms or persons who may invest in innovations although this is not their main business. Included are commercial and investment banks, insurance companies, large industrial companies and private investors.

Commercial banks and insurance companies are usually reluctant to take the high risks involved in innovative ventures. This is particularly true with regard to small and unknown companies. Contrary to companies that base their activities on mass production of standard products, the small innovative companies do not have fixed assets such as buildings, machinery and inventories that can be used as collateral for loans. Their greatest resources are the know-how, intelligence and creativity of the staff, assets that are not accepted as a base for loans.

Normally, traditional loan institutions provide money for property and equipment, in the form of secured long-term debts, after the venture has proved to be a success. Several of them also finance the earlier stages of high-risk innovations. One case from the UK is described by Spruit[13]. He refers to a bank with a special unit for 'Industrial services', consisting of 8-12 men with financial and managerial background. They cooperate with a group of external consultants. The bank usually enters the innovation process when the prototype or pilot stage has been completed. In most projects engineers play a vital role. They are competent as far as technology is concerned, but often lack managerial competence and ability to push the project ahead. In such cases the bank puts in one of its consultants, part-time or full-time, to take care of managerial or other important functions. In most cases they succeed after a year or two to organise a good management team and then gradually withdraw. Normally no more than 40-45% of the funds are provided by the bank, either as long-term loans or equity capital. In addition to this, the bank tries to increase the motivation of the managers of the firm by providing private loans to them for investment in the venture. About 50 projects are handled each year. Two-thirds fall off after a preliminary investigation. The remaining are processed further and the product is introduced in the market. Although the projects go through a severe selection procedure, about 20% of them are a failure, mostly due to insufficiently prepared marketing. Among those remaining, 50% are a moderate success and 50% a substantial success. The successful projects enable the bank to get rid of its engagement by selling it to institutional investors or to the stock market. In several countries there are banks with high-technology departments that give assistance with innovative projects.

In the UK, the British Technology Group (BTG), a combination of the National Enterprise Board and the National Research Development Corporation, provides financial support for private-sector companies seeking to develop new products and processes. The usual arrangement is to contribute an agreed proportion, up to 50%, of the expenditure incurred on a specified project up to a pre-arranged sum. BTG recovers its investment through a levy on sales of the resulting product or usage of the new process. Repayments only have to be made once the new product is generating sales revenue. The levy can be structured to meet individual circumstances, but the usual arrangement is to have a two-part levy. The first stage applies until BTG has recovered its capital with interest. The second stage, usually at a lower rate, applies for a limited period; it is this part that provides BTG with a risk premium or profit element.

Another way of providing capital from outside is to issue stocks. This is difficult in the early stages of the innovation process because of the high risks involved. One may also lose control of the company by getting new persons on the board. This can be avoided by issuing preferred stock without voting right; as compensation special advantages must be offered with regard to dividends.

Small innovative but unknown firms are not able to finance new ventures by going public. However, if they have a promising idea or invention, they may get financial support from special investors. These are persons or firms who are willing to buy stock at an early stage with the expectation of getting a high return when the innovation has materialised as a success. The innovative firm may then go public and offer shares in the open market at a much higher price than in the first issue. Among potential sources for equity financing are venture capital firms, investment banks, affluent individuals, and big firms with special departments for such activities.

10.3.3   Venture capital

A venture may take many forms, but all have in common that they are concerned with the development and/or exploitation of innovations with high profit potential.

Venture capital is provided by firms that specialise in financing innovative firms that have ideas but lack the financial strength to utilise them. They are organised and operate in different forms. According to Stuart[14], several of them have direct responsibility for managing the investments of their clients, others act as agents and only establish contacts to other sources of capital. Some firms limit their activities to managing high-risk investments of a wealthy family, a group of private individuals or a corporation. Other firms deal with a broad field of investors.

Venture capital firms may provide equity capital, loans and guarantees. Many of them give help and advice, e.g. as consultants, managers or board members. One interesting approach to venture financing is the convertible debt. According to Holland[12], this is a loan that carries a negotiated interest and payment terms. It can be converted into stock at some future date. The conversion is not required for several years, since investors desire a long period to evaluate the company's progress before making the decision. Occasionally, the conversion terms are such that the price of the stock in the early years is less than in the later years, reflecting the company's anticipated increase in value as it grows. A third form of debt investment is a loan with warrants giving the investor an option to purchase stock at some future time. Under these conditions the repayment can begin sooner than with a convertible loan, since the life of the warrant is usually independent of the terms of the debt.

A venture capital firm usually provides money for exploiting the invention, i.e. after a prototype has been made. Some of them are also willing to finance a good idea and provide necessary seed capital for evaluation of its feasibility.

The investment made by a venture capital firm in a new product can ultimately be realised by making the venture 'go public', i.e. offering the shares for sale to the public, or by sale of the venture to a larger company.

Historically, the use of venture capital started in the U.S.A., where there now are more than 600 firms working in this area. Increasingly, the concept has been adopted and applied throughout the industrial world.

10.3.4 Public funds

It is often difficult to finance high-risk technological ventures through private firms. Therefore, many governments, recognising the important role of technological innovation in economic growth and social development, have provided public funds, specialising in financing innovative projects.

One of the best systems in Europe is found in *France*. The aim is to stimulate economic and social development through technological innovation within an open and competitive industrial system. According to Saint-Paul[16], the basic policy is based on the principle that public support may be required at all stages from basic research to marketing, and that public support should stimulate private initiative when this appears to be more efficient than direct state control.

Innovation is supported directly through annual allocations of funds within the framework of five-year plans to ministries and government agencies, and from them to individual inventors and to public, semi-public and private firms. A number of selective and flexible approaches for financial support is available, including the use of public contracts. The objective is to stimulate and guide the various stages of the innovation process such as basic research, exploratory research, patents and licensing, feasibility studies and pre-development, development including prototype and pilot plant operations, manufacturing preparation, and market introduction.

Some of the funds are intended to cover specific stages, others cover the whole innovation process. Indirect support of a financial nature is given through several tax regulations. Some of them are designed to stimulate research in individual firms by means of special tax rules for deduction of expenses and capital expenditures in connection with R & D. Other regulations try to stimulate cooperative research by encouraging firms to combine their research resources, or to participate in the development of technological centres.

Another example from Europe is *Norway* where the key instruments are:

the Norwegian Consultative Office for Inventors: this gives advice to independent inventors and small entrepreneurial firms. It evaluates their ideas and inventions, and may also give financial support in connection with patent application, experiments and tests. Support is given as a grant, which has to be paid back if the invention leads to a satisfactory economic result. The office also gives assistance in connection with licensing and establishment of contacts with industrial firms that may be interested in further development and exploitation of the invention.

the Norwegian Research Council for Science and Technology: this is an independent government-financed institution. Its basic objective is to promote technological research. Among the many activities of the Council are evaluation and financing of research projects of an advanced nature. Both industrial firms, as well as public and private research institutions, may apply for support which is given as grants.

the Norwegian Industrial Fund: this is a public fund which specialises in financing innovative projects in industry. The resources of the fund consist of a guarantee authority by act of Parliament, annual appropriations through the Ministry of Industry, and basic capital and drawing facilities at the Treasury. The Fund plays an important role in the promotion of technological innovation, and is therefore treated in more detail below.

According to an information brochure[17], the Fund provides financial support for the development of new and improved products and processes, and the practical utilization of the results. Other financial resources must first be exploited, and private finance must be available for a reasonable part of the project. The most common ways of support are:

guarantees of loans: to cover medium and long-term loans for financing of buildings, machinery and other fixed assets, as well as for working capital.

equity capital: this instrument is seldom used.

subordinated load capital: provided to strengthen the capital base in connection with mergers, internal structural changes, establishment of new enterprises, and organisation of subsidiaries abroad.

loans for R & D: granted to stimulate the development of new products and processes. The loans are granted without security and will be written off fully or partly if the projects fail or are not commercially viable. The loans are normally limited to 50% of the costs of the project and paid back over 5–8 years.

direct grants: provided for adjustment projects, for implementation of new technology, for projects in special sectors of the industry, for establishment of sales companies abroad and for feasibility studies regarding international investment.

contingency appropriation: provided as grants for turnaround operations in companies with financial difficulties.

In the *U.S.A.* companies with less than 500 employees can get financial support under the Small Business Innovation Research Program. It consists of three phases:

feasibility study: awards up to $50 000 for evaluation of the feasibility of an idea;
research and development: awards up to $500 000 for development based on the results of the first phase;
commercialisation: financing from other sources is required.

Non-profit organisations and foreign based firms are not eligible to receive awards.

The *Nordic* countries – Denmark, Finland, Iceland, Norway and Sweden – provide an example of international cooperation between countries. Together they have established an industrial fund for financing of research and development projects supported by two or more of the countries. The exploitation of the R & D effort has to be financed by other sources. Support is given as grants, loans or guarantees in connection with the development of new products, processes and methods. Priorities are given to areas such as environment, health, materials and transport. Support can be given to industrial firms as well as to private and public institutions.

From the examples given above it can be seen that there are considerable differences between countries with regard to public support of innovations. This has to be taken into account, particularly when engaging in projects abroad.

10.4   THE FINANCIAL PROPOSAL

When a company does not have enough resources to finance an innovation project, it must secure capital from the outside. A key document is the financial proposal.

Financial proposals often suffer from poor presentation. This can have a negative effect on the possibility of obtaining the necessary resources. Much thought should therefore be given in order to make the proposal as good as possible.

First of all, the proposal must be written with the needs of potential readers in mind. Windle[18] recommends that a draft is made and discussed with an experienced, objective outsider. This will improve the perspective and help avoiding some of the more common pitfalls. One is likely to get best help from a successful entrepreneur, a financial expert, a management consultant, or a venture capitalist. It is also important to allow enough time to raise the money. If this is neglected, one runs the risk of not getting the money when it is needed. One may even appear so disorganised that one may not get it at all. As a rough rule, one should allow at least 90 days from the time the proposal is completed to when the money is needed.

Great care should be taken to provide a correct picture of the situation based on a realistic plan. This may require a considerable amount of work. However, the financial proposal is not only an information document for providing capital. The document, or part of it, can also be used for presenting the firm to customers, suppliers, etc. Furthermore, if the firm does not have a comprehensive business plan, the writing of the financial proposal will initiate the development of such a plan and thereby contribute to a better approach for managing the firm. The proposal is therefore an important document for the innovator. It demonstrates that careful planning has been undertaken and nothing ignored.

The importance of a well written financial proposal can hardly be overestimated, but the bargaining position of the innovating firm may also be strengthened by other means. A patent is of great value, and a working prototype is superior to written descriptions and drawings. An interesting example is the Karl Krøyer Company in Denmark, which continually makes pioneering innovations, many of them of a basic nature. The owner combines a high degree of creativity with exceptional business and entrepreneurial talents. As a young man he made several inventions. In 1950 he founded his own firm after he had succeeded in inventing the first continuous process in the world for glucose production. Among his many successes are a dry process for production of paper, a white stone material for production of light asphalt, several new materials for the building industry, a new method for raising sunken ships and several new cooking utensils. Karl Krøyer has also been innovative in financing the exploitation of his inventions. As soon as he has developed and tested a satisfactory prototype or obtained a 'techno-economic' proof through pilot plant operations, he organises a separate subsidiary. This is mostly done through a 50-50 joint venture where Karl Krøyer contributes his know-how and a partner supplies the necessary financial means for commercialisation.

Several lending institutions have their own forms or checklists. However, many of them do not fit innovative projects very well. In other situations there are no forms or guidelines available, and the innovator then has to write the proposal. The formulation depends on size and type of project − 'one should not shoot sparrows with guns'. The situation is very different for a project whose purpose is to obtain technological leadership than for a minor me-too project. If successful, in the first case one may create new needs, and even new markets, and allow for development of new companies. In the latter case, one is often able to utilise existing manufacturing and marketing resources. There is also a difference between mature markets, where existing companies have many advantages such as a large customer base and well established marketing channels, and new rapidly changing markets, where new companies may have an advantage because they are small enough to move quickly.

In general, the proposal should answer the following questions: What opportunities have initiated the project? How will these opportunities be utilised? What risks are involved? What will be the consequences of the project? What is the capability of the firm to implement the project?

The proposal may take many forms, but it should normally cover the following parts:

a summary: one, maximum two pages, written as a 'mini-proposal', i.e. a concentrate of the essentials of the proposal presented in such a way that it can be read and understood as a separate document;

a table of contents: a well organised presentation of the contents divided in sections and sub-sections;

the body: key information regarding the project, normally not longer than 20–30 typewritten pages;

exhibits: information about the firm which may in some cases be included, all or in part, in the body.

The major items to be covered in the financial proposal are presented below. The outline represents a modified and expanded version of a list presented by Windle[18]. It should be used as a guide. Working with a specific project, several items may be omitted, and others may have to be added.

10.4.1 The project staff

The perhaps most important success determinant of an innovation project is the human factor. Lending institutions pay great attention to the people, i.e. the managers, the engineers, the marketers, and other key people involved in the project.

The leader should have fighting spirit, be flexible and able to respond properly to changing conditions, and recognise that it is essential to have good teamwork where the technical, marketing and financial aspects are given full consideration.

The attitude of the leader and the team toward risk is an important factor. Higson[19] states that most people are risk averse due to 'the diminishing marginal utility of wealth'. They consider risk to be bad, something to be avoided. Such people cannot be used in high-risk innovation projects.

The amount of information to be given about the participants of the project depends on how well they are known by the lending institutions. As a checklist the following questions should be useful:

how will the project be organised?
who are the key managers?
who are the other key persons related to the project?
what are their ages, skills and experience?
what are their attitudes toward risk?
how does this relate to the success requirements of the project?
what is their track record?
how successful have they previously been?
how does this relate to the success requirements?
what staff additions related to the project are planned?
when?
what qualifications are required?
what firms, institutions and persons will cooperate in the project as partners, advisors, etc.?

In presenting the staff, it should be kept in mind that a team of people, committed to the project by investing their own time and savings, is more important than a list of outstanding people who will be available only if money is provided by others.

10.4.2   Description of the project

The whole project may be described under this heading. However, it is often practical to divide the description into several sections. Whatever approach is selected, the description must be realistic. Optimism is important among the persons involved in the project, but the description should not be dominated by coloured and over-optimistic assumptions.

All aspects should be covered in the description. The following questions may serve as a useful guide for the general description of the project:

what is the business concept, i.e. the basic idea underlying the project?
what are the major objectives?
what products are involved?
what results are expected?

what distinctive competence characterises the project?
what are the technical and marketing characteristics?
what are the chief factors that will account for success?
what arrangements have been made for exploitation of the results?
when will the project be completed?
what are the major milestones?

In some cases one may find it practical to include a short description of the most important marketing, technical and financial factors under the general description. In other cases one may prefer to have such information in separate sections.

10.4.3   Market information

Marketing has a pivotal influence on the success of the product. Both strategic and operational variables should be carefully evaluated and presented. Potential investors may be interested in:

who will be the major customers?
what markets are involved at home and abroad?
how big are they now? in five years? in ten years?
what are their chief characteristics?
what will be the major applications of the product?
what market segments will be penetrated?

For each segment, and for the company as a whole, indicate:

what are expected sales in physical units? in money?
what are the estimated sales figures for major customers? major applications?
what is the expected profitability of each product? for each major application?
what competition can be expected?
who are the major competitors?
can new competitors be expected in the near future?
what is the position of the firm in relation to competitors?
how will the competition be for each product?
how do the products objectively compare with competing products? through the eyes of the customers?

For each major application indicate:

what are the user needs?
what are current ways of fulfilling these needs?
what are the buying habits of users?
what are the advantages of using the new product considering user economics (savings per year, return on investment, internal rate of return, pay-back) and other impacts (acquisition of equipment, change in methods, change in work habits, etc.)?

Other questions that may be considered are:

have potential users been approached?
have they been exposed to a concept test?
have they seen drawings of the product?
have they tested a prototype?
what were their reactions?
what is the marketing strategy?
how will the expected market shares be obtained?
what are the plans for distribution? promotion? pricing? sales appeals? priorities among segments, applications and marketing activities?
how will prospective customers be identified?
how will it be decided which customers to contact and in what order?
what will be the level of sales effort (e.g. the number of sales persons?)
what will be the efficiency (e.g. how many calls per sales person?)
how long will each of these activities take in man-days? in elapsed time?
what will be the order size?
what evidence is available to back up the answers to the estimates above?
how much money will be required for advertising, sales promotion and market introduction?

The presentation of the marketing of the project should be concluded by a time schedule for the major activities involved.

The importance of proper market information can hardly be overestimated. In most cases the failure of innovative projects can be traced back to the fact that the marketing planning had not been satisfactorily taken care of.

10.4.4   Technical information

The technology of the product is another critical factor. First-to-the-market products are based on technological leadership. They have their strength in functional capability, whereas superior performance and special features are characteristic of follow-the-leader products. For me-too products the competitive base is design and low cost; efficient manufacturing technology is important here.

In the presentation of the technology the following elements should be considered:

what is the essence of the technology?
which companies have a technology that is similar? superior?
what are the performance requirements: functions, capacity, speed of performance, output rate, accuracy, size, weight, volume, etc.?
what are the operational needs: installation, availability, safety, manoeuvrability, producibility, operational readiness, reliability, maintainability, supportability, transportability, etc.?
what are the emotional needs involved: appearance, shape, colour, status, nostalgia, etc.?
what are the environmental requirements with regard to temperature, noise, pollution, etc.?
what are the legal requirements: existing and anticipated laws and regulations in user countries?
what is the proprietary technology?
how much is patented or copyrighted?
how much can be patented or copyrighted?
how comprehensive and how effective will the patents or copyrights be?
are there additional means of protecting the technology (e.g. secrecy, speed in putting out the product)?
how will the technology change during the next five years?
how much money is required for research, development, prototype building, testing, etc.?

In addition to the technology in the product, the manufacturing processes should be covered. The following questions may be relevant:

what are the manufacturing requirements?
how will they be met?
how much will be done internally?
by what method?
how much will be done through subcontractors?
by whom?

what are the production or operating advantages?
what are the production or operating disadvantages?
what is the present capacity?
how can it be expanded?
how much will it cost?
how much money is required for manufacturing planning, land, new
and modified buildings, equipment, tooling, etc.?
how much time will be required for test runs and debugging?

The technical information should be concluded by indicating
important milestones in connection with getting the product and the
manufacturing processes ready.

10.4.5   Financial information

A third critical factor is the financing of the project. As a starting point
the following questions may be useful:

how much capital is required at the start for R & D? for marketing
planning? for manufacturing planning? for other items?
how much will be required over the next five years?
when will it be needed?
how much of the financial requirements will be covered by borrowed
capital?
what terms are asked by the firm?
what sources will be used?
when and how will the money be paid back?
what security can be offered?
what is the expected cash flow?
how is the profitability of the project? return on investment? internal
rate of return? pay-back?
what economic advantages will the project have that cannot be
expressed with figures?
what key assumptions have been made in the plans?
how good are they?
how will they influence the outlook?
has the impact of the tax system been taken into account?

The ability to meet the financial requirements is crucial. Particular
emphasis should be given to the cash flow forecast in order to avoid
liquidity problems. According to a rough rule of thumb, $1 under-
capitalisation later has to be compensated with $3. The rule may be

questioned, but it is at least a reminder of the importance of sufficient funding.

It is important to estimate the profitability of the project. This can be expressed in several ways.

The *return on investment* (ROI) is the most widely used measure of profitability. Inside the company it is used for evaluation of the performance of the company as a whole, for appraisal of divisions, and for evaluation of project proposals. An outsider, for example a lending institution or a private investor, will be interested in the development of ROI for the company over time as well as the expected ROI for the project under consideration.

In connection with the financing of new projects the return on investment can be estimated as follows:

ROI = *expected profit* / amount invested in the project

Expected profit is the difference between expected revenues and expenses. It may be estimated before or after taxes, and before or after extraordinary items, i.e. items derived from events or transactions outside the ordinary activities of the company.

The amount invested in the project refers to the cost of assets intended for continuing use such as buildings, equipment, machinery and tools.

In estimating income and cost the impact of *inflation* should be considered. A simple approach is to assume that all items are equally responsive to inflation. It is then sufficient to determine one rate and apply it equally to all cash flows. This makes the project more attractive as the expected profit is scaled up as well.

The simple scaling of all items can give a distorted picture as the prices of the various items may vary in different ways over different periods of time. Materials tend to increase first; next come wages, and then overhead. Even in periods with high inflation, prices for some items, e.g. interest on loans and depreciation, may remain relatively stable. When investment in fixed assets is replaced with new assets, the cost of capital may increase considerably. The effect of inflation on income depends on several factors, for example the strength of competition and the extent of government price control.

The *internal rate of return* (IRR) is the interest rate that makes the value of all cash flows equal to zero. In the first period the cash flow is negative; one only pays out money. After market introduction of the new product, the money starts coming back at an increasing rate if the product is successful.

The IRR can be estimated by first determining the cash flow of the project, i.e. the stream of disbursements and income over the estimated life of the product. At this stage the engineers and the marketers involved in the project have important contributions to make. Having determined the cash flow, the net present value (NPV), also called the discounted cash flow, is calculated by discounting the various items back to the present time by means of a chosen interest rate. The IRR is then determined by finding the interest rate that makes NPV equal to zero. Expressed in mathematical terms the equation is as follows:

$$\sum_{x=0}^{x=t} \frac{C_x}{(1+r)^x} = 0$$

where t is the expected life time of the product, C the annual cash flow, and r the internal rate of return. The equation cannot be solved directly: one has to do it by a trial and error process where alternative interest rates are inserted, or by applying a table or a computer.

The *pay-back period* (PB) gives a rough measure of the profitability of a project. It shows the length of time it will take to recover the initial investment in terms of R & D, physical assets, market planning, etc., by the annual cash flow of the project. The pay-back is calculated as follows:

$$PB = \frac{\text{amount invested in the project (first cost)}}{\text{annual disbursement (annual savings)}}$$

The pay-back method is simple and easy to understand. It is also valuable that it indicates the period where unexpected events will be most harmful. On the other hand, it does not give a good representation of the expected profitability of the project if the lifetime of the product is likely to be considerably higher than the pay-back period, which it often is.

10.4.6   Risk assessment

Innovative projects are associated with uncertainty and risk. The greater the newness of the product, the greater the risk. Projects based on a first-to-the-market strategy are very risky. They are more characterised by faith, vision and courage to take risk than by systematic planning and well prepared estimates.

The traditional methods of analysis of investment projects may be useful in connection with innovative activities, but not sufficient. The risk cannot be eliminated by not referring to it. On the contrary, this aspect of the financial proposal is so important that it should be treated as a special element.

Investments in the development of new projects represent great risks; only a small percentage of new ideas and inventions results in successful innovations. On the other hand, the higher the risk, the higher, usually, is the earning potential. A firm that is willing to take the risk of a pioneering innovation, and succeeds, will get a solid grip on key parts of the new business.

The possibility of assessing the risk of a project depends on how much knowledge one has concerning the factors involved. The more radical and unfamiliar the changes, the less information is available, and the greater is the risk. Thus, there is a big difference between a first-to-the-market product and a me-too product where most technological and marketing factors are known.

The risk should match the resources and the know-how of the firm. For a big firm an error may lead to wreckage; it represents a loss that may be compensated by other profitable activities. For a small firm it may be a deadly blow.

An assessment of the risk should be based on an analysis of the various risk factors (see Section 10.1.2). In addition the following questions may be asked:

what are the critical and difficult parts of the project?
what is the technical risk? the commercial risk? the financial risk? the timing risk? other risks?
what precautions have been taken to reduce the various risks?
how are the risks related to the size and nature of the project?

In projects with low technical risk, me-too projects, and to some extent second-to-the-market projects, the risk can be quantified by corrections in the cash flow forecast or by adding a risk premium to the interest rate used in the economic estimates.

For high-risk projects one operates under extreme uncertainty about the future. Nevertheless, even in such cases the decision maker should attempt to be rational. One approach is to use the pay-back criterion. If one has to make a choice between several projects, one selects the one with the shortest pay-back period.

Faced with only one project, it may be rejected if the pay-back period is longer than an arbitrarily fixed acceptance criterion, e.g. two years. By basing the decision on pay-back, one implicitly accepts that low utility is attached to uncertain outcomes, and that uncertainty increases with time, as 'it does with distance on a foggy road'. Another approach to uncertainty in high-risk projects is *sensitivity analysis*. This is basically a method in which one studies how sensitive the estimates are to changes in the assumptions.

A simple approach is to use *scenarios*. The values in the original profitability estimate for key items such as investments, life of assets, and important income and disbursements, are used as the most likely cash flow pattern. This is then replaced by new values. The study is usually limited to two new alternatives, the best and the worst case scenarios. The first is based on a positive development of the project, the second assumes a negative development. Both must have a reasonable chance of occurrence.

Another simple approach is to change each variable by the same amount, e.g. 20%, and study the impact of these changes on return on investment, internal rate of return, pay-back or other profitability indicators. For the factors having the greatest impact, one may proceed by inserting other values.

According to a similar approach, suggested by Higson[19], one first determines the critical values of the project. These are then changed to see what effect they have on the expected value of the project as a whole.

With a complex series of annual cash flows, the sensitivity analysis has to be made by trial and error. The process can be facilitated by using a computer. Higson indicates that his approach is the equivalent of 'feeling one's way on a foggy road; by repeated touches an outline is developed of what is there'. The analysis enables the firm to use as much of the estimated data as possible in a meaningful way. It splits up the problem and makes it possible for the project leader to identify those aspects that are most at risk and that should cause most concern.

The information provided by the sensitivity analysis should be presented in a form that decision makers can easily digest and use. The expected value of the project can for example be portrayed together with a sensitivity graph showing the effect of changes in the most critical items.

10.4.7 Company information

In addition to well documented information about the project it may be appropriate to present the company with its history and pertinent data regarding present situation and expected developments (see also Method 21.2, Capability analysis).

The most important *general data* would be:

name and address of the firm and its subsidiaries,
year of foundation and brief history,
type of ownership,
composition of the board and voting rules,

major stockholders with number of shares,
other stockholder groups,
amount of stock authorised and issued.

Pertinent *organisational data* would be:

organisation chart,
name, age, education and experience of the management group,
number of employees divided in groups according to jobs, departments, sex, etc.,
age, educational background and experience of the various groups.

The major *objectives and plans* may include:

the business concept,
basic economic and non-economic objectives,
corporate strategy,
long-term plans,
strategies and policies for product innovation.

The *marketing information* may comprise:

major product lines and market shares,
customer groups and applications,
sales organisation and distribution channels,
competitive situation including the most important competitors and their market shares,
the sale of major product lines over the last five years, subdivided on markets and/or customer groups.

The description of the *product development function* may cover the following items:

organisation of the product development function,
product technology in relation to state of the art and major competitors,
results over the last five years,
new products developed,
products that have been improved,
current and planned projects for new and improved products.

The description of the *manufacturing function* may include:

type of manufacturing processes and layout,

level of manufacturing technology in relation to state of the art and major competitors.

The *financial information* about the company may include:

system for financial planning and control,
balance sheets and profit and loss statements for the last five years,
estimates of balance and income (profit and loss) for the next three years (see Methods 25.1 and 25.2),
trends of financial ratios (see Method 25.3).

The *outlook for the company* may cover:

threats and opportunities,
expected results with regard to markets, technology and financial results.

In connection with the financial statements one should recognise that there are many ways of preparing them. There is a big difference between a small company working for the home market and a large international company with subsidiaries all around the world. The form of the statements depends on laws and regulations, international and national recommendations and standards, and company practice.

One illustration is a large European company operating worldwide. The parent company and each subsidiary prepare separate financial statements. In addition a consolidated statement is prepared for the whole group. In its annual report the company gives due consideration to the recommendations given in the *Declaration and Decisions on International Investment and Multinational Enterprises* of the Organization for Economic Cooperation and Development (OECD). The company also follows the guidelines relative to multinational companies and the labour market developed by the International Labor Organization (ILO), and the United Nations organisation dealing with labour matters. The same prices established for sales to external customers are applied in intercompany sales, except that consideration is given to the absence of certain costs in intercompany transactions.

The consolidated financial statements are prepared in accordance with accounting principles generally accepted in the home country. These principles differ in important respects from accounting principles generally accepted in the United States. One example is the evaluation of assets. In its statements the company values plant and equipment at an amount in excess of cost. This procedure, under certain circumstances, is allowed according to accounting practice in several European countries. However, accounting principles generally accepted in the

United States do not permit the re-evaluation of assets in the primary financial statements.

The emphasis that should be given to the various points depends on the needs of the lending institutions and the possibility of providing the necessary data. The preparation of balance sheets, income statements, as well as cash flow statements, trends of financial ratios, budgets and financial forecasts can be facilitated by use of a *spreadsheet*, also called a worksheet. According to Schware and Trembour[20], a spreadsheet program together with a database can be used for producing 'what if', 'where if' and 'when if' scenarios. By changing certain assumptions, or adding new variables, one can construct alternative business futures.

The most well known spreadsheets are integrated in an electronic package that also contains database, graphics and a limited word processing capability to complement the other programs.

In a spreadsheet, the place where a row and a column meet is called a cell. One can put numbers, text or instructions in each cell. By means of instructions, one can assign spreadsheets to do cost accounting, consolidation accounting, cash management, financial forecasts, etc. Just by pressing a few keys on the computer one gets a five-year cash-flow analysis, a balance sheet, and a profit and loss statement.

The spreadsheet represents a simple *expert system*, i.e. a computer program that has the ability to reason, manipulate data, and solve complex problems similar to the human expert. As the systems gradually improve, they will be able to provide human expertise at low cost. Thereby small companies will have access to the same expertise as their larger competitors by buying the computer program rather than hiring a highly paid human expert. The ultimate objective is to have the expert system learn from experience and produce new rules and approaches – 'hopefully, this is what most people do'.

REFERENCES

1. Drucker, P., *Innovation and Entrepreneurship*, 277, Harper & Row, New York (1986)
2. Booz, Allen, and Hamilton, *New Product Management in the 1980s*, Booz, Allen and Hamilton, 24, New York (1982)
3. Langrish, J., *et al.*, *Wealth from Knowledge*, 477, MacMillan, Edinburgh (1972)
4. Mueller, F.W., 'The origin of the basic inventions underlying Du Pont's major product and process innovations 1920 to 1950'. In Nelson, R.R. (ed.), *The Rate and Direction of Inventive Activity: Economic and Social Factors*, 323, Princeton University Press, Princeton (1962)
5. Mansfield, E., *Research and Innovation in the Modern Corporation*, 239, MacMillan, London (1972)

6. Schoch, G., *Innovatie Processen in de Nederlandse Industrie*, TNO, 19, Delft (1972)
7. Falck, R., 'Rekordår i egenkapital', *Norges Industri*, No.2. 12–13 (1987)
8. Wilson, G.H., 'Financial assessment and control'. In Bishop, T. (ed.) *Management of Innovation*, 36, London (1974)
9. Braüling, A., *et al.*, *Toward an Assessment of Government Measures to Promote Technical Change in Industry*, 116, Institut für Systemtechnik und Innovationsforschung, Karlsruhe (1976)
10. Grasley, R.H., *The Availability of Risk Capital for Technological Innovation and Invention in Canada*, 80, Ottawa (1975)
11. Mueller, R.K., *The Innovation Ethic*, 226, American Management Association, New York (1971)
12. Holland, D.J., 'Financial deals for private funds'. In Putt, W.D. (ed.), *How to Start your Own Business*, 259, M.I.T. Press, Cambridge, Mass. (1974)
13. Spruit, J.W., *Financing for Innovation*, 130, Proceedings from 6th TNO Conference 'Organization for Technological Innovation', TNO, Rotterdam (1973)
14. Stuart, J.J., 'Sources of financing'. In Putt, W.D. (ed.), *How to Start your Own Business*, 259, M.I.T. Press, Cambridge, Mass. (1974)
15. Gibbsons, M., and Watkins, D.S., 'Innovation and the small firm', *R & D Management*, No. 1, 10–13 (1970)
16. Saint-Paul, R., *French Government Policy in Favour of Innovation*, 130, Proceedings from 6th TNO Conference, 'Organization for Technological Innovation', TNO, Rotterdam (1973)
17. Industrifondet, *The Norwegian Industrial Fund*, 1, Industrifondet, Oslo (1985)
18. Windle, J.P., 'The financial proposal'. In Putt, W.D. (ed.), *How to Start your Own Business*, 259, M.I.T. Press, Cambridge, Mass. (1974)
19. Higson, C.J., *Business Finance*, 490, Butterworths, London (1986)
20. Schware, R., and Trembour, A., *All about 1-2-3*, Dilithium Press, 128, Oregon (1983)

Part II

On the following pages 96 tools for the product innovation process are presented. Then follow 17 tools covering strategy, product planning, and organisation and financing of product innovation activities.

A detailed description is given of 88 tools; the remaining are considered well known and are therefore only briefly referred to.

1. Intelligence-Need Related

1.1 NEED CONFRONTATION (ACTIVE NEED EXPERIENCE)

1.1.1 Definition

Need confrontation is a method for the systematic study of what is unsatisfactory in a user situation by actually working on site for a period of time ('observation from within').

1.1.2 Purpose

The purpose of need confrontation is to discover new needs or needs that are not satisfactorily covered by existing solutions.

1.1.3 Description

A company wanting to create a new product may apply the need confrontation approach in the following manner:

1. *Selection of appropriate subjects for study* — this involves search and selection of one or more users or user groups willing to cooperate and having situations (processes/operations) that are suitable for study.

2. *Selection of personnel* — one or more members from the staff of the company, usually from R & D, are selected for the task.

3. *Establishment of the confrontation period* — the duration of the period must be decided upon, considering the costs involved and the time needed for getting enough experience in order to make a satisfactory assessment.

4. *Reporting* — feelings, observations and relevant facts are recorded during the entire confrontation period and presented in a report.

5. *Development of specifications* — the confrontation report is discussed with those concerned and requirements or product specifications are formulated.

1.1.4   Areas of application

The application of need confrontation requires that the situation to be studied consists of such tasks that people unfamiliar with the work are able to learn and perform it within a reasonable period of time. Thus, the method is well fitted for a company that wants to develop foundry equipment, whereas a company interested in equipment for surgery may run into great difficulties in trying to apply it.

1.1.5   Comments

In areas where it can be applied, need confrontation is perhaps the best method for discovering new needs or needs that are not satisfactorily covered. However, the advantages have to be balanced against the costs of the study and the personal inconvenience to the staff, who must be away from their regular jobs during the confrontation period.

1.1.6   References

Holt 1975, RKW Geschka 1976, Geschka *et al.* 1982, Holt *et al.* 1984, Holt 1987.

1.2   USER OBSERVATION

1.2.1   Definition

User observation is a method for the systematic study of what is unsatisfactory in a user situation by observing, recording and analysing the behaviour of those involved ('observation from outside').

1.2.2   Purpose

The purpose of user observation is to discover new needs or needs that are not satisfactorily covered with existing products.

1.2.3   Description

A study of users normally involves the following steps:

1. *Selection of appropriate subjects for the study* — this involves search and selection of one or more users or user groups willing to cooperate and having situations (processes/operations) that are suitable for study.

2. *Selection of methodology* – this involves the consideration of, and selection among, various approaches such as note taking by paper and pen, still photographs, motion pictures, tape recordings, etc.

3. *Establishment of observation period* – the duration must be decided upon, considering costs of the study and the time needed to gain a representative picture of the situation.

4. *Reporting* – this includes tabulation, analysis and presentation of the data obtained.

5. *Development of specifications* – after discussing the report of the study with those concerned, requirements or product specifications are formulated.

1.2.4   Areas of application

The most common way of applying user observation is in a real situation. However, the method may also be applied in a simulated, laboratory situation. An example is a case involving development of equipment and methods for maintenance and cleaning of hospital floors. The observation was undertaken in a motion study laboratory where both a hospital corridor and a sick room were reconstructed. The activities were carried out by hospital personnel borrowed for the purpose.

Another simulation approach is the use of an audio-visual room where the activities concerned are presented on a large screen by means of still and motion pictures, supplemented by sound recordings, statements from knowledgeable persons, etc.

1.2.5   Comments

User observation is an important tool with a wide range of applications. It is perhaps the best approach for need assessment under conditions where need confrontation is not possible.

1.2.6   References

Jones 1970, Hake 1971, Holt 1975, RKW Geschka 1976, Geschka *et al.* 1982, Holt *et al.* 1984, O'Shaughnessy 1984, Holt 1987.

1.3   USER CONTACTS

1.3.1   Definition

User contacts is a method for need assessment based on the systematic collection of relevant information from users regarding a certain task or product and what they find unsatisfactory with it.

1.3.2   Purpose

The purpose is to gain information from users regarding their situation, as a basis for discovering new or unsatisfied needs.

1.3.3   Description

Need assessment by means of user contacts involves the following steps:

1. *Selection of approach* — a number of approaches may be used to gain information from users regarding their situation. The most important are:

User panels; a carefully selected group of users meet with representatives from the company, answer questions, give their opinions and discuss relevant issues.

Employment of users; the company hires people with user experience. An example would be a manufacturer of machine tools who hires operators or manufacturing engineers with practical experience in the operations involved.

Cooperation (project) with users; the company establishes contact with one or more users who assist in assessments of needs and development of the product. An example is a shipyard which cooperates with a ship-owner and develops a ship with some unique characteristics.

Dealer questioning; the company develops an appropriate method, e.g. a questionnaire, and systematically collects information from dealers. Such information may also be collected by means of telephone surveys or face-to-face interviews. Another approach is to arrange regular meetings where representatives from R & D and marketing meet with dealers in order to discuss and evaluate needs related to present and future products. One company by using this approach had developed need specifications for future products which are updated annually.

User questioning; the company develops an appropriate method, for example a mail survey, and collects information from a sample of actual or potential users.

2. *Reporting* — the material collected is analysed and presented in an appropriate form.

3. *Development of specifications* — the report is discussed with those concerned and requirements or product specifications are formulated.

1.3.4   Areas of application

Approaches based on user contacts have a wide area of application. However, most tend to be limited to the provision of information that will lead only to improvements in existing products. Possible exceptions may be the hiring of competent people with broad user experience and cooperation with users.

1.3.5 Comments

Companies that want to base their need assessment on user contacts should carefully analyse the various approaches in relation to their particular situation. Guidelines and procedures can then be developed for the approaches selected.

1.3.6 References

Kelly 1968, Jones 1970, Scheuing 1972, Holt 1975, Stone 1976, RKW Geschka 1976, Geschka *et al.* 1982, Pessimier 1982, Holt *et al.* 1984, Pahl and Beitz 1984, Hübner 1986, Holt 1987, Kinnear and Taylor 1987.

1.4 SURVEILLANCE OF COMPETITORS

1.4.1 Definition

Surveillance of competitors is a method for assessing needs by means of a systematic study of the products, the patents and the activities of competitors.

1.4.2 Purpose

The purpose of surveillance of competitors is to develop an appropriate strategy, e.g. by adopting and improving on their products, by discovering user needs that may lead to new and better products, etc.

1.4.3 Description

Surveillance of competitors involves the following steps:

1. *Selection of competitors* — a decision is made as to which of the competitors is worth monitoring.
2. *Establishment of procedures* — this involves the following elements:

Selection of persons to be involved in actual surveillance and in utilisation of the results.
Selection of subjects to be monitored, i.e. products, marketing procedures, patents, articles in journals, advertising, lectures and other types of activities.

Selection of methods for gaining information, e.g. laboratory testing of the performance characteristics of the products of competitors, market research, brainstorming for fault finding, patent surveillance, visiting exhibitions, etc. – see also Methods 2.4 and 11.6.

3. *Development of specifications* – the findings are reported to and discussed with those concerned. New strategies are formulated, and functional requirements or product specifications for new or existing products are decided upon.

1.4.4   Areas of application

The method can be used for almost any kind of product, but appears to be most useful in connection with products where there is strong competition or rapid technological change. Typical examples would include consumer goods such as equipment related to the home, leisure time and sports activities.

1.4.5   Comments

Most methods for surveillance of competitors have a rather offensive character. However, there are also approaches based on cooperation. Participation in industrial associations is quite common. There are also companies that meet once or twice per year and exchange information, e.g. in the form of 'competitors' dinners'.

1.4.6   References

Kelly 1968, Holt 1975, Stone 1976, Geschka *et al.* 1982, Pessemier 1982, Holt *et al.* 1984, Kotler 1984, O'Shaughnessy 1984, David 1986, Hübner 1986, Holt 1987.

1.5   SURVEILLANCE OF GOVERNMENT REGULATIONS

1.5.1   Definition

Surveillance of government regulations is a method for assessment of needs by a systematic study of legislation in force, current regulations, anticipated legislation and anticipated regulations.

1.5.2   Purpose

The purpose of surveilling government regulations is to avoid developing products which are or will be violating the law and to discover needs that can lead to new or improved products.

1.5.3   Description

A systematic study of government regulations consists of the following steps:

1. *Selection of subjects* — this involves determination of the areas that should be surveyed, such as labour, environmental and commercial laws, consumer regulations, building codes, etc.

2. *Selection of personnel* — this involves the selection of the persons to be involved in the surveillance and in the use of the results.

3. *Selection of sources* — among those to be considered are laws, parliamentary documents, reports from government committees, etc.

4. *Development of specifications* — the findings are discussed among those concerned and the results formulated as functional requirements or product specifications.

1.5.4   Areas of application

Most companies operate in a rapidly changing society which attempts more and more to control operations through new laws and regulations. Companies, therefore, will have to conduct systematic legal analysis in order to modify existing products and avoid new products which in one way or another can be expected to be in conflict with the law (see also Method 5.6).

However, in addition to these negative aspects, which from a company point of view may appear to be of a rather restrictive character, government regulations may also have a positive value by stimulating the development of new products. An example is a company, in the metal working industry, which has formulated a new strategy involving growth in markets created by legislation, i.e. products which can help industrial companies conform to the regulations against pollution of air, of water and by solid waste.

1.5.5   Comments

Surveillance of government regulations has so far been neglected by many companies, but in situations where more and more government control is to be expected, the matter should be given serious consideration. If necessary, cooperation with a lawyer should be established.

1.5.6   References

Spitz 1977, Geschka *et al.* 1982, Holt *et al.* 1984, Kotler 1984, David 1986, Holt 1987.

1.6   SURVEILLANCE OF MARKET SECTORS

1.6.1   Definition

Surveillance of market sectors is a method for assessment of needs by systematic study of need patterns and changes in them within selected industries or user groups.

1.6.2   Purpose

The purpose of surveying market sectors is to discover new or unsatisfactorily covered needs which can lead to new or improved products.

1.6.3   Description

Surveillance of market sectors involves the following steps:

1. *Selection of sectors* — one starts by clarifying which branches or user groups are of current or potential interest as stimuli for new or improved products.

2. *Development of procedures* — this involves the following elements:

Selection of personnel for participation in the surveillance; at least one person should be assigned to each sector.
Determination of guidelines for the surveillance, which may include literature, competing products (see also Method 1.4), trade journals, newspapers, patents, seminars, lectures, personal contacts, etc.
Methods for reporting.

3. *Development of specifications* — the information is discussed with those concerned. Requirements or tentative product specifications are then formulated.

1.6.4   Areas of application

Surveillance of market sectors can be applied by all companies. The method appears to be most relevant for dynamic sectors with rapidly changing need patterns.

1.6.5   Comments

The surveillance requires that at least one person is assigned to each sector. The best result is likely to be obtained by using personnel from the R & D department, as this would give a direct coupling between market needs and technology.

1.6.6   References

Kelly 1968.

2. Intelligence–Technology Related

2.1 SURVEILLANCE OF TECHNOLOGY

2.1.1 Definition

Surveillance of technology is a method for systematically collecting relevant information in technological areas of interest.

2.1.2 Purpose

The purpose of surveying technology is to update existing technological knowhow in order to find the best possible technical solution for the products and the processes of the company.

2.1.3 Description

A systematic surveillance of technology includes the following steps:

1. *Selection of areas to be covered* – these will, first of all, be areas related to current products and processes, but areas of potential interest may also be included.
2. *Selection of personnel* – at least one competent person from the technical staff is selected and assigned to each area.
3. *Determination of procedures* – this involves the following elements:

Guidelines for media to be used such as books, competing products (see also Method 1.4), professional journals, patents, contact with researchers and consultants, attendance at professional meetings, trade fairs, study trips, etc.
Guidelines for reporting the results of the surveillance, e.g. by means of reports, internal seminars, informal meetings, etc.

2.1.4   Areas of application

Surveillance of technology should be applied by all companies. It is of particular importance to companies that experience rapid changes in the technological foundation for their products or processes.

2.1.5   Comments

The more sophisticated methods for surveillance of technology, e.g. use of consultants, may involve considerable costs which must be evaluated against the benefits. Smaller companies may have to rely on simpler methods, but even so, with careful choice good results can be obtained.

2.1.6   References

Stone 1976, David 1986, Hübner 1986.

2.2   DEVELOPMENT OF TECHNOLOGICAL COMPETENCE

2.2.1   Definition

Development of technological competence is a method for the systematic acquisition of technological knowhow in areas of current or potential interest.

2.2.2   Purpose

The purpose of developing technological competence is to be able to handle in a satisfactory manner the technical problems that will arise in connection with the creation, development and manufacturing of new or improved products.

2.2.3   Description

The systematic development of technological competence involves the following steps:

1. *Selection of areas to be covered* — this may include current products, but is first of all related to future products. A decision at top level, concerning strategy and policies for new products, may therefore be required.
2. *Development of procedures* — this involves the following elements:

Guidelines for approaches to be used, e.g. external and internal seminars, R & D projects, hiring of competent personnel, etc.
Selection of personnel to be involved.
Guidelines for time and costs to be involved.
Guidelines for utilisation and diffusion of new knowhow within the company, e.g. by means of reports, internal seminars, etc.

2.2.4 Areas of application

Development of technological competence should be conducted by all forward looking companies that may expect radical changes in the technological foundation of present products or want to base their competitive strategy on development of products that are new for the company or the market.

2.2.5 Comments

Development of technological competence is closely related to surveillance of technology (see Method 2.1).

2.3 SURVEILLANCE OF RESOURCES

2.3.1 Definition

Surveillance of resources is a method for systematic control of major resources of current or potential interest for the company.

2.3.2 Purpose

The purpose of surveying resources is for early warning about major changes (increases or decreases) in supply, quality or price, in order to adapt the products of the company to the expected resource situation.

2.3.3 Description

Surveillance of resources involves the following steps:

1. *Selection of resources to be controlled* — for economic reasons, only the most important resources should be systematically surveyed. Among those to be considered are:

Internal resources such as R & D competence, manufacturing competence, marketing competence, management competence and financial strength (equity capital).
External resources such as energy, raw materials, parts, manpower, consulting services, contact with research organisations, manufacturing equipment, etc.

2. *Establishment of procedures* — this will include the following elements:

Selection of information sources such as consultants, trade journals, suppliers, research organisations, industrial associations, etc.
Guidelines for collection and presentation of information.
Allocation of personnel.

2.3.4   Areas of application

Surveillance of resources should be undertaken by all companies using or expecting to use resources that are or will be in short supply, or show or are expected to show great variation in quality and price. Thus, in a period of drastic and rapid changes in the supply of raw materials, it is important to follow closely the development of the most important raw materials presently used and raw materials that may be the basis for future products.

2.3.5   Comments

In the development of a procedure for surveillance of resources, the time and costs involved must be balanced against the expected benefits. This means that smaller companies will have to use relatively simple procedures.

2.3.6   References

Kelly 1968, Riggs 1981.

2.4   INDUSTRIAL ESPIONAGE

2.4.1   Definition

Industrial espionage is the acquisition of information, often of a confidential nature, concerning competitors.

2.4.2   Purpose

The purpose of industrial espionage is to maintain or increase corporate profit by developing appropriate strategies against competitors.

2.4.3   Description

Industrial espionage involves the following steps:

1. *Selection of organisations to be covered* — here one decides which organisation is worth covering.

2. *Selection of subjects* — among those to be considered are:

Corporate and financial information.
Production information.
Marketing information.
Technical information.
Legal information.

3. *Selection of methods* — among those to be considered are:

Published material and public documents such as court records.
Disclosures made by competitor's employees, and obtained without subterfuge.
Market surveys and consultant's reports.
Financial reports, and broker's research surveys.
Trade fairs, exhibits, and competitor's brochures.
Analysis of competitor's products.
Reports from salesmen and purchasing agents.
Legitimate employment interviews with people who have worked for competitors.
Camouflaged questioning and 'drawing out' of competitor's employees at technical meetings.
Direct observation under secret conditions.
False job interviews with competitor's employees (i.e. where there is no real intent to hire).
False negotiations with competitors for licence.
Hiring a professional investigator to obtain a specific piece of information.
Hiring an employee away from the competitor to get specific knowhow.
Trespassing on competitor's property.
Bribing competitor's suppliers or employees.
'Planting' an agent on competitor's payroll.
Eavesdropping on competitors (e.g. via wire tapping).
Theft of drawings, samples, documents and similar property.
Blackmail and extortion.

The methods are listed in descending order of ethics and legality. The first eight are usually considered legal and ethical.

2.4.4   Areas of application

Industrial espionage has been more widely used in the U.S.A. and Japan than in Europe, but this may be changing. It is mostly undertaken at the international level by large organisations. Both civil and military products are covered. The area of application is limited because of both the high costs and the legal and moral issues involved.

2.4.5 Comments

The purpose of listing industrial espionage as a tool is not to encourage product innovators to engage in this type of endeavour. However, one may be exposed to it and should therefore have some knowledge of the various methods in order to take precautionary countermeasures. Some principles for countering espionage are:

Protective measures must be so designed that when information is stolen the theft becomes known as quickly as possible.

Protection of information is the responsibility of the possessor, who is the best person to organise the protection of it.

Security measures should be commensurate with the threat.

Vital information should be concentrated into as small an area as possible.

No one should be given secret information unless it is necessary for their duties.

A security system is as strong as its weakest link.

All security systems should contain an element of surprise for the spy or thief.

Quality of protective measures is more important than quantity.

Security tasks are usually irreconcilable with other tasks.

2.4.6 References

Hamilton 1967, Kelly 1968, Wade 1966.

3. Forecasting

3.1 SCENARIO TECHNIQUE

3.1.1 Definition

Scenario writing is an outlining of alternative futures, including a discussion of the events which may lead to the situations depicted; thus an attempt is made to set up sequences of events which starting from the present situation show how future states might evolve step by step.

3.1.2 Purpose

Scenario writing aims at providing pictures of future developments — based on alternative sets of assumptions — that serve as a context, in which the various options open to the decision maker can be placed, so that he can determine which one is the most satisfactory overall.

3.1.3 Description

Scenario writing consists of the following steps:

1. *Choice of a language of description* — a number of sectors or descriptors is chosen, capable at least of describing an initial plausible range of variation for the field of concern (the planning cone), and within each sector factors to describe all plausible alternatives are designated.

2. *Selection of reference scenarios* — the factors and sectors are combined in a number (3–10) of schematic, skeletal configurations of future patterns, which may plausibly exist 10–30 years ahead. The selection of relevant reference scenarios from the expansion of the sector/factor array is based on the criteria of internal consistency and the aim of exploring scenarios as different as possible and thus fairly illustrative of the planning cone.

3. *Outline of scenarios* — invention of sequences of configurations, that are coherent when viewed one at a time, and that starting from the present situation relate to each other through possible events within a plausible line of development leading to a reference scenario. The description focuses attention on benchmark and branching point events and dates, possible stake holders, and potential deviations, discontinuities and innovations.

3.1.4   Areas of application

Scenario writing is used to determine and assess higher level goals and missions in different contexts; to focus discussion on and develop familiarity with the fundamental alternatives within the different sectors of a holistic, systemic view of the future; and to analyse the importance in the development of a system of certain parameters through construction of scenarios, where their values have deliberately been exaggerated.

3.1.5   Comments

Scenario writing is one of the most effective tools in lessening 'carry over' — thinking from the present and past to the future. Scenario writing forces the analyst to deal with details and dynamics which he might easily avoid treating if he restricted himself to abstract considerations.

A reasonable time limit for scenario writing depends upon the time it takes to achieve fundamental changes within the area under consideration. The total time horizon may be divided into 3—5 temporal steps, each one of less than seven years.

Scenario writing has been the method used in France in a number of studies that relate to regional development planning problems, in particular by the French Government Agency DATAR (la Délégation à l'Amenagement du Territoire et à l'Action Regionale). Pattern and Systems International (U.S.A.), a corporation specialising in contextual and policy research, has exposed the method at several seminars and worked out contextual as well as focused projections for component areas and institutions.

3.1.6   References

Kahn 1966, Jantsch 1967, Gerstenfeld 1970, Durand 1972, Gregory 1972, Rhyne 1974, Twiss 1974, RKW Geschka 1976, Geschka *et al.* 1980, Ramo 1980, Twiss and Weinshall 1980, Geschka *et al.* 1982, Holt *et al.* 1984, Kotler 1984, O'Shaughnessy 1984.

3.2   DELPHI TECHNIQUE

3.2.1   Definition

Delphi technique is a controlled succession of iterative statements with a panel of anonymous participants interacting by letters through a coordinating staff.

3.2.2   Purpose

The purpose of the method is to elicit judgement, insights and expectations from a panel of experts within a field, to organise the items (statements), and have them evaluated by the whole group, so that a shared, broader, more structured and less biased answer to a general question is assured, e.g. the future state within a given field.

3.2.3   Description

A Delphi investigation consists of the following steps:

1. *Selection of the panel* – the panel is made up of 10–1000 persons possessing relevant knowledge within the field and having different background and training, and different organisational positions within or outside the field. By asking the participants in the letters mentioned in 2 below to rate their own knowledge of the field a subpanel of an elite group might be established.

2. *Starting the iterative process* – in a letter mailed to the participants they are asked to respond with statements to a general question, e.g. to name inventions and scientific breakthroughs which appear both urgently needed and realisable within the next 10–15 years.

3. *First iterative step* – by editing the answers from step 2 a basic list of items (statements) is drawn up. (Step 2 may be omitted and the iterative process started with an already prepared list of items.) The list of items is mailed to the panel and the participants are asked to supply their judgements and/or opinions, e.g. in what time period there is a 50–50 probability that the change will occur. The answers are combined and if possible represented in quartiles and medians on a scale.

4. *Following iterative steps* – the results from the last step are mailed to the panel and the participants are asked to reconsider their previous answers, and dissenters are invited to state their reasons. In addition, the participants may be asked questions such as: How desirable is this change? What will be the consequences if it occurs? Who can do what to promote or hinder this change? Normally 2–3 iterations are performed.

3.2.4   Areas of application

Delphi technique may be used for forecasting future technological developments within a field; for forecasting future needs and requirements within a certain area; to explore the possible consequences and ramifications of a given technological development; to reach consensus on goals at the highest level in a society or an organisation, or to develop evaluation criteria at lower levels; to reveal areas of agreement and disagreement and elaborate differences of opinion within a group.

3.2.5   Comments

The quality of the results is very sensitive to the expertise of the panel members. Thus, it is of crucial significance how the sample of experts is drawn and how their answers are combined (weighted). Experience tells that most of the change in opinions/judgements occurs after the results from the first round are reported back to the participants. Subsequent rounds may produce changes if significant new information is supplied.

The magnitude of the editing process, following the first letter and every time the panel members are invited to respond with their own statements, is much larger than generally realised. Using prestructured response statements, where possible, may significantly reduce the amount of work for the coordinating staff.

3.2.6   References

Helmer 1966, Jantsch 1967, Gerstenfeld 1970, Claude and Morize 1972, Gregory 1972, Twiss 1974, Blanchard 1976, RKW Geschka 1976, Berridge 1977, Riggs 1981, Geschka *et al.* 1982, Pessemier 1982, Tushman and Moore 1982, Holt *et al.* 1984, Kotler 1984, O'Shaughnessy 1984, Pahl and Beitz 1984, Kinnear and Taylor 1987.

3.3   TREND EXTRAPOLATION TECHNIQUE

3.3.1   Definition

Trend extrapolation is a rational and explicit method for projecting past data regarding the level of functional capability that has been reached into the future — ignoring the subtle interaction or inner working of the technology-producing system as well as the concrete technical approach used.

3.3.2 *Purpose*

Trend extrapolation aims at going beyond the growth of the current technical approach to carry out a function and forecast the level of capability which will be obtained by the successor technical approach or by a series of successor technical approaches.

3.3.3 *Description*

Trend extrapolation is divided into the following steps:

1. *Selection of a parameter* – a parameter which adequately describes the level of functional capability is chosen, i.e. an objectively measurable attribute which represents the state of the art and applies to diverse technical approaches to perform the same function (e.g. passenger miles per hour, lumens per watt).

2. *Collection of historical data* – past data must be available, preferably for two times as long a period as the forecast, and internally consistent, i.e. from the same stage of the innovation process (either first commercial introduction, or first prototype, or first laboratory demonstration).

3. *Assumption of continuity* – for the growth in the level of functional capability of a specific technical approach, or for the rate of substitution of a new technical approach for a previous approach to obtain the same function, an S-shaped (logistic, Gompertz, or von Bertalanffy) curve may be fitted. For the cumulative improvement brought about by successive innovations of increasing functional capability, an exponential curve will prove to forecast the future capability, assuming a constant rate of innovation.

4. *Evaluation of results* – by comparing the logistic limit of the present approach with the projected future level of capability, the date of innovation may be forecast. Statistical confidence limits are estimated from the past data and factors which may influence the forecast are analysed.

3.3.4 *Areas of application*

Trend extrapolation is used to forecast dates of innovation and the required future level of functional capability wherever valid and relevant historical data establish a trend line and evidence cannot be produced that today is the point of discontinuity for this particular trend, i.e. where the conditions which produced past behaviour can be assumed to produce the same kind of behaviour in the future too. (This will be the case more often for trends that reflect usage by society, than trends of technical capabilities, which again change more slowly than those telling about specific technical approaches.)

3.3.5   Comments

Make sure that the chosen parameter cannot be traded off against
another parameter and that there is no time-independent upper limit
set by some fundamental physical law (e.g. maximum possible
efficiency), or use such information to improve the forecast by combining
the trade-off parameters and revising the forecast in the limiting region
where progress is affected by the imminent limit. Trend extrapolation
is included in all courses on technological forecasting and many other
business oriented courses about forecasting the future. John McHale has
collected a catalogue of world trends in his *World Facts and Trends*, 95,
MacMillan (1972).

3.3.6   References

Cheaney 1966, Jantsch 1967, Ayres 1968, Gerstenfeld 1970, Martino
1972, Gregory 1972, Gorle and Long 1973, Twiss 1974, Blanchard
1976, Berridge 1977, Ramo 1980, Twiss and Weinshall 1980, Riggs
1981, Pessemier 1982, Tushman and Moore 1982, Kotler 1984,
O'Shaughnessy 1984, David 1986, Kinnear and Taylor 1987.

3.4   RELEVANCE-TREE TECHNIQUE

3.4.1   Definition

A relevance tree is an analysis of a system or a process in terms of
causation, levels of complexity, or levels of hierarchy, that elucidates
the degree of importance of various 'inputs' to a broadly defined future
outcome or goal.

3.4.2   Purpose

The purpose of a relevance-tree analysis is to relate objectives in the
future to strategies and tactics and to define key points, through
breaking down overall performance specifications into ever finer
detail, so that when, and only when, each of the goals at one level
are met then the goals at the next higher level are met.

3.4.3   Description

The technique may be divided in the following steps:

   1. *Specification on the number of levels* — at least three levels are
necessary. Descending from the top of the structure the levels may

specify the necessary missions, tasks, approaches, systems, subsystems, functional elements and technological deficiencies (see also pp. 34–36).

2. *Decomposing the overall objective* – the number of branches descending from different elements at a level may differ and the number of branches from top to bottom of the tree may differ for different paths, but for each element the branches descending from it must be mutually exclusive and exhaustive of all the possibilities at the next lower level.

3. *Assignment of relevance numbers* – the relative need for improvement in the elements at one level – contributing to an element at the next higher level – is evaluated. These relative numbers are normalised, so that they add up to 1.0 for each element at the next higher level. Absolute relevance numbers are computed by forming the product of the relative numbers along a path from the top of the tree down to the element.

3.4.4 Areas of application

Relevance-tree analysis may be used for clarifying the requirements which must be satisfied before an objective can be met and for defining needs (goals) for each portion of a system; to evaluate alternative solutions to a problem, and thus to allocate technical effort (money, man hours, etc.) more rationally; to identify deficiencies in relation to an objective and thus improve the R & D planning by forecasting future needs and requirements within a field.

3.4.5 Comments

How a system or process is broken down depends on the purpose of the analysis. There is no single correct relevance tree, but a particular tree might be suitable for solving certain problems. However, when subdividing the elements one should try to establish a balance in the number of branches in different parts of the tree structure. Multi-criteria evaluation techniques may be used to achieve better estimates of the relevance numbers, but it increases the man hours required to use the relevance tree method several fold.

Honeywell (U.S.A.) made the first large scale application of relevance trees to numerical analysis for decision making (PATTERN: Planning Assistance through Technical Evaluation of Relevance Numbers). Battelle Institute has applied relevance trees in giving advice on strategic decisions in a number of industries and organisations.

3.4.6 References

Esch 1965, Jantsch 1967, Cetron 1969, Gerstenfeld 1970, Gregory 1972, Gorle and Long 1973, Twiss 1974, RKW Geschka 1976, Tushman and Moore 1982.

3.5   SYSTEM DYNAMICS

3.5.1   Definition

System dynamics is a predictive and descriptive tool demonstrating how the structure of complex social systems — the way the elements interact through circular, interlocking, multiloop, amplifying, and sometimes delayed relationships — influences the behaviour over time of the system.

3.5.2   Purpose

The purpose of using system dynamics is to come to a better understanding of the inherent characteristics of complex social systems and thus their dynamic, non-linear, counter-intuitive behaviour as a basis for anticipating the long term effects of decisions, policies, organisational forms, and investment choices.

3.5.3   Description

System dynamics can be divided into the following steps:

1. *Determination of system boundaries* — a choice is made at some level of aggregation of the set of dynamic system behaviours which are of interest.

2. *Construction of a causal loop diagram* — a coarse diagram is constructed, describing the mechanisms (positive and negative loops) through which the chosen behavioural characteristics are perceived to be influenced by other variables. These variables must be included in the description of the system operation and may cause a reconsideration of step 1.

3. *Transposition into a flow diagram* — when the causal diagram is redrawn in, for example, the common DYNAMO-language, it is important to distinguish between flows with a physical and an informational reference, i.e. between flows of real quantities and flows of information or functional dependencies. Furthermore, the language distinguishes between level (or state) variable — describing the condition of the system at any particular time — and rate variables — telling how fast the levels are changing. Assumptions about the boundaries and the environment of the system are expressed in constant model elements and in levels considered of no interest.

4. *Quantification of the model* — equations specifying the functional dependencies of levels and rates are identified intuitively or on the basis of historical data. The simulation programme is completed and a first run is undertaken. Having examined the logical consistency of the results and compared them with the historical performance of the

system, the previous steps may be reconsidered and the programme revised.

5. *Policy experimentation* — simulation runs are performed to gain knowledge of the effects of random, periodic, and cumulative changes in the dependencies specified for the different variables, the effects of reaching maximum or minimum limits of different variables, the effects of changing the rules of decision, i.e. the specification of the equations in the programme or the causal structure of the model, etc.

3.5.4 Areas of application

System dynamics is used to identify the controlling variables in existing social systems; to make conditional statements about the future based on explicit and formal experiments with a model of the social system of interest; to project future performance of a system given its currently inherent forces, that is the logical consequences of a continued development based on the premises of the present; to determine operating policies which will increase the probability of a future desirable outcome (e.g. level of technical capability).

3.5.5 Comments

The most important difference between the properly conceived computer model and the mental model is in the ability to determine the dynamic consequences when the assumptions within the model interact with one another. The human mind is not adapted to sensing correctly the consequences of a mental model. In many instances it thus emerges that presumed solutions to perceived problems make the difficulties even worse, causing exactly the reverse of desired results. A properly constructed model is necessary to explain how such results can happen. Even though the estimates of many of the parameter values may be wrong — sometimes severalfold — the model may be surprisingly good in demonstrating the modes of behaviour that a system can exhibit.

System dynamics — originally named 'industrial dynamics' — was conceived by Professor J. W. Forrester, Massachusetts Institute of Technology, in the late 1950s. The breakthrough was achieved with publication of *World Dynamics* and *Limits to Growth* in 1971/1972.

3.5.6 References

Forrester 1961, Jantsch 1967, Jones 1970, Gregory 1972, Derviniotis 1973, Geschka *et al.* 1982, Roth 1982, Holt *et al.* 1984, Kotler 1984, Pahl and Beitz 1984.

3.6   STRUCTURAL MODELS

3.6.1   Definition

A structural model is a description of a process or system in terms of
a set of behaviour equations specifying its elements and their interactions.
The description of the system is made so that each equation can be
analysed separately and the results then combined in order to give
theoretical interpretations. No feedback relationships or reciprocal
causation between two or more variables are permitted (recursive
description).

3.6.2   Purpose

The purpose of describing a process or system in terms of a structural
model is to obtain an explanatory model whose parameters can be
estimated and whose fit with past behaviour can be evaluated empirically,
and that can be used to predict the future course of technology when
it is known that certain elements of the situation are going to be
changed.

3.6.3   Description

The model building involves the following steps:

1. *Choice of variables* — the set of variables relevant to the problem
are defined operationally. Unimportant and less important variables are
excluded.

2. *Specification of the model* — a distinction is made between variables whose values are taken as 'givens' (exogenous) and those whose
values are dependent on at least some other variables in the system
and thus may be deduced from a past state of the system (endogenous).
The endogenous variables are ordered so that each of them can be
expressed as a function of endogenous variables of lower order,
exogenous variables and an error term.

3. *Identification of the equations* — under certain assumptions about
the error terms unbiased (least square) estimates of the coefficients in
the set of equations may be obtained from statistical analysis of empirical
data.

4. *Forecast of the exogenous variables* — forecast of changes, or
proposed changes, in the exogenous variables are inserted in the model
in order to compute the influence they have upon the outcome (the
endogenous variables).

3.6.4 Areas of application

Structural models are used to improve 'naive' trend extrapolation by taking account of the inner workings of the process of technological growth; used in simple lead-lag models to take advantage of knowledge of advances in precursor technologies (e.g. flow of technology developed for industrial applications into domestic or residential application, military technology into civilian use); used to provide policy guidance as to what elements in the situation require change, and to what extent, so that a desired technological outcome is attained.

3.6.5 Comments

The 'best fit' criterion applied to tests on past data should not be used as the sole measure of acceptability. First, the fact that the consequences of a number of hypotheses regarding important variables and their interactions are verified does not prove the validity of the hypotheses. There may be distinctly different sets of hypotheses capable of explaining the same empirical observations (cf. discussions of multicolliniarity, spurious correlation, etc.). Second, even though an explanatory model fits past behaviour very well there is no guarantee whatsoever that it will continue to fit future behaviour, that the relations the equations express are stable, that the variables will continue to have the same correlations in the future, that variables which were unimportant in the past may not suddenly become important.

3.6.6 References

Wonnacott and Wonnacott 1970, Kotler 1984.

3.7 CROSS-IMPACT ANALYSIS

3.7.1 Definition

Cross-impact analysis is a generic term for a family of techniques by which the probability of an event or the level of a trend in a set of possible future events and trends can be adjusted in view of judgements relating to the interdependence among the events and trends — their cross impacts.

3.7.2 Purpose

The aim of cross-impact analysis is to clarify an obscure situation, where the total set of changes resulting from different developments or actions is not always exactly what was anticipated, and to identify trends and pivotal events, including deliberate actions.

3.7.3 Description

Cross-impact analysis involves the following steps:

1. *Specification of a time period* — the length of the planning period determines the time horizon, but the number of intervals into which the period is to be broken down depends on the amount of detail required.

2. *Identification of significant events* — which may occur within the time period, and trends considered important to the future within the area of interest. A probable event may occur in a time interval because it cannot be predicted with certainty or due to consciously pursued actions.

3. *Estimation of probabilities and levels* — for each time interval the probability that an event will occur within the time period and the anticipated level that a trend will have at the beginning of the time interval are estimated according to mathematical formulae. Initial estimates may be derived from Delphi studies and past time series.

4. *Estimation of the cross impacts* — for each event or trend it is estimated how much its occurrence or non-occurrence, or deviation of its value from the anticipated level, in a time interval will raise or lower the probabilities of the subsequent occurrence of other events and the subsequence level of other trends in the next time interval.

5. *'Playing' the cross-impact matrix* — sequences of events/trends are selected to occur at/deviate from anticipated levels either at random or to test alternative courses of actions; and using the estimates from step 4, the probabilities and levels in step 3 are adjusted the number of times chosen in step 1.

3.7.4 Areas of application

Cross-impact analysis is used to test the effects of alternative actions on specified events and trends; to gain insights into important causal chains of events; to identify strong 'actor' and 'reactor' events and their sensitivity; and to gain insight into key branch points and items on which current actions and policies should be focused in order to increase the likelihood of achieving a desired outcome.

3.7.5 Comments

The success of a cross-impact analysis depends on the quality of the specification of the event set as well as the impacts. All events crucial to the problem under considerstion must be included and double accounting of impacts must be avoided. So far only pairwise interactions between events are taken into consideration, not the simultaneous impact of two or more events on a third.

The number of items included should be kept small. The amount of information that must be gathered, usually on the basis of intuitive expert judgement, is enormous (growing with the square of the number of items).

3.7.6   References

Enzer 1969, Helmer 1972, Gregory 1972, Twiss 1974, Kotler 1984.

4. Development of Creativity

4.1 CREATIVITY TESTS

4.1.1 Definition

A creativity test is a tool for the measurement of creative potential of individuals, i.e. the capacity, in a specific situation, to suggest a great quantity of novel and worthwhile ideas based on different principles or approaches.

4.1.2 Purpose

The purpose is to help managers to identify idea-producing individuals capable of a creative approach to problem solving.

4.1.3 Description

The use of creativity tests involves the following steps:

1. *Selection of appropriate tests* — normally, a battery of tests measuring various dimensions supposed to be characteristic of creativity is used.

2. *Administration of the tests* — most tests require an expert to administer them. Those taking the tests have to answer a number of items for each test, often within a specified time.

3. *Scoring of the tests* — after completion the tests are scored by the administrator. The score may in some instances be the correct number of answers. Some tests require a consideration both of quantity and variety in the response.

4.1.4 Areas of application

Creativity tests can be used when hiring employees for jobs where creativity is important. They can also be used on present employees in connection with transfer and promotions, and when assigning jobs or organising groups where creative performance is required.

4.1.5   Comments

Creativity tests can indicate creative potential, but not ensure creative output. Other factors are also involved. The organisational climate must stimulate creative behaviour, and the individual must have the necessary knowledge, fit the social environment and accept the task. The introduction of creativity tests in a company requires expert assistance. The tests were introduced in the U.S.A. in the late 1950s. During the 1960s, they spread to other countries, but they still appear to be relatively little used in Europe. The administration of a battery of creativity tests takes about one to two hours. The scoring time varies from minutes to hours for each person tested, depending on the complexity of the tests.

4.1.6   References

Taylor and Barron 1963, Raudsepp 1965, Parnes and Harding 1972, Ulrich 1975, Bailey 1978, Davis and Scott 1978, Kaufmann 1980, Holt 1987.

4.2   CLIMATE MEASUREMENTS (ORGANISATIONAL CLIMATE)

4.2.1   Definition

Climate measurement is a method for assessment of the internal climate of an organisation as it is perceived by its members.

4.2.2   Purpose

The purpose of measuring the climate is to get a diagnostical tool for developing a more creative climate by spotlighting weak points, by giving a quantitative basis for discussions regarding action to be taken, and by showing the results of changes made with the intention of improving the climate.

4.2.3   Description

A climate measurement involves the following steps:

1. *Determination of scope* — here it is decided whether the whole company should participate or only certain portions, e.g. departments where creative behaviour is of especial importance.

2. *Selection of methodology* — various methods are available for climate measurements. They all have in common the characteristic that the climate is described by a number of variables which are measured

by means of questionnaires. There is, however, a great variety among them, both with regard to number and content of the variables. One method is based on the following variables:

1. Time for creative activity
2. Freedom from restrictions
3. Freedom of choice
4. Reception of new ideas
5. Attitude of supervisor
6. Attitude of the organisation
7. Recognition of creativity
8. Physical environment
9. Interaction with others
10. Composition of staff
11. Method of problem solving
12. Contact with the project
13. Type of project

3. *Implementation* — the basic measurement tool is a questionnaire in two versions, one for managers at various levels and one for employees. For each climate factor the managers indicate how they think the climate is within their area of responsibility and how they would like it to be by selecting one of five answer alternatives. The employees indicate the perceived and the desired climate for the same climate factors. All respondents list the three factors they find most important and the three of least importance.

4. *Tabulation* — this involves transfer of data from the questionnaires for processing, usually by means of a computer. After processing, climate profiles are made on an overall basis for all participants and for departments, sections and groups. Separate profiles are also made for managers and employees.

5. *Analysis* — this is perhaps the most important step. Great care should be taken in finding a good approach where all concerned are given an opportunity to participate in the analysis and discussion of the results.

4.2.4   Areas of application

Climate measurements can be used by all companies that want to improve the organisational climate. They are particularly important in departments where a climate that promotes creative behaviour is necessary, such as marketing, R & D, manufacturing planning, industrial engineering and personnel. The measurements may also be used in other departments in order to get a basis for the stimulation of creative behaviour.

4.2.5   Comments

Although the purpose of using climate measurements is normally to improve the organisational climate, they may also serve other purposes. One is for the performance evaluation of managers. Measurements will show, with quantitative data, how the situation is and to what extent managers have a correct perception of the climate within their area of responsibility. Another purpose is for management development programmes which should benefit from the focus the measurements give to the innovative aspects of the role of the managers. A better understanding of climate variables and their relative importance is useful in connection with studies of innovation, a theme which is gaining increasing importance in management development programmes.

4.2.6 References

Tagiuri 1968, General Electric 1969, Gerstenfeld 1970, Holt 1971, Peterson 1972, Holt 1972, Steele 1975, Gee and Tyler 1976, Bailey 1978, Davis and Scott 1978, Hayes and Wheelwright 1984, David 1986, Hübner 1986, Holt 1987.

4.3   MORPHOLOGICAL TECHNIQUE

4.3.1 Definition

The morphological technique is an analytic aid to creativity which assures that all possible solutions to a problem are enumerated through a systematic breakdown of a problem into parts which can be treated independently.

4.3.2 Purpose

The purpose of morphological analysis is to find new solutions to a given problem by obtaining a proper appraisal of all the facts — *boundary conditions* -- needed for the unbiased deduction of possible solutions to any given problem.

4.3.3 Description

Morphological analysis consists of the following steps:

1. *Defining and structuring the problem* — the problem to be solved must be formulated concisely in terms of all the characteristic parameters that might be of importance for the solution of the problem.

2. *The morphological box* — the parameters are analysed, and for each parameter as many significantly distinct values (solutions or approaches) as possible are devised. The number of overall solutions to the original problem are obtained by enumerating all possible combinations of the different values of the different parameters (choosing one element from each parameter).

3. *Stepwise screening of best overall solutions* — one might start systematically to rule out all solutions which are not feasible because of interactions between values on different parameters (potential

solutions to individual parts). Next, evaluate the performance value of each solution with respect to the purposes that are to be achieved, and choose the optimally suitable solutions.

4. *Random access to improved solutions* – one might start from already known solutions, or from what promise to be interesting solutions or infeasible solutions, or simply from a set of randomly chosen solutions; apply the performance criteria to determine whether improved solutions could be found in the neighbourhood, that is, by changing the values of one or a few parameters.

4.3.4   Areas of application

Morphological analysis is used to identify all possible devices to achieve a functional capability; to structure and organise thinking about a problem in such a way that new information is generated; to generate branches in a relevance tree or reference scenarios when writing scenarios.

4.3.5   Comments

It is important that the structuring of the problem is carried out so that the parameters are as far as possible mutually independent, of approximately equal importance and relevant for the analysis. As an aid in structuring the problem into parameters one may try to generalise characteristics of known solutions as far as possible. Some parameters can be expressed in absolute or relative dimensional terms, but many significant parameters are dimensionless, i.e. have phenomenological discrete values.

Morphological analysis belongs to a group which may be called *analytical creativity* techniques. These techniques are all based on a logical analysis of the problem and its various elements. Among other well known techniques in this group are *attribute listing*, where the major attributes are changed in any conceivable way, and the *input-output technique*, where all possible ways of converting available inputs into desired outputs are explored.

4.3.6   References

Zwicky 1969, Jones 1970, Gregory 1972, Twiss 1974, Ulrich 1975, RKW Geschka 1976, Schlicksupp 1977, Siemens 1977, Bailey 1978, Battelle 1979, Kaufmann 1980, Geschka *et al.* 1982, Roth 1982, Holt *et al.* 1984, Kotler 1984, O'Shaughnessy 1984, Pahl and Beitz 1984, Koller 1985.

4.4 BRAINSTORMING

4.4.1 Definition

Brainstorming is a method for creative thinking based on free association and deferred judgement.

4.4.2 Purpose

The purpose of brainstorming is to generate within a short time a large quantity of ideas, among which there will be some fitted for further use.

4.4.3 Description

The use of brainstorming involves the following steps:

1. *Selection of problem* — the problem is selected or received by the leader of the group. He may inform the participants about it some time, e.g. a week, before the start of the brainstorming session.

2. *Selection of group* — although brainstorming can be applied individually, it normally takes place in a session where six to twelve persons participate.

3. *Determination of duration* — this depends on the type of problem. A rough guideline is indicated below:

Simple problems; e.g. development of brand names, half-an-hour.
Normal problems; e.g. advertising, marketing, personnel, manufacturing, product development, one hour.
Special problems; experts from outside with relevant know-how join the group, e.g. financial, technical and organisational areas, 1½ hours.

4. *Implementation* — a session may be conducted in the following way:

Statement of the problem; this is first done by the leader, then by the group. Finally the best statement is selected.
Brainstorming; the basic rules here are: *suspended judgement* (any form of evaluation and criticism is ruled out); *'freewheeling' is welcomed* (the wilder the ideas, the better the results); *quantity is encouraged* (the more ideas, the better); *cross fertilisation* (combination and improvement on the ideas of others are sought).
Evaluation; selection criteria are formulated and one or a few ideas are selected for further processing. The duration of the evaluation period is usually 3—5 times longer than the actual brainstorming.
Reverse (negative) brainstorming; awkward questions are anticipated by investigating in how many ways the ideas selected can fail and why (also see Method 11.6).

5. *Proposal* — a brief statement is written with description of the problem, alternative ideas with advantages and disadvantages, and recommended solution.

4.4.4   Areas of application

Brainstorming has a wide area of applications ranging from minor improvements to original innovations. It can be used in connection with the generation of the basic idea at the start of the innovation processes, but is also useful during the subsequent stages.

4.4.5   Comments

From brainstorming have been developed a number of similar techniques. One of them is the Philips 66 buzz session; this is a type of competitive brainstorming where a large group is divided into small groups with five or six participants. Each group, which has a leader briefed beforehand, works on the same problem and conducts its own session. Another approach is brainwriting, a form of written brainstorming. Each member of the group writes during a short period, e.g. 3–5 min, some ideas on a piece of paper, puts it into a pool, takes back another sheet, adds some ideas, returns it to the pool, etc.

4.4.6   References

Parnes 1967, Jones 1970, Hake 1971, Gregory 1972, Parnes and Harding 1972, Holt 1973, Twiss 1974, Kleine 1975, Ulrich 1975, RKW Geschka 1976, Schlicksupp 1977, Siemens 1977, Bailey 1978, Davis and Scott 1978, Battelle 1979, Kaufmann 1980, Capey and Carr 1982, Geschka et al. 1982, Roth 1982, De Bono 1983, Holt et al. 1984, O'Shaughnessy 1984, Pahl and Beitz 1984, Holt 1987.

4.5   FORCED RELATIONSHIP TECHNIQUE

4.5.1   Definition

Forced relationship techniques are approaches for creative problem solving based on the establishment of forced relationships between two or more elements (ideas or objects) which seem unrelated according to habitual thinking patterns.

4.5.2   Purpose

The purpose of applying a forced relationship technique is to generate a number of ideas among which there will be some that are new, yet useful.

4.5.3   Description

Having selected and defined the problems to be solved, the following steps are involved:

1. *Selection of approach* — the most commonly used are the following:

The catalogue technique; from a catalogue are selected at random two elements, e.g. subjects, pictures or words.

The listing technique; a number of elements are listed and numbered.

The focus-object technique; one element is preselected with a definite purpose in mind, e.g. a product or a statement of a problem. Another element is chosen at random.

2. *Force fit* — the elements chosen are considered in all possible combinations as a basis for free association from which new and original ideas will emerge.

4.5.4 Areas of application

Forced relationship techniques can be applied to all kinds of problems. With the exception of the focus-object technique, the elements are not controlled, and the area in which the ideas are needed must be rather broad.

4.5.5 References

Parnes 1967, Parnes and Harding 1972, Ulrich 1975, Berridge 1977, Bailey 1978, Kaufmann 1980, De Bono 1983, Kotler 1984, Holt 1987.

4.6 SYNECTICS

4.6.1 Definition

Synectics is a method for creative problem solving where one attempts to simulate the thinking processes which individuals are using when they are most creative.

4.6.2 Purpose

The purpose is to find good solutions by restructuring the problem and by achieving freedom from constraints, elimination of negative responses, deferred judgement and escape from the boundaries imposed by traditional thought patterns.

4.6.3 Description

In a synectics session participate a client who has a problem which he has not been able to solve satisfactorily, and a group. At least the chairman must have experience with synectics, but also members of the group may have been trained in the method. The synectics procedure involves the following steps:

1. *Statement of the problem* – as given by the client to the group (PAG).
2. *Discussion and analysis* – this is based on the problem as given (PAG).
3. *Elimination of immediate, obvious solutions* – these usually come from preconceived ideas.
4. *Statement of the problem as understood* – PAU.
5. *Stimulation of divergent thinking* – by means of an evocative question, which calls for a solution in one of these analogies:

Personal analogy, where the problem solver identifies himself with the object or situation and imagines how he would react.
Direct analogy, where biological, mechanical or other solutions to similar problems are examined.
Symbolic analogy, in which the crucial or unclear parts of the problem are symbolised in words, pictures or other images.

6. *Analogy development* – the group plays in a leisurely way with the evocative question.
7. *Force fit* (generation of a possible solution or 'viewpoint') – if a fruitful analogy is generated, its implications are examined in detail in relation to the problem as understood (PAU).
8. *Redirection* – if no solution is found, the chairman redirects the discussion by posing a new evocative question.

4.6.4 Areas of application

Synectics can be applied to scientific, technical and managerial problems.

4.6.5 Comments

Synectics is a useful, but somewhat difficult technique. It requires about a week of formal training, but in order to achieve a reasonable competence many months of practice may be needed. A session organised for solving a particular problem brought by a client may last up to a whole day.

4.6.6 References

Gordon 1961, Jones 1970, Prince 1970, Gregory 1972, Geschka 1973, Michael 1973, Twiss 1974, Ulrich 1975, Berridge 1977, Midley 1977, Schlicksupp 1977, Siemens 1977, Bailey 1978, Davis and Scott 1978, Battelle 1979, Kaufmann 1980, Roth 1982, Kotler 1984, Pahl and Beitz 1984, Holt 1987.

4.7   ECLECTIC APPROACH FOR CREATIVE THINKING

4.7.1   Definition

The eclectic approach for creative thinking consists of using those parts of the various techniques found to be the most appropriate for the problem to be solved.

4.7.2   Purpose

The purpose of the eclectic approach is to apply a method that is best considering both the type of problem and the personality of the people involved in the problem solving.

4.7.3   Description

As the eclectic approach is tailor-made for each particular problem, no general procedure can be described in detail. However, in order to utilise the techniques for creative problem solving, motivated people from various levels and departments should be trained in their use and act as a core for problem solving groups throughout the organisation. Of particular importance is to have a good coverage of innovative functions, such as research and development, marketing, manufacturing engineering, industrial engineering and personnel. Normally, horizontal groups are most efficient. However, if one has group leaders who are able to get vertical groups working well, this is one way of breaking down status barriers between hierarchical levels.

4.7.4   Areas of application

Not only problems vary, but also people have different ways of thinking. Some prefer analytical approaches, others want to use their imagination. An eclectic approach takes this into consideration. It is flexible and has a very wide area of application, both with regard to problems and people involved.

4.7.5   Comments

In practice most problems require a mixture of analytical and associative thinking. A systematic analysis of facts is often needed in order to arrive at a correct definition of the problem, although associative thinking also may be useful. Then facts about the problem are collected and alternatives developed. During this step associative thinking may be needed in order to find as many useful ideas as possible. In order to select the final solutions, facts regarding the various alternatives must be collected and analysed in a systematic manner. This may stimulate more associative thinking, and so on.

In general, associative thinking is concerned with choice of concepts and approaches to problems. Analytical thinking is more concerned with definition and selection of problems, and processing and implementation of ideas.

4.7.6   References

Bailey 1978, De Bono 1983, Pahl and Beitz 1984, Holt 1987.

4.8   WORK SIMPLIFICATION

4.8.1   Definition

Work simplification is a special application of the method study where the employees are trained to analyse and improve in a systematic manner the work they perform or supervise.

4.8.2   References

Maynard 1963

4.9   SUGGESTION SYSTEM

4.9.1   Definition

A suggestion system is a method for utilisation of the creative potential in an organisation by collection, evaluation and rewarding of ideas and proposals conceived by the employees.

4.9.2   References

Maynard 1963, Ekvall 1971, Berridge 1977, Hisrich and Peters 1978.

5. Preliminary Study

5.1 FEASIBILITY STUDY

5.1.1 Definition

A feasibility study is a systematic study of the potential of an idea from a technical, marketing, economic, financial, social, ecological, resource and legal point of view.

5.1.2 Purpose

The purpose of the study is to get a base for determining whether the processing of the idea should go on, be postponed or discontinued.

5.1.3 Description

The procedure applied depends on a number of factors such as novelty and originality of the idea, type of product and its potential, technology, and market situation. In general, the following steps are involved:

1. *Determination of the purpose of the study* — this is concerned with an evaluation of the worth of the idea and its advantages and disadvantages. Sometimes the worth can be easily quantified. In other cases it may be valuated in terms of an increased ability for utilisation of special opportunities or markets. In areas where social values are of importance it may be very difficult to quantify the benefits of the idea.

2. *Determination of time and resources* — at this stage is decided how much time and effort should be devoted to the study.

3. *Selection of an appropriate screening method* — among those most widely used are check lists, profile charts and ranking methods.

4. *Collection of data* — normally both internal and external data are required: the approach for collection should be determined with due consideration to the purpose of the study.

5. *Evaluation of data* — the data collected must be evaluated by means of relevant criteria. The evaluation is followed by recommendations as to further processing of the idea.

5.1.4 Areas of application

A feasibility study should be applied to all ideas and proposals before a decision is made to start development work. The more novel and radical the idea is for the company, the more effort should be put into the study. In order to use resources effectively one should avoid spending too much time on studying projects that are inherently unprofitable. Effort should be given to an early and careful screening of each idea. This can best be done by a procedure involving two or more steps. A preliminary screening is made after the idea is received. This will save time and effort on making feasibility studies of ideas which are inconsistent with the objectives and policies of the company, which are not suited for technical and commercial development with the knowhow and resources available, and which do not appear to have the potential of successful innovations. At this stage, the screening must be quick, simple and cheap. It is therefore based on existing knowhow within the organisation and done without any effort to get supporting data.

Ideas which pass preliminary screening are submitted to a feasibility study.

5.1.5 Comments

A feasibility study should be short, at least an order of magnitude shorter than the development stage. The cost should also be kept low — it should not exceed the amount of money management is willing to spend if nothing comes out of the study.

5.1.6 References

Scheuing 1972, Schmitt-Grohe 1972, Twiss 1974, Kramer and Appelt 1974, Blanchard 1976, Berridge 1977, Hisrich and Peters 1978, Webster 1979, Pessmier 1982, Holt 1987.

5.2 TECHNOLOGY ASSESSMENT

5.2.1 Definition

Technology assessment is the exploration and evaluation of the full range of impacts on the environment and on the quality of life, of a technological development.

5.2.2 Purpose

The aim of technology assessment is to foster a socially more balanced and acceptable development and use of technology through systematic comparison of alternative technical options in terms of their social, economic, environmental and other (direct and indirect, immediate and delayed) consequences.

5.2.3 Description

Technology assessment involves the following steps:

1. *Description of the features* – here comes (*a*) the technology to be assessed, and (*b*) the physical and social setting into which the technology will be introduced. The choice of a concrete frame of reference for the description can only be made relative to the particular problem at hand; nevertheless, checklists, functional analysis, social theories, etc., may help avoid a biased approach by fixing the order and relevance of the problems for investigation, and the objects and patterns to be observed.

2. *Identification of the anticipated consequences* – within the specified physical and social setting of the technology, a large number of well tested propositions within the physical, social and life sciences are predicted with varying degrees of statistical accuracy. They might be supplemented with on-site observation, surveys of affected public, panels of experts, etc. Furthermore, techniques of future research, such as Delphi, trend extrapolation and simulation, might be used to eliminate flaws in the predictions.

3. *Evaluation of the consequences* (identified in step 2) – cross impact matrices, environmental impact analysis, relevance and decision trees might be used as an aid to the structured thinking involved in the evaluation of the identified consequences.

5.2.4 Areas of application

Technology assessment is used for monitoring of negative 'side effects' of existing technologies, which may emerge when the technology is brought to new uses, misused or applied on an excessive scale; for identification of new technological opportunities arising from the already available knowledge and R & D results through systematic scrutiny of scientific discoveries; and for control and management of technology, to serve explicit social, institutional or organisational goals through definition of desirable functional capabilities of innovations.

Technology assessment is applied by governments, research organisations, etc. Individual firms should use a similar approach for studying the consequences of new product ideas, e.g. by applying checklists which also cover other aspects than the technical and economic factors (see Methods 5.4 and 5.5).

5.2.5   Comments

The Technology Assessment Act, signed by President Nixon in October 1972, required that any major innovation should be appropriately evaluated before it can be introduced on the U.S. market. However, there is no set formula for doing assessments. But there is a methodology which requires an appropriate mix of methods and techniques drawn from a variety of fields. The following characteristics of this methodology should be noted: technology assessment is concerned with immediate, secondary and higher order consequences, it incorporates the needs of a wide range of social groups, it takes account of all pertinent aspects — economic, political, social, cultural and environmental — and it is ideally a policy making tool for iterative evaluation of the consequences of technological developments.

Technology assessment should be done by an interdisciplinary team for the description and valuation task. Feedback should be established from groups affected by the technology.

5.2.6   References

Cetron and Bertocha 1973, Hetman 1973, Medford 1973, Gregory 1972, Blanchard 1976, Gee and Tylor 1976, Spitz 1977.

5.3   PATENT SEARCH

5.3.1   Definition

A patent search is an investigation among patent literature, i.e. pending applications and patents.

5.3.2   Purpose

The purpose of a patent search is to collect technical and legal information relating to inventions, which otherwise may not be available to the firm.

5.3.3   Description

A patent search involves the following steps:

1. *Stating the objective of the search* — this may be:

To find technical solutions to a given problem.
To gather data for judging the novelty of an invention or the possibility of using a new product or process freely.
To reveal information about the inventive activities of a competitor.

2. *Selection of sources* – among the most important are:

Own patent library.
The library and services of the Patent Office.
Other external services, e.g. patent agencies.

3. *Distribution of material collected* – the results of the survey are analysed and forwarded to those concerned within the firm.

5.3.4 Areas of application

A patent search may be of particular interest in highly competitive industries and in industries which experience rapid technological changes.

5.3.5 Comments

It is important to note that patent literature is a comprehensive and systematically structured source of technical information. By collecting data on known technologies, much R & D work may be avoided. This means that the efficiency of the R & D department in a firm with an active patent information attitude will be superior to that of comparable firms with less patent information input.

5.3.6 References

Libesny 1972, Spitz 1977, Berridge 1977, Ramo 1980, Pessemier 1982.

5.4   ECOLOGICAL ANALYSIS

5.4.1 Definition

An ecological analysis (pollution analysis) is an investigation that aims at charting the environmental consequences of a proposed product.

5.4.2 Purpose

The analysis aims at adapting the product to the requirements and expectations presented by the environment as far as various types of pollution are concerned.

5.4.3   Description

A pollution analysis can be divided into three steps:

1. *Charting the consequences of pollution* – an investigation is made into what extent the product will be polluting. Generally, a distinction can be made between:

Air pollution.
Water pollution.
Ground pollution.

Further, consideration must be taken of the fact that the product can be polluting at different phases of its life. Distinction can be made here between:

Manufacturing phase.
Use phase.
Disposal phase.

The result of this step in the analysis shows the extent to which the product is polluting and the types of pollution which occur in the various phases of its life.

2. *Charting of requirements of the environment* – investigation is made as to what requirements are presented by the environment as far as pollution is concerned, and what requirements it can be expected to present in the future. It will also be advantageous to clarify what measures potential competitors may have taken to meet the requirements of the environment.

3. *Comparison* – here, steps 1 and 2 are compared to find out what short and long range consequences the product will have for the company. A product that is polluting during the manufacturing phase can influence the company's labour force situation or relationship with the surrounding community. A product that is polluting during use or upon disposal can lead to undesired changes in the company's image, and, thereby, affect the sales of the company's products.

5.4.4   Areas of application

Ecological analysis is a new aid which has not yet become particularly widespread. In the meantime, the problems of pollution have been so great that such analysis ought to be considered as a regular procedure in the analysis and evaluation of product ideas.

5.4.5   Comments

The scope and duration of a pollution analysis will be entirely dependent on the type of product involved. Each individual company should, based on evaluation of its special situation, develop a suitable method, such as a checklist for the study of the problem and criteria, to support the decisions which must be made. The criteria ought to be formulated so that they will contribute to simplifying the optimisation which must be carried out among the technical, ecological and economic sides of the problem.

5.4.6 References

Watt 1968, Varble 1972, Blanchard 1976, Spitz 1977, Kotler 1984, Colinvaux 1986, Hübner 1986, Harlem Brundtland 1987.

5.5 RESOURCE ANALYSIS

5.5.1 Definition

A resource analysis aims at clarifying how much energy and raw material the product will consume, how the part played by resources in production can be minimised, and the manner in which resources can be reclaimed in the disposal process.

5.5.2 Purpose

A resource analysis aims at clarifying whether there is a resource basis for realising a product and, in addition, at economising on the use of resources which otherwise could become in short supply.

5.5.3 Description

The analysis can be performed in four steps:

1. *The resource situation* — here, investigation is made as to the anticipated development of prices for energy and raw materials, whether there will be a shortage of certain raw materials, whether it is possible to produce the product with alternative resources which are not in short supply, or whether the product consumes so much of scant resources as to make it morally indefensible to start production.

2. *The manufacturing process* — one attempts to chart the extent to which resources will be used in the manufacturing process, the extent to which waste material from production can be used in other production within or without the company, and the extent to which waste material from other production can be used in the production of the proposed product.

3. *The use situation* — here, investigation is made as to which resources the product will consume during use and how the price and supply of the resources will develop.

4. *The disposal phase* — here, investigation is made as to what extent and in what manner the resources in the product can be reclaimed in the product disposal phase and, possibly, how the product should be constituted in order to make possible such reclamation (see also Method 10.8).

5.5.4   Areas of application

Systematic use of resource analysis in connection with product development has hitherto been little used. However, one is now faced with a situation characterised by a steadily increasing shortage of various natural resources. This leads not only to drastic price increases for energy and raw materials, but also increases the significance of a sensible use of the resources. Therefore, there is much that calls for a resource analysis, from the criterion both of profitability and of the responsibility the company has to society concerning the consumption of scarce resources.

5.5.5   Comments

Every company should investigate the need to develop, in the same manner as for pollution analysis, a method of analysis that is adapted to the company's special situation. The method should encompass a procedure with specific steps and guidelines for the balancing which must be undertaken for an optimal resource consumption both from a company and societal point of view.

5.5.6   References

Watt 1968, Baruch 1972, Spitz 1977, Kotler 1984, Hübner 1986, Harlem Brundtland, 1987.

5.6   LEGAL ANALYSIS

5.6.1   Definition

A legal analysis consists of clarifying whether the product will conform to the existing and anticipated legal requirements.

5.6.2   Purpose

The purpose of legal analysis is to avoid initiating undertakings which, in one way or another, are or can be expected to become in conflict with the law.

5.6.3 Description

A legal analysis, which should be performed in cooperation with a lawyer, can be divided into two steps:

1. *Legislation in force* − investigation is made as to whether or not the product will conform to the legislation that is in force during the various phases:

Production.
Use.
Disposal.

Some of the legal areas which are natural to consider are labour laws, environmental laws, licensing laws, consumer laws, building codes, patent laws (i.e. exclusive foreign rights − see also Method 5.3), and miscellaneous laws and requirements for the approval of the products by the authorities.

2. *Anticipated legislation* − the analysis ought to reveal which laws are under preparation, when a more restrictive legislation can possibly be expected, and whether or not the product will satisfy the new requirements.

5.6.4 Areas of application

Since a constantly increasing number of laws can be expected in the years to come, which will affect companies and their product development, systematic legal analysis will be necessary to adapt to this situation.

5.6.5 Comments

Every company that works on development of new products ought to establish cooperation with a competent lawyer and to include him in the evaluation of legal aspects in connection with new ideas and proposals for products.

5.6.6 References

Zallen 1974, RKW Borrmann 1976, RKW Grefermann 1976, Berridge 1977, Spitz 1977, Bailey 1978, Hisrich and Peters 1978.

6. Project Formulation

6.1.1 Definition

A project selection technique is a method for providing relevant information as a basis for deciding if an idea should be rejected, deferred or accepted for further processing, and, if so, what priority it should be given.

6.1.2 Purpose

The purpose of applying the project selection technique is to establish the best possible basis for making decisions regarding the processing of ideas and proposals for new or improved products.

6.1.3 Description

A project selection usually consists of the following steps:

1. *Definition of the problem* — the objective should be clearly indicated, e.g. to rank proposals according to priority.
2. *Description of alternatives* — this would include the following information:

A short description of each alternative, with an indication of technical feasibility (see Method 5.1).

Marketing data, such as anticipated demand and price, relationship between performance and price of proposed product and of competing products, service requirements, market trends, market potentials, expected annual sale, distribution channels, marketing costs, probability of marketing success and possible income from sale of licences.

Cost data, such as costs related to R & D, costs related to equipment and tooling, possible licensing costs, and costs related to wages, materials, etc.

The probability of technical success.
Financial data, such as capital requirements and possible sources for financing the project.
Social aspects, including positive and negative consequences of the proposals for people inside and outside the company (see also Methods 5.4 and 5.5).

3. *Choice of screening method* – this must be done with consideration to the uncertainty of the data, the costs of using the methods and the benefits to be gained. The most common approaches are checklists and payback analysis. Other methods which may be used are profile charts, profitability indices, net discounted present value and internal interest (see pp. 112–114).
4. *Choice of evaluation criteria* – based on the methods selected, technical, economic and social criteria are chosen as a guide for the final evaluation.
5. *Evaluation and decision* – based on the material from the preceding steps and personal judgement, a final evaluation is made and a decision on the further handling of each proposal is taken.

6.1.4   Areas of application

A systematic screening can be applied to all kinds of proposals for new or improved products. The approach to be used depends both on the company and on the degree of uncertainty involved in the proposals.

6.1.5   Comments

The systematic screening of an idea is important, but may hamper the innovative efforts if too much weight is given to the risk element which depends on the probabilities of technical and commercial success. The creation of an innovation idea is, to a large extent, a non-rational process. The more radical the solution, the less the predictability and the greater the risk. In order to get innovation, a systematic selection procedure should be used, but those who do the selection must be willing to accept a certain amount of risks and mistakes.

6.1.6   References

Bright 1964, Hake 1971, Gorle and Long 1973, Twiss 1974, Steele 1975, RKW Geyer 1976, RKW Brockhoff 1976, Giragosian 1978, Hisrich and Peters 1978, Webster 1979, Kaufmann 1980, Ramo 1980, Riggs 1981, Pessemier 1982, Kotler 1984, O'Shaughnessy 1984, Holt 1987.

6.2　DEVELOP/BUY ANALYSIS

6.2.1　Definition

A develop/buy analysis is a method for providing a base for deciding whether the technical solution should be bought from outside or developed within the company.

6.2.2　Purpose

The purpose of a develop/buy analysis is to determine, both for the product as a whole and at each design level, the advantages and disadvantages of developing or buying the technology involved, in order to find the optimal way for getting the technical solution both with regard to time and costs, and possible long range effects.

6.2.3　Description

A develop/buy analysis consists of the following steps:

1. *Definition of the problem* — this includes a clear statement of the objectives of the study.
2. *Description of technical alternatives* — the actual technical alternatives are listed, both with regard to development and purchase from outside. For each alternative, the following are indicated:

Technical data, such as performance/capability of those involved, quality of their work, time required for development/purchasing of the technological solution.
Economic data, such as costs for development/purchasing, economic risk, required capital, conditions of payment.
Requirements for the organisation, planning and control of the work.
Social aspects, such as the impact on hiring, lay off, transfer and training of employees.
Other aspects, such as development of technological competence, impact on other R & D projects, flexibility, reliability of outside suppliers and own organisation, risk of delays.

3. *Development of decision criteria* — this includes the selection of appropriate technical, economic and social criteria and the determination of their relative importance.
4. *Comparison of alternatives* — the various alternatives are analysed, using the established criteria, and ranked in order of priority.
5. *Selection of solution* — this is done on the basis of the material from the preceding steps and of the personal evaluation of those to whom responsibility of making the decision has been given.

6.2.4   Areas of application

A develop/buy analysis should be made by all companies that have a real choice between developing their own technology or buying it from outside.

6.2.5   Comments

In many companies there has been a tendency to have their own staff do most of the development work. However, in recent years there has been a change in attitude, and it appears that more and more companies are becoming aware of the advantages of importing technology from outside. One important factor is the great pace of change in most areas. There may be circumstances where a general policy regarding development or purchase can be developed, but in most companies the decision should be made in each case by competent people with the support of a systematic develop/buy analysis.

6.2.6   References

Gerstenfeld 1970, Hake 1971.

6.3   ACQUISITION OF LICENCES

6.3.1   Definition

The acquisition of a licence is a commercial agreement concerning the transfer of technology from outside to the firm.

6.3.2   Purpose

The purpose of acquiring a licence is to reduce time and costs involved in the development of a new product or process.

6.3.3   Description

If a company has made a develop/buy analysis and decided to acquire the technology from outside, the following steps are usually involved:

1. *Listing of relevant sources* – here may be considered:

Foreign firms; these offer the sale of technological knowhow through licences and other forms of commercial agreements. A number of information channels are used, such as exhibitions, trade fairs, trade delegations, special publications, patent offices, professional journals and newspapers.

Domestic inventors offer sale of their inventions through National Research Development Corporation, Kingsgate House, Victoria St., London SW1.

2. *Choice of source* – both the technology involved and the potential sources must be evaluated.

3. *Formulation of agreement* – this is a task requiring legal knowledge and experience. For those not having the necessary background within the firm, assistance can be obtained from outside consultants, patent lawyers and business lawyers. Help can also be obtained from an international association, License Executive Society (1225 Elbur Avenue, Cleveland, Ohio 44107, U.S.A.).

6.3.4   Areas of application

The possibilities of acquiring new technology from outside should be considered by most firms as an alternative to own development. The approach appears to be of particular importance for firms that do not have a satisfactory R & D department, for firms that want to enter a new technological field, and for firms that want to introduce a new product within a short time.

6.3.5   Comments

A licence agreement usually has a clause permitting the seller to use improvements in the technology made by the user.

6.3.6   References

Hake 1971, Gorle and Long 1973, Vaitos 1973, Twiss 1974, RKW Borrmann 1976, RKW Grefermann 1976, Berridge 1977, Spitz 1977, Pessemier 1982, Holt 1987.

6.4   LEGAL PROTECTION

6.4.1   Definition

Legal protection is used to denote the possibilities existing for the protection of products and processes against imitation as well as the measures necessary to obtain protective coverage by patent or design registration.

6.4.2 Purpose

The purpose of such protection is to prevent other firms benefitting by the inventive results of the firm and thus give the firm a monopoly for its original, new products or processes.

6.4.3 Description

To obtain a proper coverage on new products or processes, the following steps will be necessary:

1. *Selection of items to be protected* – an application for patent, in the U.K. and most other countries, implies considerable costs. Normally the firm has to restrict its activities in this area and file patent applications only for the most promising and original inventions. A set of criteria has to be established for selecting the products on which patents are to be applied for. These criteria may include:

Degree of originality, i.e. the quality of the invention or the design relative to prior art.
Economic value.
Competitive situation.
Possibility of combatting infringement.

2. *Selection of time for filing* – applications for protection should be filed sufficiently early not to be anticipated by competitors. On the other hand, the development work should have reached such a stage that enough details on the invention are available.

3. *Selection of type of protection* – patent, design registration, or both may be considered. Design registration is normally obtained for products with a new and original appearance, whereas patent is obtained for a novel idea in the technical area.

4. *Selection of geographical coverage* – as no 'world patent' exists, it is necessary to apply for patent in each country wherein protection is desirable. Normally, costs and marketing aspects will be the main criteria for choosing countries.

5. *Selection of patent agency* – although some companies find it useful to have their own patent department, most firms will have to get assistance from a patent agency.

6.4.4 Areas of application

Legal protection is usually sought in areas with great competition and not too rapid technological change. Other areas to be considered are mass produced products and high value products.

6.4.5　Comments

Legal protection may also be obtained for trade marks, ornaments, decorations, slogans, etc., through trade mark registration.

The duration of a patent is 16−20 years; in most countries an annual fee must be paid. In most countries the duration of a design registration is 15 years at most. Patents are granted by a central authority − in the U.K. The Patent Office, Dept. of Trade, 25 Southampton Buildings, WC2.

6.4.6　References

Zallen 1974, RKW Borrmann 1976, RKW Grefermann 1976, Berridge 1977, Spitz 1977, Bailey 1978, Hisrich and Peters 1978, Ramo 1980, Pessemier 1982.

7. Preliminary Analysis

7.1 QUALITY LEVEL PLANNING

7.1.1 Definition

Quality level planning means the process of preparing for the product to achieve a specific amount of user's satisfaction, either compared to full user's satisfaction or to the satisfaction offered by competing products.

7.1.2 Purpose

The purpose of quality level planning is to help those involved to develop functional specifications for the product which offer an optimal balance between user needs and technical and economic requirements.

7.1.3 Description

Quality level planning involves the following steps:

1. *Checking the need analysis* — i.e. making sure that it actually reflects the user's needs, that the needs are ranked according to their relative importance to the user, and that the minimum and ideal extents of need satisfaction are specified, when possible, and related to the price which the user will be willing to pay for a corresponding product property.

2. *Collecting information on restrictions* — limitations as to price (costs), technical factors and human factors.

3. *Deciding the quality level* — optimising all factors concerned in order to achieve the highest possible product quality (user's satisfaction) with the least possible resource consumption.

4. *Comparing the intended quality with established goals* — i.e. either for full user's satisfaction or the satisfaction offered by competing products, in order to accept or reject the proposed functional specifications.

7.1.4 Areas of application

The available techniques connected with quality level planning should be used in the early stages of the product innovation process, irrespective of the product in question.

7.1.5 Comments

In practice, some input information regarding the user's needs and the need/price relationships is hard to get. This should not, however, make anybody reluctant to undertake a systematic quality level planning, as the analysis itself will be of great value and contribute to a favourable quality level.

7.1.6 References

Kawlath 1969, Juran 1974, Blanchard 1976, Spitz 1977, Twiss and Weinshall 1980, Riggs 1981, Wilson *et al.* 1983, Hayes and Wheelwright 1984, Kotler 1984.

7.2 SCHEDULING – NETWORK MODELS

7.2.1 Definition

A network model is a graphical representation in which the various activities required for a given task are shown in such a way that both the time required for each activity and their interdependence are depicted.

7.2.2 Purpose

The purpose of a network model is to provide a basis for planning and control of complex projects, e.g. development, manufacturing, and introduction into the market of a new product.

7.2.3 Description

The use of a network model involves the following steps:

1. *Definition of objectives* – here, the major objective comes first, e.g. development of a new product with certain specifications within a specified period of time. The major objective is broken down into characteristic events representing the fulfilment of the various portions of the project.

2. *Development of the network model* – this consists of the following tasks:

Listing of the various activities required to reach the major objective of the project.

Arrangement of the activities in a network. Each activity is represented by an arrow. Each arrow starts in one node of the network and ends in another. The nodes, which are represented by circles, represent start and end events. When a start event has taken place, the activity shall be undertaken independent of all other activities.

3. *Determination of time* – how much time each activity is expected to take is determined.

4. *Determination of critical path* – the critical path is determined by analysing the network model, i.e. the sequence of activities, from the time of the start to the time of the end of the project, that cannot be changed without influencing the total time of the project. Activities along the critical path require the most attention during the planning and control of the project.

5. *Data processing* – this can be done manually when the number of activities is less than 200; for a larger number of activities, a computer may be advantageous.

7.2.4 Areas of application

A network model can be applied to the total project or to certain parts of the project that require special attention. By estimating the costs of the various activities the model can be used to determine the total cost of the project. By comparing time and cost for various alternatives, it is possible to find the optimal solution for the project, with regard to activities and their sequence.

7.2.5 Comments

Network models are important tools for the planning and control of large, complex projects. Standard programs are available for data processing using computers.

7.2.6 References

Elmaghraby 1970, Twiss 1974, RKW Geyer 1976, Blanchard 1976, Berridge 1977, Buffa 1977, Midley 1977, Siemens 1977, Spitz 1977, Bailey 1978, Kerzner 1979, Ramo 1980, Twiss and Weinshall 1980, Riggs 1981, Pessemier 1982.

7.3   SCHEDULING – GANTT CHARTS

7.3.1   Definition

A gantt chart is a graphical representation in which the various activities required for a certain task are shown in relation to a time scale.

7.3.2   References

Schmitt-Grohe 1972, Blanchard 1976, Berridge 1977, Buffa 1977, Spitz 1977, Bailey 1978, Kerzner 1979, Twiss and Weinshall 1980, Riggs 1981, Pessemier 1982, Wilson et al. 1983.

8. Market Research

8.1   USE OF INTERNAL MARKET STATISTICS

8.1.1   Definition

Use of internal market statistics means the collection, analysis and evaluation of internal data concerning marketing.

8.1.2   Purpose

The purpose is to chart the internal circumstances of a company in order to reveal the locations of the weak and strong points. The intent is to obtain a basis for introducing improvements and to build upon that foundation that has the greatest solidity.

8.1.3   Description

The procedure in the use of internal market statistics is as follows:

1. *Procuring of basic, internal data* – these are recorded for the areas that the company wishes to monitor.
2. *Analysis and evaluation* – the collation of the data concerning the internal capabilities of the company.
3. *Follow-up* – the decisions made on the basis of the analysis are implemented. The implementation is monitored and followed up.

Some areas where the use of internal market statistics can be useful are:

Position in the market: ordering and completion data. Terms of life for existing products, marketing sectors, sales districts, etc. Existing customer behaviour – loyalty to products and brands. Special strong points regarding products, distribution, communication.
Sales effort: sales data (type, quantity, period, distribution by target groups, etc.). Data concerning the effect of sales campaigns.

8.1.4   Areas of application

Internal market statistics can be used in situations where there is a desire to change the company's sales set-up or the product–market make-up.

8.1.5   Comments

If the use of internal market statistics is to be useful and applicable, it is necessary to establish close cooperation between the heads of marketing, product lines, sales, advertising, etc. Everyone involved should participate in all the phases of the surveillance.

8.1.6   References

Giragosian 1978, Ramo 1980, Kotler 1984, O'Shaughnessy 1984, Chisnall 1985, Aaker 1986, Kinnear and Taylor 1987.

8.2   USE OF EXTERNAL MARKET STATISTICS

8.2.1   Definition

Use of external market statistics means the collection, processing, analysis and application of external data concerning marketing.

8.2.2   Purpose

The purpose is to avoid involving the company in expensive collection and processing of data in areas where statistics already exist which satisfactorily illuminate, directly or indirectly, the problem in which the company is interested.

8.2.3   Description

It may be desirable, with the use of external market statistics, to undertake a survey of the following areas:

Social conditions, such as economy, population, energy, transportation, etc.
Commercial conditions, such as foreign trade, consumption, media accessibility, advertising expenses, etc.
Political conditions, domestic and foreign.

The procedure will ordinarily be:

1. *Problem clarification* — one sets out, concretely, what one desires to attain with the use of the external statistics.

2. *Collection of information* — one must search out the correct sources. A number of alternatives are cited below:

Foreign sources

Arthur D. Little, Cambridge, Massachusetts, U.S.A. (Subscription arrangement with reports on technology, information, letters, etc.).

Battelle Memorial Institute, Columbus, Ohio, U.S.A.

The Brookings Institution, Washington, D.C., U.S.A.

Bureau d'Informations et de Previsions Économique (BIPE), Neuilly-sur-Seine, France.

The Diebold Group, Inc., New York, U.S.A. (Specialist in information technology.)

Hudson Institute, New York, U.S.A. (Future studies.)

National Planning Association, Washington, D.C., U.S.A.

The Rand Corporation, Santa Monica, California, U.S.A.

Société d'Études et de Documentation Économiques Industrielles et Sociales, Paris, France.

Standford Research Institute, California, U.S.A. (Research economics, technology and social development. Subscription possible on Long Range Planning Service.)

Institut für Zukunftsfragen, Vienna, Austria.

Zentrum Berlin für Zukunftsforschung, Berlin, West Germany.

Institute for Future Studies, Copenhagen, Denmark.

3. *Analysis of information* — the information relevant to the problem of interest is extracted and compared.

8.2.4 Areas of application

External statistics can be of help for companies that have their attention directed toward the changes occurring around them and are disposed to analyse and plan future activities on the basis of the best possible data base.

8.2.5 Comments

An individual or a small group should be assigned the responsibility of seeking out and selecting the sources that are the most pertinent under the circumstances.

8.2.6 References

Hake 1971, Gorle and Long 1973, Berridge 1977, Spitz 1977, Kotler 1984, O'Shaughnessy 1984, Chisnall 1985, Aaker 1986, Kinnear and Taylor 1987.

8.3   CURRENT MARKET STUDIES

8.3.1   *Definition*

Current market studies mean regular investigations in the market to obtain data concerning market conditions.

8.3.2   *Purpose*

The purpose of current market studies is to monitor parameters which change rapidly and which have great consequences for the company's activities.

8.3.3   *Description*

The procedure in current market studies is as follows:

1. *Clarification of the problem* — statement of the purpose of the investigation and what one desires to attain.
2. *Identification of relevant parameters* — some of the parameters which can be pertinent are:

The market; demand analysis and customer research, advertising media, residential structure and demography, distribution structure.

General development of economy; trends in the development of the gross national product, the relationship between investment and consumption, between public and private consumption, development of business conditions and prices, inflation, changes in productivity, population growth.

Competition; the product's life cycle, new products, share of the market.

Governmental regulations; the government's attitude towards business-men, public planning, tax, fiscal, money and credit policies.

Cultural distinctions; life style, leisure time, family size, educational system, value structure.

International; economic integration (EEC), trade agreements (GATT), etc.

3. *Planning for implementation* — decisions for where, how, when, and by whom the investigation shall be made.
4. *Data processing* — collection and tabulation of the mass of information elicited.
5. *Evaluation* — analysis of the material and the working out of forecasts, premises and plans.
6. *Action* — implementation of plans and checking of the actions implemented.

8.3.4 Areas of application

Current market studies provide the company with a comprehensive view of its surroundings and information on which to base market related decisions.

8.3.5 Comments

The responsibility for current market studies should be assigned to a definite unit in the organisation, e.g. the marketing department or the financial department.

8.3.6 References

Hake, 1971, Kotler 1984, O'Shaughnessy 1984, Chisnall 1985, Aaker 1986, Kinnear and Taylor 1987.

8.4 SPECIAL MARKET STUDIES

8.4.1 Definition

Special market studies are isolated studies performed to procure data on market conditions in connection with special projects or enterprises.

8.4.2 Purpose

The purpose is to obtain information for the evaluation of a new enterprise such as the possibility of a new export market, the market acceptance or the sales potential for a new product, etc.

8.4.3 Description

The procedure with special market studies is:

1. *Clarification of the problem* — the statement of why the investigation is to be made; what is desired to be attained. Pertinent questions could be:

Which group is of interest, i.e. the target group for the investigation?
What has brought about the investigation?
What type of decision, and of what importance, shall be made on the basis of the results of the investigation?
Which questions must be answered for a correct decision to be made?

How far shall one go to obtain detailed information about subgroups and what requirements of precision are there in this connection?

What earlier investigation results and general experience does one have in the area, and how can they be improved and be helpful in the planning of the current investigation?

When should the results of the investigation be complete and when must it be presented, at the latest, so that a correct decision can be taken at the right time?

2. *Identification of relevant parameters.*

3. *Planning of implementation* — decisions on where, how and when the investigation shall be performed. Included here are the preparation of questionnaires, schedule and cost planning, requirements for precision, etc.

4. *Data processing* — consists of data collection and tabulation of the mass of information elicited.

5. *Evaluation* — consists of the analysis, the interpretation of the results, and decision for possible action.

6. *Implementation* — launching and supervision of the necessary actions.

8.4.4   Areas of application

Special market studies can be used to advantage by companies that desire information about how a new product can be expected to be received on the market, how an established product is viewed, its application areas and 'image'. These studies can also be used in the evaluation of new markets, such as in connection with export, by the measurement of the company's 'image', etc.

8.4.5   Comments

Special market studies are relatively expensive. Therefore, one should place great emphasis on the definition of the anticipated goal, and weigh the anticipated advantages against the expenses to which the study will lead.

8.4.6   References

Hake 1971, Scheuing 1972, Gorle and Long 1973, Design Council 1975, Gee and Tylor 1976, Berridge 1977, Hinterhuber 1977, Giragosian 1978, Hisrich and Peters 1978, Webster 1979, Ramo 1980, Pessemier 1982, Tushman and Moore 1982, Kotler 1984, Aaker 1986, Kinnear and Taylor 1987.

9. Cost Estimates

9.1 RISK ANALYSIS

9.1.1 Definition

Risk analysis is an aid for the calculation of the risk entailed by a project.

9.1.2 Purpose

The purpose of risk analysis is to calculate, as closely as possible, the value of a project, considering the uncertainty of the available information, and the accompanying risk.

9.1.3 Description

The procedure in the use of risk analysis may be as follows (see also pp. 114–116):

1. *Collection of relevant data* – data collection begins with the clarification of which parameters, because of their great uncertainty, shall be included in the analysis.
2. *Determination of subjective probability distribution* – this is done for the uncertain parameters. One can use two values per factor. A more time consuming procedure is the use of log-normal distribution which is well suited for cost as well as income distribution.
3. *Risk simulation* – this is done for the uncertain parameters. Monte Carlo simulation is much used and is well suited for calculating the total risk profile of the project. The simulation sequence is as follows:

Random selection of values for development costs, sales price, etc.
Calculation of internal interest with the aid of randomly selected values.
Calculation of pay-back period.
Repetition of the procedure with newly selected random values, and recalculation of internal interest and pay-back period.

The procedure is repeated several hundred times and each value is stored.

4. *Working out the probability* – this is done for the internal interest and the pay-back period.

5. *Analysis of curve for the probability distribution* – involves calculation of the mean value and standard deviation.

6. *Judgement of risk* – this takes place on the basis of the complete material set forth.

7. *Final decision* – consideration is also taken here of the non-quantifiable factors.

Relevant data for the calculation of the project's risk are the following:

The market; number of units sold, sales price, introductory price, sales and administration costs, other income (licensing, etc.), influence of earnings on the other products of the company.
Development; costs of product development.
Manufacturing; investments, unit cost, starting costs.

9.1.4   Areas of application

Risk analysis can be applied in the following areas:

Evaluation of individual projects (is it worthwhile gambling on Project X?).
Establishing priorities for various projects (is X better than Y?).
Evaluation of various technical alternatives.
Evaluation of various manufacturing and marketing strategies.

9.1.5   Comments

The risk analysis method described is inapplicable at the beginning of product development because at this stage one can seldom predict, with sufficient reliability, the course of the phases to come in the product development work. Alas, at this stage the uncertainty of most of the quantitative data is very great; the spread of probability figures will be too great to be a usable measure.

9.1.6   References

Strassmann 1959, Hertz 1964, Jantsch 1967, Luch 1972, Steele 1975, Blanchard 1976, Gee and Tylor 1976, Hussey 1976, Stone 1976,

Berridge 1977, Spitz 1977, Hinterhuber 1980, Ramo 1980, Riggs 1981, Pessemier 1982, Hayes and Wheelwright 1984, Kotler 1984, O'Shaughnessy 1984, Pahl and Beitz 1984, Holt 1987.

9.2 PROJECT COST

9.2.1 Definition

The expression *project cost* is understood to mean the estimating of the costs which a product/project will entail before it is ready for regular production.

9.2.2 References

Bierman and Smidt 1966, Lombares 1969, Schmitt-Grohé 1972, Beenhakker 1973, Blanchard 1976, Gee and Tylor 1976, Hussey 1976, Berridge 1977, Clark and Lorenzoni 1978, Kerzner 1979, Ramo 1980, Riggs 1981, Pessemier 1982, Prosjektplan 1982, Hayes and Wheelwright 1984, Hübner 1986.

9.3 PRODUCT COST (PRICING)

9.3.1 Definition

The expression *product cost* (*pricing*) is understood to mean determining total cost, gross profit margin or price of a product.

9.3.2 References

Schmitt-Grohe 1972, Wilson 1973, Blanchard 1976, Hussey 1976, Berridge 1977, Buffa 1977, Hinterhuber 1977, Giragosian 1978, Hisrich and Peters 1978, Webster 1979, Hinterhuber 1980, Ramo 1980, Riggs 1981, Pessemier 1982, Kotler 1984, David 1986.

9.4 INVESTMENT COST AND PROFITABILITY

9.4.1 Definition

The expression *investment cost and profitability* is understood to mean estimating facility costs and profitability of investment in technical equipment.

9.4.2 References

Jantsch 1967, Schmitt-Grohe 1972, Wilson 1973, Beenhakker 1975, Blanchard 1976, Hussey 1976, Stone 1976, Berridge 1977, Buffa 1977, Siemens 1977, Ramo 1980, Riggs 1981, Pessemier 1982, Prosjektplan 1982, Hayes and Wheelwright 1984.

10. Design

10.1.1   Definition

Applied research is the systematic creation and application of knowledge through the organised effort of people working toward a specific commercial objective.

10.1.2   Purpose

The purpose of applied research is to find a solution in principle (design concept) for a new or improved product, process or material, or to find a new application of an existing product, process or material.

10.1.3   Description

Applied research may be required both in connection with finding the basic solution and during the development stages. In general terms the following approach may be used:

1. *Determination of the objective* − e.g. to demonstrate that a technical idea is based on a principle that can be implemented in practice.
2. *Study of existing information* − this will include utilisation of the knowhow and experience of the researchers assigned to the project. Further, the experience of others is gleaned through consultation with knowledgeable people inside and outside the organisation, and through systematic search of relevant literature and patents.
3. *Development of an experimental model* − this is concerned with determination of key parameters and confirmation of the technical practicability of the proposed solution, whereas the efficiency, economy and user acceptability remain uncertain. It may be practicable to use the following steps:

On the basis of rough sketches the necessary parts are made and put together into a laboratory model (*mock-up*). The model is tested, improved and modified.

The model is evaluated.

Design and production of a model for experimental and operational tests. These tests are done under simulated natural conditions in a laboratory or in an actual user situation.

10.1.4   Areas of application

Applied research can be used in both a *defensive* and an *offensive* manner.

The aim of defensive research is to maintain or increase the market position of existing products through improvements in raw materials, product design, or manufacturing operations.

The aim of offensive research is to develop and market products that are new not only for the company, but that also have functional characteristics with features new for the market.

10.1.5   Comments

Although there are differences among industries, there appears to be a trend away from chance occurrences and the output of practical inventors without theoretical knowledge toward innovations based on applied research.

10.1.6   References

Bright 1964, Villars 1964, Jones 1970, Morton 1971, Holt (ed) 1973, Gorle and Long 1973, Blanchard 1976, Ramo 1980, Riggs 1981, Capey and Carr 1982, Pessemier 1982, Tushman and Moore 1982, Hübner 1986, Holt 1987.

10.2   STYLING (SHAPE AND COLOUR)

10.2.1   Definition

Styling concerns the determination of the appearance of the product; the basic concern is shape, colour and surface.

10.2.2   Purpose

The purpose of styling is to develop a product that satisfies the aesthetic requirements of potential customers as well as possible within the technical and economic constraints.

10.2.3 Description

There is no standard procedure available for styling. The approach
depends on the type of product and the attitude towards the aesthetic
aspects of the product. In some cases styling is done after or near the
end of the development stages, in other cases parallel with the technical
development. There are also cases, particularly when concerned with
mass produced consumer goods, where one starts with the styling.
The approach may then be:

1. *Creation of basic style concepts* – this can be done in terms of
pictures or mock-ups.
2. *Testing consumer acceptance* – this is done by showing alternative
concepts to potential users.
3. *Choice of design concept* – having established relevant criteria,
the final design concept is chosen.

10.2.4 Areas of application

Styling often has a decisive influence on market acceptance of consumer
goods such as home appliances, automobiles, consumer electronics,
furniture, etc. However, in other products also, such as industrial
goods and building products, the style is of importance and requires
special attention during development of the product.

10.2.5 Comments

Styling is in many cases done by the engineers responsible for development and engineering design. However, with the strong market
orientation which is now taking place in more and more industries,
many companies have started to use specially trained industrial designers
for the styling of their products. These designers take an active part
in the whole innovation process from the beginning, based on the view
that a good style cannot be imposed on the outside of the product,
but has to be built into it.

There now appears to be a trend towards increasing the scope of
modern industrial design. The underlying philosophy is that in order
to get a good product one has to consider the product as a whole. The
industrial designer therefore recognises that he should not be concerned
only with the style of the product, but also with its functional aspects
and manufacturing requirements. In close cooperation with the
marketing and engineering staffs he attempts to integrate the aesthetic
with the functional requirements derived from user needs and the
manufacturing requirements stemming from available manufacturing
equipment.

10.2.6 References

Van Doren 1954, Cross 1972, Fraser 1972, Papanek 1972, Design
Council 1975, Stone 1976, Pessemier 1982, Roth 1982, Holt 1987.

10.3   CATALOGUE AIDED DESIGN

10.3.1   Definition

Catalogue aided design is a systematic search in prearranged catalogues for possible solutions to problems concerning the working principle, the basic configuration and the design of machine parts, components and systems.

10.3.2   Purpose

The purpose of catalogue aided design is to obtain a solution to a specific design problem described in functional terms, by a systematic search through catalogues describing possible solutions based upon known principles. The main purpose of the technique is therefore:

To avoid reinvention of already known principles, solutions and designs.
To be able to investigate a large number of possible solutions.
To increase the probability of finding a satisfactory solution within a reasonable time.

10.3.3   Description

Catalogue aided design may be used at different stages in the design process, illustrated by the following examples:

Search for kinematic principles (e.g. spinning machine mechanisms).
Search for design solutions (e.g. previous designs).
Search for machine elements (e.g. roller bearings).

When using the method, the problem must be formulated in accordance with the structure of the catalogue (or data base) available, so that a routine search made by special assigned personnel or a computer is possible. The output is the description of the solution which meets the input requirements.

10.3.4   Areas of application

Catalogue aided design may in principle be used in any design office concerned with machine design, as long as comprehensive catalogue material is available, in standard form and/or as a result of own systematic collection and classification. However, the large quantity of information involved will in practice require the use of a computer. Catalogue aided design is therefore best considered as an integral part of a larger computer aided design system.

10.3.5   Comments

Catalogue aided design assumes the existence of structured information concerning the specific field of engineering in question. For the most detailed design level, information may be available in catalogues describing machine elements such as roller bearings, fasteners, profiles, etc. For the higher and less detailed levels concerned with mechanisms and working principles for transmission of force and energy, etc., information is less readily available in systematic form. It is therefore necessary to build up a collection of structured information in the form of a data base.

Catalogue aided design is an algorithmic process, which in itself contains no creative elements.

10.3.6   References

Blanchard 1976, Roth 1982, Pahl and Beitz 1984.

10.4   ALTERNATIVE DESIGN APPROACHES

10.4.1   Definition

An alternative design approach is a method which develops the *functional tree* of a product, taking each level at a time, and for each level searches for alternative solutions having properties which satisfy the functional requirements on that particular level (see pp. 34–36).

10.4.2   Purpose

The purpose of an alternative design approach is to help the designer developing the product to avoid being tied too much to previous solutions and concepts, to consider the product as a system, and to offer the designer a tool for handling the large number of variables in a complex product.

10.4.3   Description

The use of alternative design approaches involves the following steps:

1. *Start with the main functional requirements* – this is for the product as a whole, using pure functional terms, without preassuming any particular solution or product design.
2. *Find as many possible solutions (design concepts) as possible* – systematic search may be used, morphological methods, catalogue aided design, brainstorming and other methods.

3. *Reject unsatisfactory solutions* − reject solutions which:

Do not satisfy functional requirements.
Are made impossible by boundary conditions.

4. *Evaluate the solutions* − this involves ranking the remaining solutions and the choice among the most promising.

5. *Analyse the remaining solution(s)* − on the next level of resolution, state the functional requirements which are a consequence of the chosen solution(s).

6. *Repeat the above steps for all levels of resolutions* − this should be done until the resolution has reached the level of single parts or vendor components. In order to limit the number of alternatives to be investigated, it is necessary to eliminate alternative solutions at the highest possible level, i.e. lowest possible degree of solution.

These sets may be considered as an algorithm, which may be applied on each level of detailing (resolution).

10.4.4   Areas of application

Alternative design approaches are of particular use in designing mechanical products and systems of considerable complexity, where the product could be considered as a system, and the design process takes the form of an optimisation process.

10.4.5   Comments

All design will in the end depend on the ingenuity and creativity of the designer himself, and no method or automatic design could replace a good designer. However, tools like the one described will help the designer in performing his task and relieve him of much tedious work.

10.4.6   References

Jones 1970, Blanchard 1976, Pahl and Beitz 1984.

10.5   COMPUTER AIDED DESIGN

10.5.1   Definition

Computer aided design (abbreviated CAD) is the use of computers in the design process and in related activities. The computer is used to perform calculations of various kinds, and to work as a data library by storing and retrieving data. CAD is usually considered a tool to be used as part of the larger product development process.

10.5.2   Purpose

The purpose of CAD is to reduce cost and elapsed time and to improve the design. This is mainly attained by:

Letting the computer perform routine work, leaving the associative and creative work to the designer.

Giving the designer the possibility of performing more extensive and more accurate calculations by introducing new methods and raising his computational power by a factor in the range 10^3-10^5.

10.5.3   Description

CAD is a tool continuously under development. At present it is found in three basic configurations:

Several small, independent function blocks (routines). Each block can perform a specific function, such as calculating critical rev/min for an axle given the shape, or performing a stress analysis of a beam or a frame, given the necessary data.

Design system. Several function blocks connected to a common data base form a set of design tools and a communication system.

Interactive type of work. The user is 'discussing' his problem with algorithms in the computer. The designer is supplying ideas, proposing different solutions to a problem. The computer answers (most often in a graphical way) by giving some of the interesting consequences.

10.5.4   Areas of application

CAD and CAD-like systems may be used in development functions where calculations are required and other product characteristics in the form of data are to be handled (stored, distributed, etc.).

10.5.5   Comments

CAD is mainly useful where repetitive routine work is involved, or where complex and accurate calculations are to be performed. It may make design jobs more interesting by permitting the designer to concentrate on his problems instead of doing routine work.

10.5.6   References

Blanchard 1976, RKW Nees and Ströhe 1976, RKW Wessel 1976, Newman and Sproull 1976, Encarnacao 1983, Pahl and Beitz 1984.

10.6   DESIGN AND TESTING OF MODELS

10.6.1   Definition

Design and testing of models is a method of obtaining essential product information by exposing a simplified or scaled model to external conditions as equivalent as possible to those of the real product.

10.6.2   Purpose

The purpose of the design and testing of models is:

To determine functional and dimensional quantities like stresses, deformations, vibrations, thermal behaviour, fatigue life, etc., in those cases where (a) it is too expensive, or in practice impossible to carry out theoretical analysis, (b) it is desirable to check the validity of an analytical model (or computer model).
To check the product or product parts for proper functioning.
To determine maintenance and service requirements.

10.6.3   Description

The design and testing of models involves the following steps:

1. *Determine which physical parts are to be tested* — this also involves parameters to be investigated through the testing, according to the purpose of the test.
2. *Apply model laws* — this also involves the determination of model dimensions and the value of the test parameters.
3. *Make a detailed plan for the testing* — one should take particular care in arranging a systematic sequence of the variation of the parameters.
4. *Implement* — carry out the test according to plan.
5. *Evaluate the results* — it may be necessary to carry out a repeated testing, when the test reveals needs for changes in model, design, test parameters or test plan.

10.6.4   Areas of application

Design and testing of models are of primary importance where only a single specimen or a very small series of a product is expected to be produced. It is also of importance where it is desirable to isolate certain parts, parameters or environments, or where an expensive product or product-part may be replaced by an equivalent cheaper model.

10.6.5   Comments

The design and testing of models require considerable skill, and quite often also expensive test equipment and laboratory facilities. The use of external laboratories and research institutions is therefore in many cases a practical alternative or supplement to testing in the producing firm's own facilities.

10.6.6   References

Langhaar 1951, Kleine 1965.

10.7   STANDARDISATION

10.7.1   Definition

Standardisation involves methods for the development and use of internal and external standard specifications for materials and components.

10.7.2   Purpose

The purpose of standardisation is to reduce costs by simplified develop-ment, design, manufacturing and warehousing, improved communi-cations and coordination, improved or more even quality, etc.

10.7.3   Description

The procedure for preparation of company standards is mainly as follows:

1. *Analysis of requirements and standards* – a working group analyses the requirements for raw materials and components used by the company as well as relevant external standards. Among the sources of external standards are the following:

National standards:
   American Standards Association (ASA).
   German Standards Committee (Deutscher Normenausschuss) (DIN).
Industry standards: these concern specific industries.
Regional standards: examples are standards prepared cooperatively by:
   – standards organisations in the four Scandinavian countries (INSTRA)
   – EFTA and EEC (which have founded their own organisation, CEN).
   – British Standards Institution, and International Standards Organisation.
International standards: an example is the principal organisation, the International Standards Organisation (ISO).

2. *Preparation of the proposal* – this is presented to the management which then sends it to everyone who might be affected in some way, within and without the company, requesting commentary, within a given time limit, if there is any disagreement with the proposal in whole or in part.

3. *Revision of the proposal* — after receipt of critical comments and possible suggestions for changes, the group prepares a final proposal which is then presented to management for approval.

4. *Distribution* — the approved standards are published and distributed to the affected parties.

10.7.4   Areas of application

Standardisation is applied in connection with the company's product development and related activities. Standardised components and raw materials can lead to significant reductions in cost. Furthermore, standardisation can encompass dimensional and quality requirements, and also involve testing, functional and safety requirements in connection with products and systems.

10.7.5   Comments

It is important that those who are to work on standardisation have a clear understanding of the difficulties of innovation and the demands it makes on the company's organisation and procedures. One must beware of pushing standardisation so far as to hamper further development so that one is no longer able to adapt oneself in a rational manner to the requirements resulting from changes in the environment.

A decision to standardise often leads to changes in the departments concerned — primarily in purchasing, product development, manufacturing and marketing. Extensive standardisation can lead to substantial expenses, but on the other hand the advantages attained by the simplification of work is often so great that it can well pay to make the effort.

10.7.6   References

Jones 1970, Glie 1972, Sanders 1972, Blanchard 1976, Riggs 1981, Pahl and Beitz 1984, Koller 1985.

10.8   DESIGN FOR DEMANUFACTURING (RECYCLING)

10.8.1   Definition

Design for demanufacturing is a design method whereby special attention is given to disposal or re-use of the product at the end of its normal use.

10.8.2 Purpose

The purpose of design for demanufacturing is to reduce the problem of solid waste.

10.8.3 Description

Design for demanufacturing can be undertaken in the following ways:

1. *Definition of the problem* – a clear statement is made here as to what one wishes to attain.

2. *Consideration of design approaches* – in developing alternative technical solutions one should consider the following approaches:

Choice of materials which can be decomposed easily at the end of the life of the product.

Choice of materials that can be recycled at the end of the life of the product.

Development of products and components which can be used for other purposes at the end of the useful life.

3. *Choice of solution* – this involves the establishment of relevant criteria and the selection of the best alternatives based on the criteria and on the personal judgement of those concerned.

10.8.4 Areas of application

Design for demanufacturing should be considered by manufacturers of products and packages of metals, plastics, glass, wood, etc.

10.8.5 Comments

Modern society suffers increasingly from solid waste caused by scrapped products and packages. The systematic application of design for demanufacturing should help to reduce this problem. However, the technique is new, and there is little outside assistance obtainable at present in terms of advice, training, or literature. A pioneering effort of a creative nature is therefore required in order to get results.

10.8.6 References

Baruch 1972, Blanchard 1976, Spitz 1977, Roth 1982, Koller 1985.

11. Design Evaluation

11.1 VALUE ANALYSIS

11.1.1 Definition

Value analysis is an organised, creative method attempting to take care of the functions of a product at lowest possible cost.

11.1.2 Purpose

The purpose of value analysis is to optimise the profitability and competitive capability of a product. This is attained by:

Estimating the costs of the various product functions.
Making a choice among alternatives based on their value (value = function/cost).
Avoiding unnecessary costs.

11.1.3 Description

A value analysis involves the following steps:

1. *Collection of information* − this includes materials, tools, market situation, competitors, cost estimates, etc.
2. *Functional analysis* − this consists of the following steps:

Listing of all intended functions of the product.
Listing of the major functions.
Listing of those secondary functions which are absolutely necessary.

3. *Determination of the basic value* − here one attempts to find the cost of the simplest possible solution for the major function. This is the basic value; it gives the theoretical lowest limit for the cost of the product.
4. *Generation of ideas* − by using brainstorming or other methods for creative problem-solving one produces a great number of original ideas.

5. *Evaluation of ideas* — having established relevant criteria, the ideas are compared and the best one selected and formulated as a proposal.

6. *Follow up* — in order to prevent the established cost/function relationships from being changed during the progress of the project, a follow-up procedure should be established.

11.1.4   *Areas of application*

The major area of application of value analysis is industrial products. It can be used both for improvements in existing products and for development of new products. Among other areas of application, service functions, office routines, transportation, communications and organisation can be mentioned.

11.1.5   *Comments*

Closely related to value analysis is *value engineering*. Some use the terms in the same sense. Others make a distinction; value engineering then usually refers to the activities preceding actual manufacturing (cost prevention), whereas value analysis refers to the activity subsequent to initial manufacturing (cost reduction).

11.1.6   *References*

Jones 1970, Siemens 1971, Miles 1972, Ulrich 1975, RKW Jung 1976, Berridge 1977, Davis and Scott 1978, Roth 1982, Kotler 1984, O'Shaughnessy 1984, Pahl and Beitz 1984, Chisnall 1985, Holt 1987.

11.2   RELIABILITY ANALYSIS

11.2.1   *Definition*

Reliability analysis is a method for predicting the ability of an item (system or product) to perform a required function under stated conditions for a given period of time.

11.2.2   *Purpose*

The purpose of reliability analysis is to predict the probability of satisfactory function of a proposed design in order to compare the reliability of alternative design solutions, improve the reliability or reduce the manufacturing costs, i.e. the cost of components.

11.2.3   Description

The use of reliability analysis involves the following steps:

1. *Describing the design by means of a reliability diagram* — i.e. visualising which components are in series, which are in parallel.
2. *Working out a mathematical model of the system* — i.e. a model based on the probability theory.
3. *Determining the failure rates for each component* — this information may be collected from reliability data banks, or from one's own experience or tests.
4. *Calculation of the system's probability of function* — this is done by inserting the failure rates in the mathematical model.
5. *Transformation of the probability of function to a convenient reliability criterion* — for instance mean-time-between-failure (m.t.b.f.).

11.2.4   Areas of application

Reliability analysis was originally developed for electronic systems and hence has mostly been applied to such systems. A number of reliability data banks for electronic components are available.

The analysis is, however, also applicable to hydraulic, pneumatic, electrohydraulic and electropneumatic systems. The method is at last being used even for purely mechanical systems, even though the estimation of component failure rates in this area is more difficult.

11.2.5   Comments

Reliability analysis is often executed as a part of more extended analysis (see Method 11.7).

11.2.6   References

Calabro 1962, Ireson 1966, Thomason 1969, Jones 1970, Blanchard 1976, Pahl and Beitz 1984.

11.3   ERGONOMIC ANALYSIS

11.3.1   Definition

An ergonomic analysis is a method for a systematic study of the psychological and physiological requirements for a product and its manufacturing processes from a human point of view.

11.3.2 Purpose

The purpose of the analysis is to provide a basis for developing products and manufacturing processes which are fitted as well as possible to human capabilities and limitations.

11.3.3 Description

An ergonomic analysis in the creation, development and manufacturing of a product involves the following steps:

1. *Clarification of human capabilities* — this involves the determination of the physiological and psychological capabilities of the people using the product, with consideration given to sex, age, anthropometric characteristics, education, working habits, etc.

2. *Determination of load* — this includes the following elements:

Physiological load (heavy, medium or light).
Psychological load (stress, perceptual load).
Environment (heat, cold, noise, vibration, dust, chemical substances).

3. *Formulation of requirements for products and processes* — on the basis of a comparison of capabilities and loads, requirements and criteria are formulated for the product and its manufacturing processes from a human point of view.

11.3.4 Areas of application

An ergonomic analysis should be performed by any company making products intended to be operated or handled by people, whether for personal use, e.g. home appliances, cars, etc., or in the employ of a company.

11.3.5 Comments

The analysis may be undertaken repeatedly during the product innovation process. Even at the idea generation stage such an approach may be helpful for certain products for assessment of user needs and formulation of need requirements. Ergonomic considerations may be appropriate at any time during development. All companies, whatever type of product they make, will benefit from ergonomic analysis in the planning of the manufacturing facilities, including equipment, tooling, processes, operations and work environment.

11.3.6   References

Jones 1970, McCormick 1970, Van Cott and Kinkade 1972, Shackel 1974, Blanchard 1976, Buffa 1977, Pahl and Beitz 1984, Holt 1987

11.4   USEFUL LIFE ANALYSIS

11.4.1   Definition

Useful life analysis is a method for predicting the average period of time during which an item (system, product or component) can be expected to operate under normal circumstances without being worn out.

11.4.2   Purpose

The purpose of the analysis is to help the R & D group to choose the right components, i.e. components that will contribute to the fulfilment of the useful life requirements stated in the functional specification, at minimum costs.

11.4.3   Description

Useful life analysis may involve the following steps:

1. *Identifying the main functions of the system* — this is done by means of the need specification and the functional specification.

2. *Identifying the critical components* — i.e. those components in which a failure will result in the fall-out of one or several main functions. This may be done by means of a failure modes and effects analysis (f.m.e.a.) (see Method 11.8).

3. *Calculating the number of operations, revolutions, etc., per hour of system operation* — this is done for the critical components only.

4. *Choosing components* — i.e. specifying component types that will just meet the operating requirements. Ideally, all components should be worn out at the same time during use, i.e. at the end of the stated useful life time.

11.4.4   Areas of application

Useful life analysis may be carried out for all products which will probably experience technical wear-out in some of their components before replacement of the product for other reasons, e.g. economic reasons.

11.4.5   Comments

The method is frequently used in several industries, for instance in the car industry, in the electrical industry and in mechanical engineering. It has a certain resemblance to reliability analysis (see Method 11.2).

11.4.6   References

Eisner 1972, Zemanick 1972, Koller 1985.

11.5   MAINTENANCE ANALYSIS

11.5.1   Definition

Maintenance analysis is a method which determines the consequences of different design alternatives on the future maintenance of the finished product with respect to technical, economic and administrative aspects.

11.5.2   Purpose

The purpose of the analysis is to reduce the total product cost (service life included), increase reliability, and reduce down times through a proper design and dimensioning of the product, taking maintenance and service requirements into consideration during the design phase.

11.5.3   Description

A typical maintenance analysis may consist of the following steps:

   1. *Selection of preliminary design to be analysed.*
   2. *Analysis of maintenance requirements* − this implies:

Specification of maintenance objects.
Determination of changes in state and function.
Determination of the causes of maintenance requirements.

   3. *Adaptation to maintenance* − this implies:

Determination of suitable methods for registration of state and diagnostics.
Determination of necessary maintenance actions, such as lubrication, cleaning, adjustments, repair, etc.

4. *Redesign for maintenance* — this means to make the product easy to maintain, where maintenance is still necessary after trying to 'design away' the maintenance causes, or to increase the product's abilities to stand the causes. This step implies:

Incorporation of possibilities for measurement.
Incorporation of possibilities for adjustment.
Design which makes the necessary maintenance operations easy to perform.
Consideration of maintenance intervals.
Development of maintenance routines.
Design of necessary emergency systems.

  5. *Determination of spare part requirement.*

11.5.4   Areas of application

Maintenance analysis is of particular importance for products where a failure or an unexpected temporary shut-down due to maintenance needs, may expose human health to danger, or implies risk of pollution, loss of materials, etc.

11.5.5   Comments

Maintenance analysis is a method which should be regarded as an element in a larger system called *terotechnology*.

11.5.6   References

Blanchard 1976, Riggs 1981, Pahl and Beitz 1984.

11.6   FAULT ANALYSIS BY BRAINSTORMING

11.6.1   Definition

Fault analysis by brainstorming is a creative method which helps to discover faults and fault possibilities in new products before they are introduced on the market.

11.6.2   Purpose

The main purpose of the analysis is to improve the quality of the product, and thereby reduce the number of reclamations and the service cost.

11.6.3 Description

A fault analysis by brainstorming involves the following steps:

1. *Selection of product* – a product is selected that has not yet been introduced on the market.
2. *Brainstorming* – a group of six or seven persons is used. The group is given the task of finding out as many faults and accidents as possible which may occur with the product.
3. *Evaluation* – all proposals from the preceding stage are evaluated.
4. *Laboratory tests* – all fault possibilities which cannot be clarified by an evaluation alone are examined by means of laboratory tests.
5. *Improvements* – the experience gained during evaluation and the test programme should be transformed into concrete improvements.

11.6.4 Areas of application

Fault analysis is especially useful when applied on products used by technically unskilled people, e.g. household appliances.

11.6.5 Comments

The most important stage at which the analysis should be carried out is when the prototype is in its final form and consequently corresponds with the final production model in all details. On an earlier stage, when working with different design concepts, the analysis may be used as a means of choosing the most favourable solution.

The brainstorming group should be formed with people of different professions. Some members should be persons who have not earlier worked on the project.

11.6.6 References

Holt 1973.

11.7 FAULT ANALYSIS BY LOGICAL METHODS

11.7.1 Definition

Fault analysis by logical methods is a tool for predicting all kinds of events and combinations of events which may cause functional failure in a system, or human injury.

11.7.2 Purpose

The purpose of this analysis is to avoid failures and/or human injury during regular or irregular use of the product by taking appropriate precautions during the design and production phase.

11.7.3 Description

1. *Selection of appropriate methods* — the methods mainly used are fault tree analysis (f.t.a.), failure modes and effects analysis (f.m.e.a.) and hazard analysis (h.a.) (see Method 11.4). Often one or several of these are used in combination with a reliability analysis (see Method 11.2).

2. *Designing a theoretical model of the system* — this may be a fault tree, a pneumatic, hydraulic or electrical diagram, a reliability diagram, etc.

3. *Analysing the model* — there are two approaches:

By f.t.a., defining unwanted conditions of the system, and by logical means detecting which events, component failures or operations may cause a system failure or hazard.

By f.m.e.a., defining the system effect of a failure of each specific component.

4. *Taking necessary precautions* — by means of altering the system design, choosing more reliable components, or enforcing a better quality control during regular production.

11.7.4 Areas of application

Fault analysis may be executed by all kinds of systems — electronic, hydraulic, pneumatic, mechanical — and by combinations of these. The greatest usability, however, is with complex systems with a great number of possible failure combinations.

11.7.5 Comments

There are several other fault analysis methods available, for instance failure modes analysis (f.m.a.), failure modes, effects and critical analysis (f.m.e.c.a.), and critical analysis (c.a.). These methods all originate from the f.m.e.a., however, and thus only reflect small modifications of the f.m.e.a.

11.7.6 References

Hammer 1972, Eisner 1972, Zemanick 1972, Riggs 1981, Pahl and Beitz 1984.

11.8   DESIGN REVIEW

11.8.1 Definition

Design review is one or a series of meetings organised to evaluate the product design, conducted by a team consisting mainly of specialists who are not directly associated with the development of the design in question.

11.8.2 Purpose

The purpose of this review is early detection and remedy of design deficiencies which could jeopardise successful performance during use, low cost production and low cost, prompt field maintenance.

11.8.3 Description

The use of formal design reviews involves the following steps:

1. *Planning and scheduling* – design review is conducted at several phases in the design and at several levels of the product hierarchy (system, subsystem, etc., down to specific parts). Meetings should for the most part be scheduled when making the project plan.

2. *Selecting the review team* – the team should consist of a core membership such as the project manager, a product designer, a reliability engineer, a production engineer, a sales engineer and a field service engineer. Other specialists should be called in as needed.

3. *Preparing the meetings* – agendas and documentation should be prepared and sent out in advance.

4. *Executing the meetings* – the project manager is usually the chairman. The design reviews are mandatory, either through customer demand or through upper management policy.

5. *Follow-up* – minutes of meetings are prepared and circulated. Follow-up action should likewise be formalised.

11.8.4 Areas of application

Design reviews will be advantageous both for new product designs and for changing old designs, presupposing that the review team together possesses more technical knowledge than the designer alone. This usually means that the design either involves new technology to the company, is of a certain complexity, or requires special production or field knowledge.

11.8.5 Comments

The purpose of a design review is not to criticise the work performed by the designer, but rather to act as a source of good ideas in order to achieve an even more perfect design. The early warning concept is essential. In executing the meetings, the use of creative techniques may be helpful.

11.8.6 References

Juran 1974, Blanchard 1976, Pahl and Beitz 1984.

12. Design Calculation

12.1 STRESS CALCULATION

12.1.1 Definition

Stress calculation is the determination of the dynamic and static external forces a design will be exposed to, and how these forces will affect internal stresses, deformations and the expected life of the design. The calculation may be analytical or numerical, and may involve the use of computers.

12.1.2 References

Timoshenko and Goodier 1970, Zienkiewicz 1977.

12.2 MECHANICAL VIBRATION CALCULATION

12.2.1 Definition

Mechanical vibration calculation is the method of determining the expected response of a design which is exposed to a vibratory force or movement, including the determination of the different modes of vibration and the corresponding resonant frequencies.

12.2.2 References

Den Hartog 1956, Bishop and Johnsen 1960.

12.3 FLOW CALCULATION

12.3.1 Definition

Flow calculation is the method of determining flow characteristics of a fluid (such as flow rate, pressure and pressure gradient, velocity profiles, friction and friction work) for fluids which form an integrated element in a mechanical design or system.

12.3.2 References

McAdams 1954, Schmidt 1963, Olson 1980.

12.4   THERMAL CALCULATION

12.4.1 Definition

Thermal calculation is the method of determining the internal thermal state of a design, and the heat exchange with its surroundings. The calculation will include parameters like heat flow, temperature fields and transient temperatures.

12.4.2 References

McAdams 1954, Schmidt 1963, Sonntag and van Wylen 1982.

12.5   CYBERNETIC CALCULATION

12.5.1 Definition

Cybernetic calculation is the adaption and application of mathematical models and tools originally developed within the field of cybernetics, or mechanical or mixed systems, in cases where feedback of information is involved in control and stability analysis.

12.5.2 References

Lewis 1962, Shinners 1979.

13. Quality Verification

13.1 LABORATORY TESTING

13.1.1 Definition

Laboratory testing is a method for testing a design under prescribed and controlled conditions of use in an environment which may or may not simulate operational conditions.

13.1.2 Purpose

The purpose is to verify that a proposed or final design is applicable, i.e. has the expected properties.

13.1.3 Description

Laboratory testing usually involves the following steps:

1. *Making a model of the design to be tested* — most often a prototype or samples from test runs are used.
2. *Simulating the operational conditions* — i.e. trying to copy the conditions under which the product is actually going to be used in the market.
3. *Evaluating the test results* — i.e. evaluating the quality of design (the ability of the design to meet the functional specifications), and making a decision with respect to necessary alterations.

13.1.4 Areas of application

Laboratory testing always involves a higher degree of uncertainty than user testing. The method is therefore most applicable when user testing is impossible or impracticable — usually for economic or time reasons — provided it is possible to simulate actual use in the laboratory.

13.1.5   Comments

Laboratory testing should, when executed, be succeeded by user testing.

13.1.6   References

Cronstedt 1963, Juran 1974, Blanchard 1976, Hisrich and Peters 1978, Pessemier 1982, Tushman and Moore 1982, Kotler 1984, Kinnear and Taylor 1987.

13.2   USER TESTING

13.2.1   Definition

User testing is a method for testing a new product's fitness for use by letting one or several potential buyers make regular use of it, before regular manufacturing and marketing.

13.2.2   Purpose

The purpose is to minimise the risk of a large number of unexpected claims and other kinds of adverse reactions towards the product.

13.2.3   Description

User testing may involve the following steps:

1. *Producing a sufficient number of products which are representative for regular production* – this can be done by mass production, by a pilot run, or by a number of prototypes.
2. *Selecting users* – this includes determination of size and composition of the sample.
3. *Distributing the products* – the product should be accompanied by a letter stating purpose and expected characteristics.
4. *Follow-up* – i.e. executing the technical checking of the products in use and exploring the users' evaluation of the product.

13.2.4   Areas of application

User testing is especially valuable for the launching of products or designs which are new to the company. It can be applied to both industrial and consumer goods.

13.2.5   Comments

User testing is a last check of the validity of the need analysis, the quality of design and the quality of conformance before regular marketing. Major changes in the design at this stage would indicate insufficient quality planning, and should not occur.

13.2.6   References

Kotler 1972, Luch 1972, Scheuing 1972, Blanchard 1976, Pessemier 1982, Tushman and Moore 1982, Kotler 1984, O'Shaughnessy 1984, Holt 1987, Kinnear and Taylor 1987.

14. Manufacturing Preparation

14.1 MAKE/BUY ANALYSIS

14.1.1 Definition

A make/buy analysis is a method for providing a basis for deciding whether a complete product, or some of its components, should be bought from outside or manufactured within the company.

14.1.2 References

Wilson 1973, Blanchard 1976, Buffa 1977, Hinterhuber 1977, Twiss and Weinshall 1980, Gibson 1981, Pessemier 1982, Hayes and Wheelwright 1984, Holt 1987.

14.2 EQUIPMENT AND TOOLING

14.2.1 Definition

Planning of equipment and tooling involve development and analysis of alternative solutions for the manufacturing operations, and choice of the final solution by means of relevant criteria.

14.2.2 References

Wilson 1973, Blanchard 1976, Buffa 1977, Ramo 1980, Toffler 1980, Twiss and Weinshall 1980, Riggs 1981, Tushman and Moore 1982, Wilson *et al.* 1982, Hayes and Wheelwright 1984, David 1986, Hübner 1986, Holt 1987.

14.3 PROCESS AND OPERATION PLANNING

14.3.1 Definition

Process and operation planning involves development and analysis of alternative methods for the manufacturing, and assembly of components, and choice of the final solution by means of relevant criteria.

14.3.2 References

Wilson 1973, Buffa 1977, Ramo 1980, Toffler 1980, Twiss and Weinshall 1980, Riggs 1981, Tushman and Moore 1982, Wilson *et al.* 1982, Hayes and Wheelwright 1984, David 1986, Hübner 1986, Holt 1987.

14.4   MATERIAL PLANNING

14.4.1 Definition

Material planning involves an evaluation of material specifications and the determination of quantities and delivery schedules for materials and components.

14.4.2 References

Blanchard 1976, Hussey 1976, Buffa 1977, Riggs 1981, Hayes and Wheelwright 1984, David 1986.

14.5   QUALITY CONTROL PLANNING

14.5.1 Definition

Quality control planning involves analysis and determination of procedures for routine operations in quality control.

14.5.2 References

Wilson 1973, Blanchard 1976, Buffa 1977, Ramo 1980, Hayes and Wheelwright 1984, David 1986, Holt 1987.

14.6   DESIGN FOR MANUFACTURING

14.6.1 Definition

Design for manufacturing (*detailed design, design review, producibility engineering*) is a method where material and manufacturing knowhow, experience from prototype testing, etc., are used to design the product, determine quality performance and tolerances, etc., for cost reduction and manufacturing efficiency.

14.6.2   References

Cronstedt 1963, Gregory 1972, Design Council 1975, Blanchard 1976, Buffa 1977, Roth 1982, Koller 1985.

15. Marketing Preparation

15.1 DISTRIBUTION

15.1.1 Definition

The expression *distribution* is understood to mean the methods used to direct the stream of goods and services from the producer to the consumer.

15.1.2 Purpose

The purpose in the planning of a distribution scheme is to find the most appropriate channel for distribution of the product.

15.1.3 Description

The most important phases in planning for distribution are the following:

1. *Data collection* – this primarily encompasses data about pertinent markets. An analysis of customers is undertaken with the aid of available statistics or by one's own investigations; pertinent data are the type, numbers and location of customers as well as the buying and decision making characteristics of the various groups. In addition are data on sales grouped according to product, area, customer group, season and size of sales.

2. *Statistical analysis* – the collected material is analysed. Special emphasis is placed on variations in the median values since these, to a great extent, influence the dimensioning of the resources.

3. *Charting the storage (warehousing) function* – in addition to physical processes, the costs of storage and handling are analysed.

4. *Charting the transport function* – special emphasis is placed on the connection between internal and external transport as well as the costs entailed.

5. *Analysis of alternative channels of distribution* – alternatives are developed, and the effects of different solutions are investigated. The

analysis can include storage locations, transport methods, and administrative routines as well as the size of the storage facility and the rate of turnover (which determines the company's flexibility and ability to meet customer's desires). The various alternatives should also be evaluated in terms of what competitors have done and what they can be expected to do in the future. Factors that have an influence on the development of the distribution channels and which the company must consider in the analysis phase are:

The company's marketing horizon; this relates to how far the company will commit itself toward the customer in the distribution process.

Activities performed in distribution; these include activities of a sales promoting character ('order getting'), activities accompanying the filling of orders received ('order filling') and activities concerning the negotiation of payment ('order billing').

Main types of middlemen used; middlemen might be relevant here who assume ownership of the goods and who, thereby, constitute a customer horizon; e.g. wholesalers, importers and exporters. It can also be pertinent to evaluate the use of firms specialising in order getting, order filling, or order billing.

The number of participants in individual activities; mass distribution, selective distribution and exclusive distribution are relevant here.

Terms and conditions; this deals with the economic relations among the activities.

15.1.4   Areas of application

Distribution planning can be necessary upon introduction of a new or improved product. It can also be pertinent to revise the distribution apparatus upon changes in the competitive circumstances.

15.1.5   Comments

Selection of a distribution channel is a long-range decision which will have a great influence on other marketing efforts.

15.1.6   References

Kotler 1972, Scheuing 1972, Stone 1976, Giragosian 1978, Hisrich and Peters 1978, Ramo 1980, Toffler 1982, Kotler 1984, O'Shaughnessy 1984, David 1986.

15.2   SALE OF LICENCES

15.2.1   Definition

Sale of licences is a method for the sale of rights to use a technical idea or an invention, including description, drawings and other forms of knowhow.

15.2.2   Purpose

The purpose of selling licences is to put technical ideas and inventions to as good use as possible by giving other firms the opportunity to exploit them in market sectors not covered by the selling company.

15.2.3   Description

A sale of licence usually consists of the following steps:

1. *Selection of products and processes* — these will be technical solutions which the company itself does not want to exploit fully:

Products which the company is not able to exploit for special reasons, e.g. lack of financial resources.
Products which the company for strategic or other reasons does not want to offer to all geographical areas or to all user groups.

2. *Search for and choice of licence takers* — this requires considerable thought and effort, as the choice will have a great impact on the company for a long time. It is important to find firms with sufficient financial strength, manufacturing capability and marketing power. In order to get in touch with interested firms, the following channels may be used:

Trade fairs and exhibitions.
Trade delegations.
Professional journals and newspapers.
Special publications.
Patent offices.
Direct contact with firms that appear to be of potential interest.

3. *Formulation of agreement* — a task that requires legal knowledge and experience. For those not having the necessary background within the firm, assistance can be obtained from outside consultants, patent lawyers and business lawyers.

15.2.4   Areas of application

Sale of licences is of particular interest for innovation firms with too limited resources for operations in international markets.

15.2.5 Comments

Sale of licences will have much in common with purchase of licences (see Method 6.3).

15.2.6 References

Schmidt 1969, Hake 1971, Gorle and Long 1973, Vaitos 1973, Twiss 1974, Zallen 1974, RKW Borrmann 1976, RKW Grefermann 1976, Berridge 1977, Spitz 1977, Giragosian 1978.

15.3 ADVERTISING

15.3.1 Definition

Advertising involves communication methods to create, maintain, or increase the demand for a product.

15.3.2 References

Kotler 1972, Scheuing 1972, Zallen 1974, Berridge 1977, Spitz 1977, Giragosian 1978, Hisrich and Peters 1978, Webster 1979, Kotler 1984, O'Shaughnessy 1984, Chisnall 1985, Kinnear and Taylor 1987, Rossiter and Percy 1987.

15.4 SALES PROMOTION

15.4.1 Definition

Sales promotion is a method for supporting salesmen and dealers.

15.4.2 References

Kotler 1972, Scheuing 1972, Stone 1976, Berridge 1977, Spitz 1977, Giragosian 1978, Hisrich and Peters 1978, Webster 1979, Kotler 1984, O'Shaughnessy 1984, Rossiter and Percy 1987.

15.5 SALES PLANNING

15.5.1 Definition

Sales planning involves the estimating of expected sales during a definite period according to product and district.

15.5.2   References

Kotler 1972, Scheuing 1972, Hinterhuber 1977, Giragosian 1978, Hisrich and Peters 1978, Webster 1979, Kotler 1984, O'Shaughnessy 1984.

15.6   TRADE MARKS

15.6.1   Definition

A trade mark is a symbol, often protected by official registration, used for product identification.

15.6.2   References

Medcalf 1967, Scheuing 1972, Spitz 1977, Hisrich and Peters 1978, Kotler 1984.

16. Test Marketing

16.1 USE OF TEST AREA

16.1.1 Definition

Use of test area involves the selection of, and the selling of a product in an area which is representative of the marketing area that will be used upon launching the product in full scale.

16.1.2 Purpose

The purpose of using a test area is to reduce the risk by obtaining better knowledge of how consumers will receive the product and to test which sales set-up is best suited.

16.1.3 Description

Test marketing can be performed in a test area using the following procedure:

1. *Determination of the test area* — this area must be as representative as possible of the principal market, considering factors such as age distribution, income distribution, type of shops, etc. Furthermore, one must have access, in the test district, to advertising media corresponding to those intended to be used when the product is launched in full scale.
2. *Determination of the test period's duration* — there are three factors that must be considered:

Purchase frequency; this depends on whether the product is capital ware or consumption ware. For consumption wares the test ought to last long enough to cover two or three purchases, since it is the repeat purchases that are decisive.

Consideration of competitors; this implies that the test period must be as short as possible. Competitors will observe the results of the test and will take countermeasures. These can consist of copying the product, and indeed, launching the copy in full scale before test marketing is terminated.

Testing expenses; these often vary according to the duration of the test period, and consist of (a) expenses associated with the administration of the test itself, (b) earnings lost by delaying launching.

3. *Determination of the information desired* – three sets of information are desired:

Quantity of the product to be delivered to the test areas.
Placement of the wares in the shops, and, with consumption wares, the frequency of purchase.
Purchasing subgroups; which subgroups will remain loyal, and which subgroups will purchase only once.

4. *Collection of data from consumers* – the alternatives are:

Investigation of selected groups, wherein new groups of purchasers are selected and interviewed, say, every fortnight during the test period.
Panel data, wherein contact is maintained with the same selected group during the entire period.

16.1.4   *Areas of application*

Test marketing in selected areas is used mostly by companies in the consumer market. In the institutional market one often has direct contact and can test the product on a limited number of users.

16.1.5   *Comments*

The decisive factors in whether or not to test market are the competitive circumstances and the possibility of quick copying or imitation.

16.1.6   *References*

Kotler 1972, Luch 1972, Scheuing 1972, Berridge 1977, Midley 1977, Spitz 1977, Giragosian 1978, Hisrich and Peters 1978, Pessemier 1982, Tushman and Moore 1982, Kotler 1984, O'Shaughnessy 1984, Holt 1987, Kinnear and Taylor 1987.

16.2   USE OF TRADE FAIRS

16.2.1   *Definition*

Through the use of trade fairs for test marketing one can measure the interest in improved or new products by letting the public inspect and try them.

16.2.2 Purpose

The purpose of fairs for test marketing is to reduce the risk by obtaining information about the public's interest in the new product and to promote sales; the sales can occur directly or through the contact established.

16.2.3 Description

A firm that decides to participate in an exhibition or fair should have a clear purpose. Participation should not be planned as an isolated phenomenon, but rather, entered into as a part of the overall marketing effort. The following procedure indicates the major steps to be undertaken in preparation for participation:

1. *With a one year lead-time* — one investigates through one's industry association or the British National Export Council or the Confederation of British Industry about exhibitions or trade fairs that are pertinent. Further, information about the fair's significance is obtained as well as brochures and entry blanks.

2. *Nine to ten months before the fair* — one decides on the products to be exhibited and the space requirements. One also goes through the entry blank folder for the fair and enters into the checklist the deadlines for ordering electricity, furniture, water, etc. The entry blank is completed and sent, the deposit for the rental of booth space is paid, and hotel rooms are reserved.

3. *Six to seven months before the fair* — one ensures that there are sufficient brochures in stock, decides who is to man the booth, prepares press releases, and contacts the decoration firm. If the exhibition is in a foreign country, representatives, if any, are informed.

4. *Four to five months before the fair* — one ascertains which booth one has been assigned, goes through the fair regulations, and decides on the layout of the booth. Further, one checks that the brochures and press releases are in order, makes a media list for the press releases, and, if it is a trade fair, a list of the customers and contacts who should receive information and an invitation to the booth. Agreement is made with the forwarding agent about shipping and the necessary customs documents, and a check is made to confirm that the foreign representatives have received information about the participation.

5. *Three months before the fair* — one checks that the decorator is well ahead with the preparation of the booth and sends press releases to the fair's press office.

6. *Two months before the fair* — one informs the fair management about who is to man the booth, sends press reports to those on the media list, and decides the forwarding date for the wares for the fair.

7. *One month before the fair* — one makes arrangements for dismantling the booth and for return shipment of the wares to be returned, and checks that everything to accompany the shipment to the fair is ready.

8. *Three weeks before the fair* — one sends out invitation cards to customers and contacts, and checks that the shipment is going according to plan.

9. *Two weeks before the fair* — one has a meeting of the booth staff and goes through demonstration technique, customer relations, etc. Further, all requisites for the booth are made ready.

10. *One to two days before the opening* — one informs the main office about how things are going, gives the booth number, telephone number, etc.

16.2.4   Areas of application

An exhibition or fair can be used by all companies wishing to undertake market investigations, test a new product, train the firm's collaborators, disseminate information and create an 'image' of the company.

16.2.5   Comments

Gallup polls show that a significant proportion of industry uses the permanent, recognised trade fairs. One of the reasons is that a fair is one of the few media that brings the buyer and the seller into direct contact with each other. As far as orders are concerned, normally it is only after the second or third participation that sales results appear.

16.2.6   References

Kotler 1984.

17. Introduction

17.1 SELECTION OF STRATEGY FOR INTRODUCTION

17.1.1 Definition

Selection of strategy for introduction involves selection of activities and means for the launching of a product as well as of the duration and the intensity of the campaign.

17.1.2 Purpose

The purpose of the selection of strategy is to obtain maximum results by devoting resources to the dissemination of information, to dealers and the ultimate consumer, about the product, qualities, sales locations and prices.

17.1.3 Description

The procedure in the selection of strategy for introduction can be as follows:

1. *Preparation of plans* — this includes sales, methods of distribution, employment and training of salesmen, preparation of advertising material, demonstration set-ups, special publicity efforts, etc.
2. *Decision on size of the introduction campaign* — this depends on the type of product, expected sales, competitive situation, and the degree to which the product is new.
3. *Decision on the form of introduction* — it is decided here whether to test market or to launch the product in full scale. The decisive factors are the competitive situation, the possibility of quick copying or imitation, and the risk.

During the preparation of the plans one must also make a decision on the market persuasion policy. This involves:

Establishment of sales policy; guidelines can be mentioned for the size of the investment in sales, sales arguments and sales appeals, sales volume, salesmen, progression of sales intensity, areas of operation and timing of effort, as well as claims, exchanges and returns, etc.

Establishment of advertising policy; this includes the total advertising expense (advertising budget), the principal sales arguments and sales appeals, advertising style, advertising agencies, advertising media, dissemination, timing of the effort and its duration, and check-up on the advertising, technical as well as on the basis of results.

17.1.4   Areas of application

The methodology for the selection of strategy for introduction can be used by all companies that consciously enter into planning, implementation, and checking of the various activities in connection with the launching of new products.

17.1.5   Comments

The preparation of plans for market introduction should be begun parallel with technical planning. With a new product it is sensible to think about the product's profile from the very first moment. It is here that the basic idea is central. It is, therefore, important to give all coworkers complete understanding of this, and to see to it that their cooperative effort builds on the same idea and supports it.

17.1.6   References

Luch 1972, Midley 1977, Hisrich and Peters 1978, Kotler 1984.

17.2   RECORDING OF ACTUAL SALES

17.2.1   Definition

The recording of actual sales means the systematic measurement of the amounts sold per period (day, week, etc.) during the introduction period.

17.2.2   References

Hisrich and Peters 1978, Kotler 1984.

18. Registration of Manufacturing and Marketing Data

18.1 REGISTRATION OF QUALITY PARAMETERS

18.1.1 Definition

Registration of quality parameters means collecting and analysing cost data related to the quality of conformity.

18.1.2 Purpose

The purpose is to control important parts of manufacturing costs in order to obtain the optimum conformity level.

18.1.3 Description

The registration of quality parameters involves the following steps:

1. *Selection of appropriate quality parameters* – i.e. internal failure costs, preventive quality costs and inspection costs.
2. *Designing a registration system* – quality costs not being reported by the accounting system should be recorded by means of special registration sheets.
3. *Registration and analysis of data* – this includes calculation of the total quality costs (i.e. the previously mentioned costs plus the external failure costs), analysis of the figures for significant trends, and decision on actions to be taken in order to reduce total quality costs.

18.1.4 Areas of application

Registration of quality parameters may and should be executed by all kinds of production.

18.1.5   Comments

The registration system should be designed to fit each specific company, and may hence be a simple manual registration of failure rates during production, or an almost complete registration of all quality parameters by means of electronic data processing.

18.1.6   References

Juran 1974, Blanchard 1976, Ramo 1980, Riggs 1981, Hayes and Wheelwright 1984, Holt 1987.

18.2   QUANTITY

18.2.1   Definition

The expression 'quantity' relates to methods for systematic recording and analysis, at regular intervals, of the quantities of the product manufactured during the preceding period.

18.2.2   References

Blanchard 1976, Buffa 1977, Ramo 1980, Riggs 1981, Kotler 1984.

18.3   SALES

18.3.1   Definition

The expression 'sales' relates to the systematic recording and analysis, at regular intervals, of the quantity sold of the product during the preceding period. (This is not to be confused with recording of actual sales, Method 17.2, which refers only to sales during the introduction period.)

18.3.2   References

Riggs 1981, Kotler 1984.

18.4   COSTS

18.4.1   Definition

The expression 'costs' relates to the systematic recording and analysis, at regular intervals, of cost and efficiency of manufacturing operations, capacity utilisation in manufacturing departments, etc.

19. Methods for Evaluation of Products and Processes

19.1 FIELD REPORTS

19.1.1 Definition

A field report involves obtaining information, in the form of complaints and claims, about the reception and acceptance of the product by users.

19.1.2 Purpose

The purpose of field reports is to obtain the best possible basis for decision making with regard to improving the suitability of the product for the market by altered marketing practice or by product improvement.

19.1.3 Description

A general procedure for complaints and claims could be:

1. *The returned product or consignment is recorded* – this consists of entry into a claims book with the date, customer's name, statement of the reason for the complaint, and other details as necessary to permit returning to the complaint upon reminder by the customer.

2. *Copy of receipt* – this is sent to the sales department, which adds to it information on credit standing, etc. If the reason for the claim is for late delivery, a copy of the order and the delivery date is obtained. This is presented to management for sales, which, in the case of obvious unreasonableness, takes the matter up with the customer, either directly or through the salesman. If the claim is sustained, this is so entered on the receipt. A more thorough handling of the case is then necessary.

3. *Statement of proceedings* – ordinarily, the product/consignment is sent to the quality control department. This department enters its commentary on the receipt, which is returned to the sales department who then take up the matter with the customer.

In connection with claims, it is important that:

The proceedings are given high priority. The customer ought to get a reply as soon as possible, preferably within a few days. A quick and effective handling can turn the situation into a sales advantage instead of a sales hindrance.

Monthly statistics are worked out on the basis of the claims book. Norm figures should be worked out. If too great a deviation one must decide what should be done to improve the situation.

Appropriate routines exist. This concerns the internal handling of complaints as well as the field personnel.

19.1.4   Areas of application

Field reports should be used by all companies wanting a rapid and satisfactory handling of claims and complaints from their customers.

19.1.5   Comments

It is important that both claims and complaints are handled by both the sales department and the salesmen. Handling includes many aspects which do not necessarily have anything to do with quality, such as general customer relations, the customer's pre-established attitude toward the ultimate consumer, confidence, delivery time, competitive situation, the relative quality of competitors, etc.

19.1.6   References

Kotler 1984.

19.2   PROJECT EVALUATION

19.2.1   Definition

A project evaluation is a critical analysis undertaken after the completion of a project in order to assess the results obtained.

19.2.2   Purpose

The purpose of the evaluation is to achieve a basis for evaluation of the project; to discover weaknesses and strengths in the project planning and control processes; to learn from experience for planning and implementation of future projects.

19.2.3   Description

A project evaluation involves the following steps:

1. *Determination of objectives* – the emphasis may be on evaluating departments involved, on the recording and assessment of experience, or on both.
2. *Determination when to make the evaluation* – the evaluation may be undertaken one or more times at any time between the end of the introduction period and the end of the life of the product.
3. *Selection of subjects to be studied* – depending on the objectives, these may include:

Technical results.
Marketing results.
Economic results.
Financial results.
Time and costs.
Methods of planning and implementation.

4. *Collection and analysis of data* – relevant data are collected, reported and analysed by those concerned. The analysis may include comparisons of results with objectives, assumptions and expectations at the start of the project, comparisons with similar projects, accuracy of estimates and forecasts, attitude and behaviour of the departments and personalities involved, etc.

19.2.4   Areas of application

A project evaluation should be considered for all projects concerned with new products and major improvements in existing products.

19.2.5   Comments

As indicated, the evaluation may be undertaken one or more times. The most correct picture of the degree of success can be obtained only when all relevant data are available, i.e. at the end of the life of the product. However, for a more timely, though less accurate picture it is usually desirable to perform an evaluation at a much earlier date.

19.2.6   References

Jones 1970, Blanchard 1976, Kotler 1984.

20. Elimination Analysis

20.1 PRODUCT–MARKET MATRIX

20.1.1 Definition

An elimination analysis with the aid of a *product–market matrix* is a graphic method in matrix form that, for existing as well as improved and new product, shows alternative possibilities such as continued sales in existing, or new markets, as well as product elimination.

20.1.2 Purpose

The purpose of an analysis of the product–market matrix is to provide a basis for managing the company's product mix by regularly and systematically evaluating the various possibilities that exist.

20.1.3 Description

The procedure in the use of a product–market matrix can be as follows:

1. *Preparation of the matrix* – on the product side of the matrix, the existing products, improved products, and new products are listed; on the market side, in addition to product elimination, existing and new markets in the form of customer groups or geographic areas are listed.

2. *Analysis of products* – in connection with the matrix it is pertinent to investigate the position of the product in its life cycle, use area, comparison with products using competitive technology, comparison with products using similar technology, advantages for the user, production capacity, seasonal dependency, percentage of the total sales of the company, sensitivity to business conditions, the gross profit margin for the product, and the gross profit ratio (gross profit margin/net sales). The last two values are evaluated relative to previously established profitability criteria.

3. *Analysis of market sectors* – pertinent considerations for each market sector will be the company's position in the sector, general public purchasing power, the business cycle, consumption and purchasing

habits, competitive conditions, legislative and social conditions, and the gross profit margin and gross profit ratio from sale in the sector. The last two are evaluated relative to the company's profitability criteria.

20.1.4   Areas of application

A product–market matrix can be a useful tool for companies that pay attention to the systematic monitoring of their product mix, including the elimination of existing products.

20.1.5   Comments

Companies that would like to start analysing their product mix with the aid of a product–market matrix, either because of an acute situation or as a regular monitoring operation, would profit by taking only the most important products and markets at the beginning and later expanding the matrix gradually.

20.1.6   References

Holt 1987

20.2   LIFE CYCLE ANALYSIS

20.2.1   Definition

An elimination analysis by means of the life cycle of a product is performed to clarify where on the time scale the product is located within its anticipated economic lifespan.

20.2.2   Purpose

The purpose of the method is to obtain a basis for evaluation of when elimination of a product ought to be planned and implemented.

20.2.3   Description

In order to obtain knowledge of the life cycle's form, the rapidity with which this curve is traversed, and when the market is saturated, it is necessary to study market acceptance of the product. Such a study usually involves:

1. *Analysis of the development of factors influencing demand* – this includes economic and technological trends, long range changes in

consumption patterns and consumer tastes, changes in the social environment, and developments in competing companies and products.

2. *Analysis of the product's position* — this includes people's knowledge of the product (its existence and capabilities), people's attitudes toward the product (the product's justification for existence and its asserted advantages or disadvantages relative to other products), the manner in which people are informed about the product, what is especially noticeable about the product, plans for buying the product in the future, and which consumer groups appear to be the most interested in the product.

20.2.4   Areas of application

Analysis and monitoring of the life cycle of a product, conducted regularly, can be pertinent for companies that engage in systematic market planning and forecasting.

20.2.5   Comments

The method is time consuming, and there can be considerable uncertainty in estimation of trends and future developments.

20.2.6   References

Gerstenfeld 1970, Hake 1971, Kotler 1972, Luch 1972, Gorle and Long 1973, Twiss 1974, Blanchard 1976, Gee and Tylor 1976, Stone 1976, Berridge 1977, Hinterhuber 1977, Spitz 1977, Hisrich and Peters 1978, Webster 1979, Twiss and Weinshall 1980, Riggs 1981, Pessemier 1982, Roth 1982, Tushman and Moore 1982, Kotler 1984, O'Shaughnessy 1984, Chisnall 1985, Holt 1987.

20.3   SALES TRENDS

20.3.1   Definition

An elimination analysis with the aid of *sales trends* is a quantitative method with major emphasis upon changes in sales volume.

20.3.2   Purpose

The purpose of such a survey is to create a quantitative basis to evaluate whether or not an unprofitable product should be abandoned.

20.3.3   Description

A procedure that can be useful for localising weak products in the product mix is:

1. *Investigation of the product's share of the company's total sales* – the investigation is performed on a running basis, but with reference to definite periods. If it shows a decline, one should:

Look at the sales volume for the product, adjusted for seasonal variations; is there a decline during the period?
Find the product's market share for the period; is there a decline?
Consider the variable costs in per cent of the price; are they increasing?
Analyse the product's contribution to covering overhead costs; does it show a decline for the period?

If the answer is 'yes' on one or more points, it can be useful to dig deeper to see whether the product should be eliminated, e.g. with the aid of an *ad hoc* group composed of representatives from various departments such as purchasing, product development, marketing, manufacturing and accounting.

2. *Product evaluation* – the following considerations may be relevant here:

What are the total sales in the market for which the product is intended? Are the sales increasing or declining?
Is there any possibility for focusing effort upon special market sectors?
Is it possible to make product changes which can lead to increased sales or reduced costs?
Has the product any consequences for the manufacturing and sales of other products? Does it have an inhibiting or an encouraging effect?
Can elimination of the product occur without causing dissatisfaction among dealers and customers?
Is the product necessary to maintain employment?
Do obvious alternatives for the product exist?

3. *Preparation of a plan for possible elimination* – if the evaluation says that the product should be abandoned, then:

A plan is set up for how this is to be done.
Investigation is made as to the extent of the obligation to maintain a stock of spare parts, and for how long.
The possibility is evaluated for the selling or turning over of the product and the service activity to other companies.

In order not to lose good will, consideration is made to giving the dealer special support for the selling out of the remainder.

20.3.4   Areas of application

The method can be used for all types of products sold in quantities.

20.3.5   Comments

The method is based on recording changes in the product's position from period to period. The length of the period that should be used (months, half-year, year) depends on the size of the product selection and how quickly it changes. The method is adaptable to electronic data processing, so that the products that should be examined are routinely separated out.

Quantitative information will considerably aid the evaluation, but other considerations can also become manifest. Should there be extraordinary success for one product, one would immediately be more attentive to the possibility of eliminating other products. Should one experience a decline in business accompanied by poor sales of all products, it could become far more difficult to eliminate a product, since one is concentrating on selling whatever can be sold in order to maintain activity.

20.3.6   References

Spitz 1977, Pessemier 1982, Kotler 1984.

20.4   PROFIT DATA

20.4.1   Definition

An elimination analysis with the aid of *profit data* is a quantitative method where the emphasis is upon profit and cost data.

20.4.2   Purpose

The purpose of using profit data is to focus attention on the economic aspects on the situation when making an elimination analysis.

20.4.3 Description

Basically one can distinguish between two different approaches based on profit data:

The cash return method; the earnings of the product are here defined as the cash income that would be lost by elimination less the cash expenses that would be avoided thereby. The investment base is calculated by finding the net disposal value of the investment that would be released by the elimination. By comparing the cash return with some minimum rate of return, one achieves a basis for the elimination decision.

The book return method; here the net profit of a product, i.e. the difference between its sales income and expenses, is divided with the net book investment devoted to it. This gives the rate of return of the product, which is compared with a desired rate of return.

20.4.4 Area of application

The method can be a useful tool in companies who have a system for budgetary control which can provide the necessary cost and profit data.

20.4.5 Comments

The profit method should be used with care. In addition to the economic profitability, there are other factors, mostly of a social nature, that may come into the picture. Thus, there may be situations where the company would support a product that yields less than the standard return because other considerations make it desirable.

20.4.6 References

Shillinglaw 1957, Spitz 1977, Pessemier 1982.

21. Strategy Formulation

21.1 GAP ANALYSIS

21.1.1 Definition

Gap analysis is an aid to determine the future gap between the growth objective of the firm and future results predicted on the basis of current products and new products planned for introduction.

21.1.2 Purpose

The purpose of a gap analysis is to formulate a concrete, quantitative objective for strategy formulation.

21.1.3 Description

A gap analysis may be undertaken in the following way:

1. Determination of a quantitative growth objective, e.g., a certain increase in annual turnover or profitability, as a function of time.

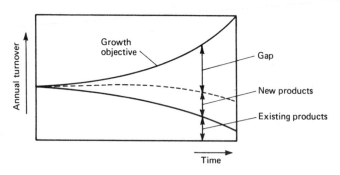

2. Possible correction of the objective for price changes due to influences of the business cycle (inflation, deflation, recession).

3. Development of sales forecasts, e.g., over a five-year period, for current and new products (products under development, and products planned for development or acquisition). The forecasts may be based on historical sales trends, business forecasts from nation and international organisations, predictions from dealers and customers, etc.

4. Presentation of the data in a diagram as indicated above.

21.1.4   Areas of application

Gap analysis is an important analytical tool for firms which frequently have to introduce new products.

21.1.5   Comments

The gap diagram and its underlying data should be updated regularly or for special occasions, e.g., when deciding upon the introduction of a new major product.

21.1.6   References

Gerstenfeld 1970, Kramer and Appelt 1974, Sveriges Mekanförbund 1974, Gee and Tylor 1976, Hussey 1976, Geschka 1978, Holt 1978, Hinterhuber 1980, Kotler 1984, O'Shaughnessy 1984, Holt 1987.

21.2   CAPABILITY ANALYSIS

21.2.1   Definition

Capability analysis is a method for evaluating the human, physical and financial resources of the firm in terms of strengths and weaknesses.

21.2.2   Purpose

The purpose of a capability analysis is to obtain a basis for a quantitative and qualitative evaluation of the potential of the firm.

21.2.3 Description

A capability analysis may be undertaken as follows:

1. Determination of *factors* to be studied (the following checklist may serve as a starting point):

Management; business concept, strategy; size, education, experience, age distribution and special competencies of top management; attitude, risk willingness and orientation towards the future; type of leadership, participation; management development, organisational development, creativity development; information, communication; organisation for current and future oriented activities.

Marketing; policies; size, education, experience, age distribution and special competencies of staff; technical, economical and social characteristics of products; structure and importance of competition; market share and trend of market growth; relation to customers, dependence on specific customer groups; image of the firm from a customer point of view; distribution of sales on product lines and products; organisation of sales, distribution, service and export; sales promotion, advertising and public relations; methods for the assessment of user needs; logistics including stores and transport.

R & D/engineering; policies, size, education, experience, age distribution and special competencies of staff; R & D in percent of annual sale; organisation and procedures for processing of projects; new products developed in the last five years, current projects.

Purchasing; policies, size, education, experience, age distribution and special competencies of staff; organisation and procedures for purchasing and raw material storage; capital tied up in raw materials.

Manufacturing; policies, size, education, experience, age distribution and special competencies of staff; type of manufacturing; organisation and procedures; logistics; industrial engineering; quality control; maintenance; waste disposal; environment pollution; buildings and equipment;

Finance; policies, size, experience, age distribution and special competencies of staff; organisation and procedures for financial and cost accounting; capital structure; profitability, liquidity, solidity and capital reserves; short-term obligations; possibilities for borrowing.

2. Evaluation of *strengths and weaknesses* of capability factors with regard to status and trends.

3. Summarisation of results by focusing upon the most pertinent strengths and weaknesses. These may be presented graphically as a *capability profile chart*. Data for the strongest competitors may also be indicated in the chart.

21.2.4 Areas of application

A capability analysis is used in connection with decisions related to strategy formulation, diversification and product planning. It provides both a general background as well as a foundation for development of search and evaluation criteria.

21.2.5 Comments

The capability analysis should be repeated and the conclusions modified when major changes in relevant data have occurred. One should aim for solutions which capitalise upon specific strengths and avoid weaknesses. Special attention should be given to the *driving force*, i.e., the factors which keep the firm in a certain direction. Further, one should be careful in excluding relevant solutions because of existing capability deficiencies if these can be changed into positive contributors.

21.2.6 References

Geschka and Pausewang 1974; 1978, Kramer and Appelt 1974, Gee and Tylor 1976, Stone 1976, Hinterhuber 1977, David 1986.

21.3 COMPETITIVE STRENGTHS — MARKET ATTRACTIVENESS MATRIX

21.3.1 Definition

The CS-MA matrix is an aid for determining the relative position of product lines and diversification projects based on an analysis of their competitive strength and the attractiveness of their markets.

21.3.2 Purpose

The purpose of CS-MA matrix is to provide an analytical basis for strategic decisions concerning resource allocation (including possible elimination) for existing product lines as well as for decisions concerning diversification into new business areas.

21.3.3 Description

A CS-MA matrix is made in the following way:

1. Determination of competitive strength factors such as market share, market capability, product quality, technological advantages, manufacturing capability, raw material and energy availability, etc.

2. Determination of relative competitive strength of product lines or diversification options by comparing the strength factors of the firm with the strongest competitors.

3. Determination of market attractiveness by means of factors such as overall size, growth rate, profit potential, segmentation potential, ease of entry, diversity, number and strength of competitors; role of technological, social, political and economical aspects such as ecology, laws and regulations, direct government interference, foreign exchange, impact of the business cycle, etc.

4. Design of the matrix. This includes selection of scale, e.g., 0–60 or 0–100, and division into fields, e.g., 2 × 2 or 3 × 3. By using a 0–60 scale as indicated in the figure, the maximum score on both

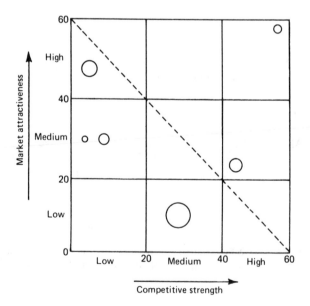

dimensions would be 120 points. This equals the upper right-hand corner.

5. Determination of a scoring scale, e.g., low, medium and high. One may also use a quantitative scale. If there are six strength and six attraction factors and the matrix has a 0–60 scale, each factor will have a 0–10 scale. Usually the factors are given the same weight, but one may refine the approach by using a special weighting scheme.

6. Scoring of product lines or diversification projects and allocation to fields in the diagram. Annual turnover of each product or project may be indicated by means of the size of each circle as indicated in the figure.

7. Analysis of possible strategies based on the position of the product lines or diversification projects. Those below the diagonal have low competitive strength in markets with low attraction. Divestment and elimination strategies are here relevant. On the other hand, for product lines above the diagonal, investment and growth strategies are most appropriate. Selective strategies should be applied to product lines close to the diagonal.

21.3.4 Areas of application

The CS-MA matrix is first of all a tool for the analysis and formulation of strategies concerning existing products. It may also be used for analysis of different units in a firm, e.g., divisions or profit centres. Other applications are related to analysis of competitors and decisions concerning diversification into new business areas including options such as internal development, licensing, acquisition, and joint ventures.

21.3.5 Comments

The CS-MA matrix represents a flexible and tailor-made approach as it is designed according to the particular needs and characteristics of the firm using it. When major changes in the firm or its environment occur, the matrix should be updated by means of adjustments in the factors and their scaling. The matrix should be used with an open mind; in some situations factors not reflected in the matrix may have great influence.

21.3.6   References

Hinterhuber 1977, Bruce Merrifield 1978, Nichols-Manning 1978, Thackray 1978, Hinterhuber 1980, Pessemier 1982, Tushman and Moore 1982, Kotler 1984, O'Shaughnessy 1984, Chisnall 1985, Holt 1987.

21.4   MARKET SHARE — MARKET GROWTH MATRIX

21.4.1   Definition

The MS-MG matrix is an aid for determining the relative position of product lines based on their relative market share and the growth patterns of their markets.

21.4.2   Purpose

The purpose of the MS-MG matrix is to provide an analytical basis for strategic decisions concerning support or elimination of product lines.

21.4.3   Description

The MS-MG matrix represents a simplification of the CS-MA matrix. It is made in the following way:

1.   Design of the matrix. The basic procedure is the same as for the CS-MA matrix (see 21.3.3). However, the MS-MG matrix is easier to make; the two dimensions, as shown in the figure, are represented with only one factor each. Thus, competitive strength is replaced by relative market share, i.e., the market share of the firm in relation to the market share of the strongest competitor. In the same way, market attractiveness is replaced by the rate of market growth. The method is further simplified by using only four fields as shown in the figure.

2.   Analysis of possible strategies based on the position of the product lines in the matrix. As a rough guide, the following may be indicated:

Stars; product lines with high market share in a high growth market should be given strong support in order to keep their market shares and improve profit; most often investments are required in order to improve manufacturing or marketing operations.

Cash cows; product lines with high market share in a slow growth or declining market should be given enough support to maximise net cash flow without major investments.

Dilemma ('problem child'); product lines with low market share in a high growth market should be supported, for example by means of acquisition or cooperation with other firms with the aim of fast growth in market share, or divested.

Dogs ('cash trap'); product lines with low relative market share in a slow market growth should be divested and eliminated with the aim of minimising the loss.

21.4.4   Areas of application

The MS-MG matrix is used for the analysis and formulation of strategies concerning existing products. The underlying assumption is that it is not the absolute size of the firm that determines its profitability, but the relative size in terms of market share in a given market segment. There are indications that this is true in many cases. Thus, several studies show that the market leader also has the highest profitability. However, a high correlation between market share and profitability cannot always be taken for granted. In each case therefore, one must determine whether the underlying assumption is correct before using the MS-MG matrix.

21.4.5 Comments

The MS-MG matrix is easier to apply and requires much less work than the 'competitive strength-market attractiveness' matrix. One weakness is that it does not take technological factors into account, factors which may have a significant influence on the competitive strength of a firm (see also Comment 21.3.5).

21.4.6 References

Moose and Zakon 1971, Rhenman 1973, Buzzel *et al*. 1974, Normann 1977, Hinterhuber 1977, Merlino 1978, Tushman and Moore 1982, Kotler 1984, O'Shaughnessy 1984, Chisnall 1985, David 1986, Holt 1987.

21.5 PRODUCT/MARKET — STRATEGIC OPTION MATRIX

21.5.1 Definition

The PM-SO matrix is an aid for the determination and analysis of strategic alternatives.

21.5.2 Purpose

The purpose of the PM-SO matrix is to facilitate the search for strategic alternatives.

21.5.3 Description

The matrix is made in the following way:

1. Determination of possible product/market combinations.
2. Determination of possible options.
3. Design of the matrix; one example is indicated on the next side.
4. Analysis of the matrix; one should note here that not every option is appropriate for every product/market combination.

21.5.4   Areas of application

The PM-SO matrix can be applied in any situation where a company has to formulate a new strategy in order to reach its major objectives.

21.5.5   Comments

The PM-SO matrix indicates all strategic combinations. It can be simplified by combining options, e.g., 'mergers, acquisitions and joint ventures', and enlarged by expanding product/market combinations, e.g., subdividing 'new products' into 'new products for the firm' and 'new products for the market'.

At one extreme in the matrix are improvements in connection with the production of existing products for existing markets. Such an

Product/ market combinations
Strategic options	Existing products			New products		
	Existing markets	New broad markets	New specialised markets	Existing markets	New broad markets	New specialised markets
Improvement						
Purchase of licenses						
Mergers						
Acquisitions						
Joint ventures						
Internal R & D						
External R & D						
Subcontracting						
Distribution through others						
Distribution for others						
Manufacturing for others						
Selling of licenses						
Divestment						

improvement strategy may be implemented by new manufacturing processes, a new approach to distribution, change in advertising methods, etc. At the other extreme is a strategy based on a pioneering technological effort through the internal or external development of new products which are sold in new, specialised markets.

21.5.6 References

Scheuing 1972, Steele 1975, Hussey 1976, Holt 1987.

21.6 PERFORMANCE CRITERIA

21.6.1 Definition

Performance criteria are an aid for analysis and evaluation of the performance of the whole company as well as of its major activities.

21.6.2 Purpose

The purpose of using performance criteria is to provide a basis for judging the quality of management, for evaluating diversification proposals, and for making strategic decisions concerning support or elimination of product lines.

21.6.3 Description

Performance criteria are established and used for strategic purposes in the following way:

1. Selection of performance criteria against which each division, unit or diversification proposal is to be measured, e.g. sales in percent of total corporate sales, return on invested capital, annual earnings in percent of sales, competitive advantage through technology, proprietary products or market dominance, and quality of management.
2. Formulation of standards for each criterion; for the first one listed above it may be, for example that each unit should at least generate 10% of corporate sales.
3. Comparison of actual or estimated performance with standards, and decisions regarding possible action to be taken.

21.6.4   Areas of application

Performance criteria provide a basis for analysis of diversification proposals as well as for decisions concerning support or divestment of various divisions or units of a firm.

21.6.5   Comments

In connection with diversification proposals it should be taken into consideration that it may take some time before a satisfactory performance is reached. Also in connection with evaluation of existing divisions or units, the criteria should be used with care. Thus, if a division or unit does not satisfy certain of the criteria, one should investigate if the situation can be improved in a reasonable time and at an acceptable cost.

21.6.6   References

Nicholson 1979.

22. Diversification Studies

22.1 NEED – TECHNOLOGY – CUSTOMER MATRIX

22.1.1 Definition

The N-T-C matrix is an aid for an analysis and determination of the type of diversification required, based on considerations concerning existing and new needs, technologies and customers.

22.1.2 Purpose

The purpose of the N-T-C matrix is to give firms who want to diversify a framework for analysing and determining the type of diversification to be undertaken.

22.1.3 Description

The diversification analysis is based on the matrix below, which shows all possible alternatives. If a more detailed analysis is preferred, one may, in the matrix, distinguish between technologies new to the firm and new to the market, and between broad and narrow customer groups.

At one extreme in the matrix is market preservation, i.e., the sale of existing products to existing customers. At the other extreme, which represents the highest degree of change, is a lateral diversification where a new product, both in terms of needs and technology, is sold to new customers. This alternative has the highest risk, but offers the greatest profit potential if successful.

The various alternatives should be analysed and the consequences evaluated taking into account the human, financial and economic factors as well as the risks involved.

Needs or functions	Technology	Customers	
		Old	New
Existing	Existing	Market preservation 1	Market expansion 2
Existing	New	Technology change 3	Technology/ customer diversification 4
New	Existing	Need diversification 5	Need/customer diversification 6
New	New	Need/technology 7 diversification	Need/technology/ 8 customer diversification

22.1.4   Areas of application

The N-T-C matrix should be used early in a diversification study. It will provide thereby, a better basis for a top management decision on the type of diversification to be undertaken. Such a decision will help to limit the search area and thus facilitate search and selection of diversification ideas.

22.1.5   Comments

In the N-T-C matrix alternatives are presented according to increasing degree of change and novelty. The three listed first are concerned with exploiting the potential of existing products, whereas the remaining ones represent various degrees of diversification. To a certain degree, the arrangement of the matrix reflects the degree of risk, although in the long run great risks may also be involved in concentrating all resources upon the manufacturing, improvement and marketing of existing products.

22.1.6   References

Hirschmann and Kramer 1974, Geschka and Pausewang 1974; 1978, Hussey 1976, Holt 1987.

22.2   DIVERSIFICATION AREA — CAPABILITY MATRIX

22.2.1   Definition

The DA-C matrix is a tool for the systematic search and selection of ideas for new business areas.

22.2.2   Purpose

The purpose of the DA-C matrix is to assist the firm in the search stage of the diversification process by arriving at one or a limited number of relevant diversification areas.

22.2.3   Description

The following procedure may be used:

1.   Determination of relevant sectors for diversification; one may for example, select one or more among the following ones: the public sector, the industrial sector, the institutional sector, or the private consumer sector.

Search / Strengths Weaknesses	SECTORS		
	Public	Industrial	Consumer
Know-how in steel structures and mechanical transmissions			
Lack of know-how in electronics			
Efficient manufacturing facility			
Efficient purchasing organisation			
Lack of sales organisation and professional marketing staff			

2. Subdivision of the sectors selected according to search areas in terms of products or markets. The public sector may, for example, be subdivided into government, defence, health, education, roads, etc.

3. Determination of major strengths and weaknesses of the firm (see Method 21.2).

4. Design of the matrix, based on the results of the preceding steps, as indicated below.

5. Selection of one or more diversification areas by capitalising upon strengths and avoiding weaknesses. Areas of potential interest may be indicated in the matrix by, for example, the sign +.

22.2.4   Areas of application

The DA-C matrix is one of several approaches that may be used for the generation of ideas in connection with the search for and selection of diversification areas.

22.2.5   Comments

The DA-C matrix is a well-structured search approach. The determination of search areas is based on personal judgement of those involved, on the use of creative techniques, or by means of standardised product classifications.

The DA-C matrix facilitates the evaluation and final selection of the diversification area as relatively few, yet well-founded, ideas are generated.

22.2.6   References

Geschka and Pausewang 1974, Hirschmann and Kramer 1974, Stone 1976.

22.3   SCREENING PROCEDURES

22.3.1   Definition

A screening procedure is a systematic multistage approach for the selection of the best one among several ideas.

22.3.2 Purpose

The purpose of a screening procedure in connection with diversification studies is to arrive at the best idea for a new business area among a number of possible alternatives.

22.2.3 Description

The following procedure may be used (see also Method 5.1).

1. Grouping ideas for new business areas, if relevant and practical, into classes according to product areas, product lines, market areas, market segments or part of market segments.
2. Improvement and modification of potential valuable ideas before being evaluated.
3. Formulation of screening criteria related to marketing, technical, economical and social factors. Particularly during the early screening stages great attention should be given to factors such as market growth, market potential, competition and user needs. One should take into consideration the fact that those ideas should be eliminated that do not fit the business concept of the firm or its objectives with regard to profit, growth, public image, etc. Ideas accepted should be compatible with available know-how and human, technological (R & D), marketing, financial and manufacturing resources. When selecting criteria one should also take into consideration the effect of the diversification on employees of the firm, on venders, customers, and on society in general.
4. Screening through a step-wise reduction process where ideas are progressively eliminated, e.g., from 100 to 40 ideas, from 40 to 12, from 12 to 5, and from 5 to 1 idea. One single criterion, that can be answered by yes/no, or a simple checklist should be used during the early stages. If the selection is done by a group, one may base the first step on an overall judgement and only accept for further processing, ideas that are unanimously approved. Costly information should be used only in the last stages. The final screening may require a special feasibility study of the technological, marketing, financial, economical and social aspects of the problem. The study may also include a detailed profitability calculation with risk analysis and clarification of the consequences of the solution for groups inside and outside the firm.

In the first screening stages one or two experts may be used. Later an expert group with know-how concerning technological, marketing, financial and other relevant factors may be used. In the last stages the group may, for important projects, be supplemented by external expertise.

22.3.4 Areas of application

A systematic multistage screening procedure should be used in connection with diversification studies where one has to select one from among a large number of ideas that are generated simultaneously. A simplified approach may be used for evaluation or selection in cases where one has only one or, at most, a few diversification ideas.

A screening procedure similar to the one described should be used when one has to determine what products to make within the area selected for diversification.

22.3.5 Comments

In firms performing frequent or continuous diversification studies, it is most practical to use a fixed screening procedure. This procedure should be reviewed and updated from time to time in order to be compatible with internal and external factors. For firms that undertake diversification rather seldom, the best approach may be to tailor-make the procedure according to the particular situation.

22.3.6 References

Gerstenfeld 1970, Scheuing 1972, Holt (a) 1973, Twiss 1974, Ceschka and Pausewang 1974; 1978, Steele 1975, RKW Geyer 1976, RKW Brockhoff 1976, Stone 1976, Berridge 1977, Spitz 1977, Giragosian 1978, Hisrich and Peters 1978, Webster 1979, Pessemier 1982, Kotler 1984, Chisnall 1985, Holt 1987.

23. Product Planning Tools

23.1   PRODUCT PROPOSAL FORM

23.1.1   Definition

Product proposal refers to a tool that can be used for a systematical written presentation of proposals for new or improved products.

23.1.2   Purpose

The purpose of the product proposal is to secure that proposals are based on a systematical analysis of relevant technical, marketing, economical and social factors.

23.1.3   Description

A product proposal may be developed in the following way:

1.   Describe, and if possible and practicable, improve the product planning system.
2.   List the key persons who participate in evaluation and decision on product proposals and determine their information needs.
3.   Develop a practical form with space for relevant information. The head of the form may in addition to date, name and department of the person making the proposal, have information concerning routing of the proposal. The form may further have information concerning the following factors:

The product; what is it (precise description or sketch), what are the primary and secondary functions, what technologies may be used, how can it be made?
Costs; what costs will be required for development, tooling and marketing? What is the estimated product cost?

The market; what are primary and secondary target groups? What are their needs? What are possible applications? Who are main competitors? What are the advantages and disadvantages compared with competing products? What price can be expected? What is the size of existing and potential markets? How much can be sold per year?

Resources; what will be required of know-how, capital, raw materials, personnel, equipment and time before introduction?

Other information; here is reserved space for other items that the proposer feels is relevant for evaluation of the proposal.

4. Test the form through simulation or actual use during a test period.

5. Finalise the design of the form and issue relevant information to those concerned for motivation and proper use of the form.

6. Determine responsibilities for reception and further processing of proposals.

23.1.4   Areas of application

The product proposal can be designed to include information for new and improved products. It may also cover manufacturing processes if a separate form is not preferred for this purpose.

23.1.5   Comments

The design of the form should be adopted to the project selection technique used (see Method 6.1) and the practical possibilities of obtaining or estimating relevant data with reasonable accuracy.

23.1.6   References

Sveriges Mekanförbund 1973, Sveriges Mekanförbund 1974, Holt 1978, Holt 1987.

23.2   PRODUCT COUNCIL

23.2.1   Definition

The product council is an organisational device composed of high-level managers with functional responsibilities related to the central product planning and development activities.

23.2.2   Purpose

The purpose of the product council is overall co-ordination of activities related to product planning and development. It may include formulation of strategies and policies, decisions and recommendations concerning introduction of new and improved products, as well as elimination of old products, and control of major product innovation activities.

23.2.3   Description

The organisation of a product council may be done as follows:

1.   Describe, and if possible improve the product planning system.
2.   Discuss the need for a product council and possible alternatives with the chief executive and/or key managers as well as with key representatives of employees participating in product innovation processes.
3.   Develop and collect comments for at least two alternatives from those concerned.
4.   Develop and get approval from the chief executive of the final design of the product council.

23.2.4   Areas of application

A product council may be used in firms with frequent changes in its product spectrum for co-ordination, recommendation, decision making, and control of product innovation activities.

23.2.5   Comments

If the firm has other co-ordinating devices for product innovation activities, such as product managers, product coordination units, etc., this will influence the responsibility and composition of the product council.

In defining the responsibilities, special attention should be given to limiting the work of the council to activities having a major impact on the success of the product innovation effort.

The efficiency of the product council can be increased by using regular meeting dates or early call for meetings, well-defined agendas, short written summaries of decisions, and indication of responsibilities for action.

23.2.6 References

Sveriges Mekanförbund 1973, Sveriges Mekanförbund 1974, Holt 1978.

23.3 DEVELOPMENT ORDER (SPECIFICATIONS)

23.3.1 Definition

A development order is an aid for providing the information that is needed in order to start R & D on new or improved products.

23.3.2 Purpose

The purpose of the development order is to secure that the product will correspond to the technical, marketing, economical, social and legal requirements that have been determined during the idea generation stage.

23.3.3 Description

Content and procedures related to the development order should be developed in close co-operation with managers and operating staff from R & D, marketing, manufacturing and finance. The following steps may be included:

1. Development of a checklist with items to be specified. Among those to be considered are the following:

Performance requirements; functions, capacity, speed of performance, out-put rate, accuracy, size, weight, volume, etc.
Operational needs; installation, availability, safety, manoeuvreability, producibility, operational readiness, reliability, maintainability, supportability, foolproofness, etc.
Ergonomic requirements; physiological and psychological requirements related to the man—machine interface.
Appearance; shape, colour, surface, etc.
Environmental requirements; humidity, temperature, noise pollution, etc.
Legal requirements; existing and anticipated laws and regulations in user countries.

Technological requirements; solution concept, patents, know-how, etc.

Manufacturing requirements; equipment, subcontractors, etc.

In addition to the requirements listed above one may consider to include one or more of the items listed below:

Economic factors; anticipated revenue, life-cycle cost (all expected costs for development, investment, operation, support and disposal), sales price, quantity, product value for user, etc.

Marketing factors; type, size, stability and duration of market, time and methods for market introduction, description and evaluation of important competitors and their products.

In connection with the development order is usually undertaken a detailed planning of the project. The results of this planning in terms of a budget and a time schedule may, in condensed form, be included in the development order;

2. Determine responsibilities for provision of the information that is required.

3. Development of a procedure for provision and processing of the required information.

23.3.4 Areas of application

A development order is a useful tool in connection with most product innovation activities whether they take place continuously, or from time to time.

23.3.5 Comments

The development order should be complete and clear. However, one should be careful in specifying too much details, as this may hamper the possibility of creative behaviour of the R & D staff.

The core of the development order is information related to the requirements of the users. Therefore, one should study, and possibly improve, the approach used for need assessment, as well as the method used for converting needs into realistic specifications.

23.3.6 References

Holt 1978, Sveriges Mekanförbund 1974, Ramo 1980, Pahl and Beitz 1984, Koller 1985, Holt 1987.

23.4   PRODUCT CALENDAR

23.4.1 Definition

A product calendar is an aid for scheduling major activities related to development of the product spectrum.

23.4.2 Purpose

The purpose of the product calendar is to plan and control timing of development of new products, improvement of existing products, and withdrawal of unprofitable products.

23.4.3 Description

In co-operation with those concerned a product calendar may be developed in the following way:

1.   Determination of type and size of projects to be included.
2.   Determination of responsibility of those involved in provision of information, and in planning and control of progress.
3.   Determination of time-scale and tools to be used, e.g. gantt charts, planning boards, etc.

23.4.4 Application

Product calendar is mostly used in firms where product planning is a continuous activity and/or several projects take place at the same time.

23.4.5 Comments

The product calendar normally is limited to product development projects and product withdrawal projects. However, one may benefit from using it as a control device for the whole product life cycle. This can be done by indicating information related to irregular quality, decreasing sales, decreasing profitability, needs for product improvements, etc.

23.4.6   *References*

Holt 1978.

24. Product Innovation Organisation

24.1 PREPARATION CHECKLIST

24.1.1 Definition

A preparation checklist is an aid for analysing and planning projects concerned with the improvement of existing and the development of new product innovation organisations.

24.1.2 Purpose

The purpose of the preparation checklist is to provide an analytical basis and to tailor planning to the needs of the firm concerned.

24.1.3 Description

The following procedure may be used for preparing the study:

1. The promoter of the project, i.e., the person who initiated it or supported its initiation, should see to it that a qualified project manager is appointed for the planning of the project.

2. The project manager, in co-operation with the promoter, should analyse and plan the project by means of the following checklist:

Needs; how important are product innovations? Will they be more important in the future? What is the present organisation like? What weaknesses does it have? What changes are needed?

Timing; how urgent is the need for change? Is *now* the right time? Are key persons too occupied with other projects at present? Should the study be postponed until a more appropriate time?

Participants; who is the promoter of the study? What is his motivation? What persons with supervisory or operating responsibilities for product innovation activities will be directly influenced by change in the organisation? Who will indirectly be influenced by the study or the implementation of the results?

Engagement; how should the various groups of participants be involved? What resistance can be expected? How can acceptance and support of the project be gained? What information should be given and how? What training activities are needed as preparation?

Resources; what financial and human resources are required for the study? How much can be provided?

Organisation; should the study be organised as a project? Should a full-time or a part-time manager be used? Should he report to an executive or to a steering committee? Should an advisory board be established? How should it be composed? Should task forces be used? Should external or internal experts be used?

Approach; do available resources allow for a study of the whole product innovation process? If not, which of the four modules — integration, structural design, generation of ideas, or realisation of ideas — should be studied, and in what sequence?

Experimentation; do those concerned recognise the limitations in the theoretical background for the study? Are they willing to experiment with various solutions? Do they recognise the inherent risk in any solution?

Planning; how can the project be broken down into tasks? What procedures should be used for planning and monitoring the project? What provisions should be made for unforseen events? When should the planning stage be finished? When should the implementation stage be started, and when should it be finished?

Because of the innovative character of the study, it is not possible to develop detailed plans. Ample time should be provided for contingencies. There should be a flexible budget subdivided into months or quarters. The project should be subdivided into major activities e.g., by means of a gantt chart. An example of such a subdivision would be preparation of the study, situational analysis, problem definition, integration module, structural design module, module for generation of ideas and module for realisation of ideas.

24.1.4 Areas of application

The checklist can be used for the improvement of existing product innovation organisations as well as for the planning of new ones.

24.1.5   Comments

Design of an organisation for product innovation is a complex process that must be adapted to the individual company's special situation. As success to a large extent depends on the acceptance of the results by those concerned, great attention should be given to their involvement from the beginning. When appointing the project manager, a decision should be made as to whether he or another person should be responsible for the implementation of the project, which is characterised by less creative and theoretical thinking and more logical and action oriented thinking.

24.1.6   References

Morton 1971, Geschka 1975, Kleine 1975, Hussey 1976, Kilman *et al.* 1976, Strutz 1976, Blanchard 1976, Child 1977, Holt 1977, Khandwalla 1977, Kieser and Kubicek 1977, Siemens 1977, Bailey 1978, Kotter 1978, Capey and Carr 1982, Tushman and Moore 1982, Prosjektplan 1982.

24.2   FACTOR CHECKLIST

24.2.1   Definition

A factor checklist is an aid for analysis of the most important factors, comprising status as well as future developments, that will influence the design of a product innovation organisation.

24.2.2   Purpose

The purpose of the factor checklist is to serve as a basis for a systematical analysis of the situation of the firm, an analysis that involves a description, definition and indication of the impact of the most important factors on the design of the organisation for product innovation activities.

24.2.3   Description

The following procedure may be used for the analysis of the factors:

1.   The project manager, assisted, if necessary, by internal or external experts, should familiarise himself thoroughly with the key factors in the situational analysis.

2.   Together with those involved, the situation of the firm should be analysed by means of the following checklist:

The business concept; what is it? Should it be changed? Is it possible to change it with the present management?

Objectives, strategies and policies; how do they relate to product innovations? Are changes required? Can they be effected?

Management; who are the key decision makers? What is their attitude towards change and innovation? Is anybody hampering change? What can be done to remove negative management influences?

Employees; what is the employee attitude towards change and innovation? What can be done in terms of information and training to create a positive attitude towards the project?

Social and political changes; what changes can be expected? What will the impact on the innovation activities of the firm be? What are the organisational consequences?

Marketing and technological changes; what is the nature and rate of change of these factors? What is their impact on product innovations with regard to needs and approaches?

Economic changes; what is the impact of structural and cyclical changes? What changes are expected? Will they hamper or foster the development of an effective product innovation organisation?

Company size; what is the size of the company? What has been the rate of growth? What is expected in the future? What is the impact on the design of the organisation?

Market strategy; what is the strategy with regard to diversification? What is the competitive strategy of the firm? What are the customer types? Should any changes be made in the strategy? What are the organisational consequences?

Product factors; how many product lines does the firm have? How long are the average life-cycles of the products? What is the technological level? What changes are expected? What are the organisational consequences?

Project factors; what is the average number of product innovation projects processed simultaneously? What is the average project size? Are changes expected in this? What are the organisational consequences?

24.2.4   Areas of application

A situational analysis by means of the checklist should be undertaken whether the project involves minor changes or the design of a completely new product innovation organisation. The factors studied and the effort put into the work should be adapted to the size and importance of the project.

24.2.5   Comments

Whenever possible, one should try to quantify the factors considered most important. However, available knowledge is rather limited with regard to measurement of the various factors and their impact on the design. One may therefore, to a large extent, be compelled to rely on subjective assessments and 'educated guesses' supported by whatever knowledge is available of a theoretical or practical nature.

24.2.6   References

Burns and Stalker 1961, Burns 1975, Steele 1975, Kilman *et al.* 1976, RKW Ducker 1976, RKW von Lilienstern 1976, RKW Warnecke 1976, Stone 1976, Strutz 1976, Child 1977, Holt 1977, Khandwalla 1977, Kieser and Kubicek 1977, Giragosian 1978, Kotter 1978, Capey and Carr 1982, Tushman and Moore 1982, Prosjektplan 1982.

24.3   PROBLEM DEFINITION CHECKLIST

24.3.1   Definition

A problem definition checklist is an aid for determining what the real problem is in connection with the development of an efficient product innovation organisation.

24.3.2   Purpose

The purpose of the product definition checklist is to establish objectives for the study in terms of requirements and constraints.

24.3.3   Description

The following procedure may be used for problem definition:

1. The study should be based on an analysis of the particular situation of the firm (see Method 24.2).
2. The requirements incumbent on the product innovation organisation due to external and internal conditions, as well as existing constraints, should be determined by the following checklist:

External conditions; what is required of the organisation with regard to operational and strategic response? Must the organisation be able to adapt its structure to changing circumstances?
Internal conditions; what is required of the organisation with regard to creativity, flexibility, speed, motivation and willingness to take risks? What are the requirements for control at the various stages of the innovation process?
Constraints; what is the impact on the project of constraints with regard to financial and human resources? What is the impact of time and other constraints? Can the product innovation process be studied as a total system or is a divided approach necessary?

If it is not possible to study the whole system because of the lack of time or resources, one should limit the scope of the study by first dividing the product innovation organisation into subsystems or modules such as integration, structural design, generation of ideas, and realisation of ideas, and then assigning priorities to them.

24.3.4   Areas of application

Whatever the scope of the study, enough time and energy should be devoted to finding out what the real problem is before starting to study organisational models and develop solutions.

24.3.5   Comments

A major part of the effort made in connection with the development of an efficient product innovation organisation will be spent on the analysis, comparison and combination of various organisational models. Although the aim should be to find an optimal solution, this is hardly possible in actual practice. However, by participating in the analysis of the situation and the definition of the problem, those concerned will not only be mentally prepared, but they will also have acquired insight and knowledge regarding the problem with which they are faced. This will provide them with a good basis for the implementation of the study, which is concerned with the development of alternatives for organisation of product innovation activities and with the selection of the best one among them.

24.3.6   References

Morton 1971, RKW Geschka 1976, Bailey 1977, Child 1977, Holt 1977, Capey and Carr 1982, Prosjektplan 1982, Hayes and Wheelwright 1984, Holt 1987.

24.4   INTEGRATION CHECKLIST

24.4.1   Definition

An integration checklist is an aid for analysis and planning of the integration module in the product innovation organisation.

24.4.2   Purpose

The purpose of the integration checklist is to provide an analytical basis for development of a module that will effectively integrate the various activities in the product innovation process.

24.4.3   Description

The following procedure may be used:

1.   Clarification of the need for integration and the importance of the module for the product innovation process.
2.   Development of alternatives and selection of solution for the module by means of the following checklist:

Co-ordination unit; should a separate unit be organised? If so, what should be the size? What background is required of the staff? Can the solution be implemented immediately?

Self-coordination; what training activities should be used to promote self co-ordination? Should a job rotation programme be introduced? Can better methods for conflict resolution be applied? Is it possible to improve self co-ordination by better physical location of the participants in the product innovation process?

Documentation; to what extent are procedures with written documentation needed? How should specifications at key transfer stages in the product innovation process be formulated? What is required with regard to drawings? Can printed forms be useful? Where can they be used? How should they be designed?

Transfer of personnel; can co-ordination be obtained through transfer of persons among the various stages of the innovation process? Where in the process should they be used? Who should be selected for this purpose?

Permanent committees; should one or more committees be organised for co-ordination, control and decision making? Should they supplement, or can they be an alternative to, a co-ordination unit? How should they be composed?

Ad-hoc committees; should temporary groups be organised for co-ordination of the effort in product innovation projects? Where should they be used? How should they be composed?

Solution; how can the various co-ordination devices be combined into realistic alternatives? What criteria or considerations should be used in determining which alternative is best from a theoretical point of view? Can the best alternative be implemented or are changes required considering available staff?

The core of the product innovation process is to provide a coupling between a user need and a technology. An effective integration of the activities involved in this process is considered to be so important to the final result that normally the integration module should be studied first if no specific reason indicates otherwise. Thus, the key persons in the co-ordination activities will be able to participate actively in the development of the other modules.

24.4.4   Areas of application

The integration checklist is applicable in connection with all organisational studies, whether they are concerned with improvements or the creation of new organisations.

24.4.5   Comments

In general, it is recommended that a special staff should be organised for the co-ordination of product innovation activities. In small companies one person may be enough. As the firm grows, or more activities are added, one may increase the size of the staff or introduce other co-ordination devices such as committees, written procedures, etc. This provides a flexible solution which can be adapted easily to changing circumstances. The core will be the special unit. In large firms, or in firms where several projects are processed simultaneously, the unit may be organised as a product planning department. In divisionalised firms each division may require a separate co-ordination unit.

Although there are strong arguments favouring a special unit, there are exceptions. One exception would be a small, high-technology firm where the chief executive is actively engaged personally in managing the product innovation effort. Another would be a firm where changes in the product mix are limited to minor improvements of existing products. Also in engineering firms, where products are based on customer specifications, the need for overall integration may be so small that it does not justify a special integration unit.

24.4.6 References

Gerstenfeld 1970, Morton 1971, Scheuing 1972, Steele 1975, Gee and Tylor 1976, Kilman *et al*. 1976, Strutz 1976, Child 1977, Holt 1977, Kieser and Kubicek 1977, Midley 1977, Spitz 1977, Giragosian 1978, Hisrich and Peters 1978, Kerzner 1979, Ramo 1980, Pessemier 1982, Tushman and Moore 1982, Hübner 1986, Holt 1987.

24.5   STRUCTURE CHECKLIST

24.5.1 Definition

A structure checklist is an aid for analysis and planning of the structural module in the product innovation organisation.

24.5.2 Purpose

The purpose of the structural checklist is to provide an analytical basis for the development of the module that comprises the basic structure of the firm.

24.5.3 Description

The major steps in the development of the structure of the firm can be as follows:

1.   Clarification of relevant principles for grouping the tasks that have to be performed in the firm. Examples of such principles are function

(type of task), product (object), innovation (current/future-oriented activities), project (new activities), localisation (geographical area), technology (equipment/processes), type of customers (market segments), and combinations.

2. Development of alternatives by means of the following checklist:

Type of structure; what type is currently in use? Can more innovation-oriented solutions be developed? Would a concentration of all product innovation activities in one unit be advantageous? Is a partial concentration a better solution? Will application of dual responsibilities be advantageous? What would be the consequences of the various alternatives?

Degree of centralisation; at what organisational levels does the product innovation process take place? Is it possible to design realistic alternatives based on 100% centralisation, partial centralisation, or 100% decentralisation? What would be the advantages of a decentralised innovative organisation with centralised control? What would be the consequences of the various alternatives?

Degree of formalisation; what is the degree of formalisation in the departments that participate in the product innovation process? What changes should be considered? Would a more organic management system be advantageous? Is a differentiation of the degree of formalisation according to department required? What would be the consequences of the various alternatives?

Subsidiary; could product innovation activities be transferred to a separate company? What are the relevant alternatives? What would be the consequences of them?

Solution; how can the various elements related to the structure of the firm be combined into realistic alternatives? Which is best from a theoretical point of view? Can it be implemented or are modifications required considering available staff?

When selecting the final solution, great attention should be given to finding a proper balance between current and future-oriented activities. The goal is to create an organisation that is able to efficiently handle current operations and at the same time has sufficient innovative capacity to respond in a proper way to changes in the environment.

Current activities require a rather mechanical structure, since, to a large extent they consist of programmed and routinised activities. On the other hand, innovative activities require a more open and flexible organisation that stimulates experimentation and learning. The latter pulls in the direction of an organic structure, particularly for the first part of the innovation process.

24.5.4   Areas of application

The structure checklist is applicable in connection with improvements as well as with the creation of new organisations for product innovation activities.

24.5.5   Comments

In most firms the basic structure has been designed for efficiency in manufacturing, marketing and improvement of current products. This will not necessarily provide the best solution for the processing of product innovation projects. One should therefore investigate the possibility of changing the structure in order to obtain an optimal solution with respect to the requirements from both the current and innovative activities of the firm.

24.5.6   References

Morton 1971, Scheuing 1972, Steele 1975, Gee and Tylor 1976, Kilman *et al.* 1976, Stone 1976, Strutz 1976, Blanchard 1976, Child 1977, Holt 1977, Khandwalla 1977, Kieser and Kubicek 1977, Midley 1977, Spitz 1977, Giragosian 1978, Hisrich and Peters 1978, Kerzner 1979, Hinterhuber 1980, Ramo 1980, Gibson 1981, Riggs 1981, Pessemier 1982, Prosjektplan 1982, Tushman and Moore 1982, Kotler 1984, O'Shaughnessy 1984, David 1986, Hübner 1986, Holt 1987.

24.6   IDEA GENERATION CHECKLIST

24.6.1   Definition

An idea generation checklist is an aid for analysis and planning of the idea generation module in the product innovation organisation.

24.6.2   Purpose

The purpose of the idea generation checklist is to provide an analytical basis for organisation of the idea generation activities of the firm.

24.6.3　Description

The following procedure may be used for development of the idea generation module:

1.　Recognition of the fact that idea generation requires proper training of the staff in the use of creative techniques as well as an organisational climate which stimulates creative behaviour.

2.　Development of alternatives by means of the following checklist:

Need assessment; is proper user information transmitted to technologists? Can communication lines between users and technologists be improved? Are proper methods applied for the assessment of user needs? Who should be trained in the application of these methods? What can be done to improve the situation? What are the organisational implications?

Problem solving; What creative techniques should be used? Who should be given training in this context? How should the methods be utilised? Should special innovation groups be organised? What are the organisational consequences?

Proposal formulation; how should proposals be presented? Should specific forms be used?

Idea evaluation; what methods and criteria should be used for evaluation of ideas during problem solving and after reception of proposals? What should be the role and content of feasibility studies? What are the organisational consequences?

Project formulation; how should accepted proposals be described? Who should be responsible and who should participate in the formulation of the project? What are the organisational consequences?

Organisational climate; is the climate perceived as satisfactory by the staff? What should be done in order to improve it? What measures should be taken in order to utilise the capabilities of highly creative persons? What are the organisational implications?

Solution; how can the organisational requirements of the various activities in the idea generation stage be combined into realistic alternatives? Which is best from a theoretical point of view? Can it be implemented, or are changes required considering available staff?

The solution selected for organisation of idea generation activities should have a rather organic structure, particularly in the first stages.

24.6.4　Areas of application

Idea generation activities can be organised in several ways. However, whatever the situation of the particular firm, the idea generation check-list will provide an analytical foundation for developing the solution.

24.6.5   Comments

The foundation for a product innovation is a creative effort which results in an idea for a new or improved product. Under favourable circumstances an innovative idea may occur intuitively as a happy combination of inspiration and relevant information. In most cases, one has to work purposefully and systematically in order to obtain good results. When analysing various solutions, one should take into account the fact that not only the various steps should be appropriately organised, but that all idea generation activities must be integrated in such a way that they will provide a stream of potentially useful ideas.

24.6.6   References

Scheuing 1972, Michael 1973, Geschka 1975, Ulrich 1975, RKW Geschka 1976, Holt 1977, Kieser and Kubicek 1977, Midley 1977, Schlicksupp 1977, Giragosian 1978, Batelle 1979, Pessemier 1982, Prosjektplan 1982, Tushman and Moore 1982, Hübner 1986, Holt 1987.

24.7   IDEA REALISATION CHECKLIST

24.7.1   Definition

An idea realisation checklist is an aid for the analysis and planning of the idea realisation module in the product innovation organisation.

24.7.2   Purpose

The purpose of the idea realisation checklist is to provide an analytical basis for the organisation of the idea realisation activities of the firm.

24.7.3   Description

The following procedure may be used for development of the idea realisation module:

1.   Theoretical study of areas of application as well as advantages and disadvantages of principle models for organisation of projects.

2.   Development of alternatives and selection of solution by means of the following checklist:

The technology; to what extent should external sources be used for development and exploitation of the technology? Should a policy be established in this area, or should a decision be made in each case? What are the organisational consequences of these alternatives?

The product innovation project; can a common classification be used for all projects, or should they be classified in well-defined groups? What are the characteristics of the projects with regard to size, number, level of technology, and degree of novelty? What is the impact of these parameters on the organisational design?

Models; for which classes of projects will the basic structure, the matrix organisation and the independent project organisation be best fitted? What are the advantages and disadvantages of these approaches? What kind of planning and co-ordination devices are required for the various approaches?

Solution; how can the various approaches be combined into realistic alternatives? What criteria or considerations should be used for comparing the alternatives? Which alternative is best from a theoretical point of view? Can this alternative be implemented, or are modifications required considering available staff?

Whatever solution is selected, great attention should be given to the development of a proper procedure for the planning and monitoring of projects.

24.7.4   Areas of application

The idea realisation checklist can be used in connection with all problems related to the organisation of innovative projects.

24.7.5   Comments

As the name indicates, idea realisation is concerned with the utilisation of an innovative idea. The idea must be transformed into a physical product that can be manufactured and sold in a competitive market. This will involve the provision of an appropriate technology, as well as the planning and implementation of manufacturing and marketing operations. The realisation stages require a rather structured organisation, the following of an orderly and programmed procedure, and an increasing amount of control as the project approaches completion.

24.7.6   References

Scheuing 1972, Steele 1975, Ulrich 1975, Gee and Tyloɾ 1976, RKW Dathe 1976, Holt 1977, Hinterhuber 1977, Kieser and Kubicek 1977, Midley 1977, Geschka and Pausewang 1978, Kerzner 1980, Ramo 1980, Gibson 1981, Riggs 1981, Pessemier 1982, Prosjektplan 1982, Tushman and Moore 1982, Hayes and Wheelwright 1984, Hübner 1986, Holt 1987.

25. Financial Tools

25.1 THE BALANCE SHEET

25.1.1 Definition

The balance sheet is a statement of the assets, liabilities and shareholders funds at a particular date (see *Figure 25.1*).

ASSETS	
Cash and bank deposits	1
Short-term receivables	2
Inventories	3
CURRENT ASSETS	
Shares in consolidated subsidiaries	4
Other shares, bonds and securities	5
Receivables from group companies	6
Other long-term receivables	
LONG-TERM RECEIVABLES AND INVESTMENTS	
FIXED ASSETS	7
TOTAL ASSETS	
LIABILITIES AND EQUITY	
Bank overdrafts	
Current payables	8
Dividends	—
Corporate taxes	9
CURRENT LIABILITIES	
Long-term debt with group companies	
Mortgate loans	10
Other long-term debt	11
LONG-TERM LIABILITIES	
CONDITIONAL TAX-FREE FUNDS AND RESERVES	12
Share capital	13
Other non-distributable equity	14
Distributable equity	15
SHAREHOLDERS' EQUITY	
TOTAL LIABILITY AND EQUITY	

Figure 25.1 Assets and liabilities

25.1.2 Purpose

The purpose of the balance sheet is to give a true view of the financial position of the company with regard to share capital, reserves, provisions (depreciation, doubtful debts), liabilities, fixed assets, current assets and other assets.

25.1.3 Description

The balance sheet may take many forms. One example is indicated in *Figure 25.1*.

25.1.4 Areas of application

The balance sheet is used both for individual companies and for groups of companies. In the latter case a balance sheet is made for each subsidiary and a consolidated statement is prepared for the group.

25.1.5 Comments

The balance sheet gives a concentrated snapshot of the financial situation. It can be more or less detailed. The interpretation of it often requires the study of several pages of explanatory notes.

25.1.6 References

Blanchard 1976, Ramo 1980, Parker 1983, David 1985, Higson 1986, Imdieke 1987.

25.2   THE INCOME STATEMENT

25.2.1 Definition

The income statement, also called a profit and loss statement, shows the company's revenues, expenses and profit or loss for the financial year.

25.2.2 Purpose

The purpose of the income statement is, according to law, to give a true and fair view of the economic result.

25.2.3 Description

The income statement may take many forms. An example is given in *Figure 25.2.*

	NOTES
OPERATING REVENUES	1
Cost of raw material and energy	2
Salaries, wages and social expenses	3
Other operating, selling and administrative expenses	4
Ordinary depreciation	5
OPERATING EXPENSES	
OPERATING PROFIT	
FINANCIAL INCOME AND EXPENSES	6
INCOME BEFORE EXTRAORDINARY ITEMS	
Extraordinary items — current year	7
Extraordinary items — accounting and policy changes	8
EXTRAORDINARY INCOME AND EXPENSES	
INCOME BEFORE TAXATION AND YEAR END APPROPRIATIONS	
TAXES	9
MINORITY INTERESTS	10
YEAR-END APPROPRIATIONS	11
INCOME AFTER YEAR-END APPROPRIATIONS	12

Figure 25.2 The income statement

25.2.4   Areas of application

Like the balance sheet the income statement is used for both individual companies and groups of firms.

25.2.5   Comments

The form of the income statement depends on the legal requirements of the country concerned and the needs of the company. Normally appropriations of profit are included. The interpretation of the statement often requires the study of extensive notes.

25.2.6   References

Blanchard 1976, Ramo 1980, Parker 1983, Kotler 1984, David 1985, Higson 1986, Imdieke 1987.

25.3   FINANCIAL RATIOS

25.3.1   Definition

A financial ratio is a tool for analysis and interpretation of financial data, expressed as a percentage or by the number of times one figure can be divided into another.

25.3.2   Purpose

The purpose of financial ratios is to provide a base for comparisons with past performance, or with industry data.

25.3.3   Description

Among the most common financial ratios are:

profitability
>   dividends/stocks issued
>   net profit/equity capital
>   net profit plus interest on borrowed capital/total capital

    net profit/total assets
    net profit/sales

liquidity
    current ratio ('bankers ratio') = current assets/current liabilities
    quick ratio ('acid test') = quick assets (cash, bank deposits, short-term receivables)/current liabilities

solidity
    equity capital/total assets
    equity capital, 50% of untaxed reserves, and minority interest of consolidated subsidiaries/total assets

changes in inventories
    inventories/sales

price-earning
    current stock price/net profit

25.3.4   Areas of application

The analysis of ratios has rather limited value if based on the performance in an isolated year. The main benefit comes from studying the development of the ratios over time. Many firms present five or ten year comparisons in their annual reports. As standard for the comparison, the first year, an average year, or a normal (typical) year is used. If data are available from other companies, the ratios can also be used for company comparisons.

25.3.5   Comments

The analysis of financial ratios is an important tool for lending institutions when considering applications for financial support. The ratios can also be a useful device for internal financial planning and control.

25.3.6   References

Blanchard 1976, Ramo 1980, Parker 1983, Kotler 1984, David 1985, Higson 1986, Imdieke 1987.

Appendix 1 Scansteel — Case Study

The best way to learn is through ones own experience, e.g. by working in a relevant environment for a certain period of time. However, this ideal situation is seldom available for educational purposes. As a substitute one can simulate the situation by working with a realistic case. The following is created for this purpose. The case will facilitate learning, develop understanding and create a more realistic attitude towards concepts, models and methods than just reading and discussing them in general terms.

A case is a written description on an organisation with information about its history, environment, objectives, strategy, structure, functions, etc. It does not have complete information. In this respect the situation is the same as in real life. A manager or a staffer never has all the facts that are needed in order to develop a solution or make a decision. The missing information may not exist or it may be too costly to get.

Scansteel is a fictitious name of a real company. The description gives a true picture of the company and its major problems. A few minor changes have been made in order to facilitate the use for educational purposes.

The utilisation of the case will depend on the interest and background of the teacher, the content and duration of the course, and the motivation of the participants.

Typical examples of various uses of the case can be mentioned:

A one-term (54 hours) introductory course in Industrial management for engineering students; here 11 hours are spent on the case.

A concentrated two-days seminar (18 hours) on Product planning for experienced marketers and technologists; here nine hours are devoted to the case.

A 24-hour post-graduate course on 'Methods for product innovation' (duration four weeks) for engineers, marketers, economists, etc.; here five hours are devoted to the case.

In addition to the scheduled hours indicated above come individual work and/or group discussions.

A case can be used in several ways depending on the teaching/learning situation. A general approach is recommended first to study one or several topics individually and/or in groups. Such a study normally includes definition of the problem, development of alternatives and choice of recommended solution. Then follow plenary presentation of solutions and discussion based on input from one or several reporters under the guidance of the instructor or one of the participants. Best results are usually obtained when the students play the role of consultants. If a large group of participants is involved and the time is rather limited, one may base some of the plenary discussions on a presentation by the instructor.

In order to benefit from the case, the participants should prepare themselves, before or during the course, individually or in groups, by:

Reading the case, underlining important information, and listing/discussing unclear points, disagreements, etc.

Reading the case once more and determining strengths and weaknesses of the company (Method 21.2).

Making a gap analysis (Method 21.1).

Making a portfolio analysis (Method 21.4).

Identifying changes/trends in the environment with regard to technological, marketing, economic, political and social factors.

Identifying opportunities and threats in the environment.

Getting acquainted with morphological technique (Method 4.3) and brainstorming (Method 4.4).

The case may be used for discussion of topics such as attitudes, business concept, major objectives, formulation of strategy, diversification planning, selection of products, assessment of user needs, creation of solution concepts, formulation of proposals, formulation of R & D projects, organisation structure, organisation of product innovation activities, and marketing of industrial goods.

In order to get maximum benefit from the case, each individual should, when a topic is finished, orient the knowledge acquired to previous knowledge along the lines indicated in Appendix 4.

The depth of the analysis of the case depends on available time, and of motivation and knowledge of the student. The general approach referred to on the first page is rather simple and can be performed in a relatively short time. A more penetrating study may require an iterative process. Thus, one may start and define the problem by formulating a tentative objective considering the needs of those involved and existing restrictions. Then one may proceed by selecting and/or collecting relevant facts regarding the situation, analyse these facts by means of appropriate models and techniques, move back and redefine the problem, collect and analyse more facts, develop alternatives and selection criteria, determine consequences of the various alternatives, select solution, plan implementation, redefine the problem, get new facts, a.s.o. When facts are missing, one must make explicit assumptions. Selection criteria may be derived from the following key criteria: technical feasibility, economic profitability, and social acceptability. The weight given to the various criteria will depend on experience, judgement and values of the problem solver.

I HISTORY OF SCANSTEEL

Scansteel was founded in 1975 through a merger between two Norwegian firms. Lico was a family firm, founded in 1895, which worked for the home market. In the period 1920-1950 the main products were lifts and industrial cranes. In both fields the company dominated the market and obtained an excellent image and good profitability. However, the company lost ground during the 1950s and 1960s. The lift business was dropped in 1974. The crane business, more and more was losing its market share to other national and foreign competitors – a process which continued up to 1975. The main reason for the problems was a lack of understanding that meeting increasing competition required specific measures. Active product innovation, systematic marketing and development of an export-oriented firm might have been the solution.

Norweld was founded in 1932 by a self-made man with great skills in metal working processes. He was a strong leader and built and managed the company up to the late 1960s with a typical one-man leadership. The company, which was working for the home market, was a general engineering company with product design and manufacturing as key functions. The company succeeded only to a small degree to develop its own product lines, although the owner through numerous attempts, based on innovative ideas, tried to change the firm from general service to product concentration. The difficulties of Norweld came from structural changes in the industry, which made the policy of being a general service workshop making taylor-made products for individual customers difficult. This was recognised by the management, but development of new products and markets was not accomplished fast enough.

The new company Scansteel, founded in 1975, consisted basically of plant and employees from Norweld, and products, markets and design from Lico. The integration process was performed by an investment company which supplied financial resources and put in a new top management. Based on the Lico market contact and existing know-how in design and the skilled work force of Norweld, the investment company decided to invest some years in Scansteel in order to create a competitive enterprise. This process, which started in 1977, has been performed with various degrees of success. Some of the goals have been achieved, but the basic problem of profitability has not been solved.

II BUSINESS CONCEPT AND MAJOR OBJECTIVES

The business concept is reflected in the following guidelines formulated by the managing director:

to develop the activities of the firm in the electro-mechanical field;

to concentrate on areas requiring a high degree of design and application know-how as basis for products and services offered to the market;

to develop its own manufacturing capability as opposed to extensive use of sub-contractors; this is based on the recognition of the importance of accumulating production know-how as part of developing competitiveness;

to establish good human relations capable of recruiting, keeping and developing qualified personnel at all levels.

A consequence of these guidelines is that the company will have a relatively high cost level. It is therefore important that one selects products and markets which can justify this cost level, and use management resources and manufacturing technology in such a way that it results in competitive production.

In 1977 it was decided to concentrate the effort on existing product lines:

slewing cranes for harbour and shipbuilding applications;
gates and hatches for hydro-electric power systems.

It was recognised that the hydro-electric products were limited to the home market whereas the cranes had potential for a considerable export. The following objectives were established:

increase total sales to 60 million crowns within three years;
obtain 50% of the home market for the hydro-electric products;
export at least 50% of the crane production;
increase the manufacturing capability with 50%.

It was recognised that a strong marketing effort would be needed in order to reach these objectives. It was also necessary with increased R & D capability, improved production planning, and improved budgetting and cost control.

The main objectives were achieved by the end of 1980. Annual sale had grown from 20 to 62 million, the export percentage was 65. These results were mainly reached through a tremendous effort of the managing director who had spent a considerable part of his time visiting potential customers in foreign markets.

The remarkable increase in annual sale had not been accomplished by a similar development of profitability. It was unsatisfactory, and the company was still faced with great financial risks. This was due, to a large extent, to the willingness of the company to adapt the design of its products to special needs of individual customers. In order to improve profitability one agreed that it would be necessary in the future to concentrate the effort upon marketing of standard products.

After extensive discussions at board level it was decided that the major objectives for the coming years should be to maintain the growth rate and improve profitability.

III   STRATEGY

In order to reach the major objectives one recognised that the main strategy in the next years should be an extensive effort in developing new markets, especially outside Europe. Presently efforts are made in Brazil, Argentine and South Korea.

It has become clear that marketing abroad will involve local production in foreign countries for a substantial part of the products. Therefore one must prepare necessary arrangements for license production and/or use of sub-contractors.

An analysis of the market potential and competitive situation, both in Europe and in over-seas markets, has indicated that sale of existing product lines is not enough for meeting the major objectives. Through a series of top management discussions one has discussed the possibility of increasing the competitiveness by improvement of the efficiency of current operations, by expanding the sales volume of current products, and by market segmentation, i.e. finding a niche where the company would be able to satisfy the needs of a limited group of users. However, one finally arrived at a conclusion that the only way to solve the problem would be to embark on a diversification programme for development of products that are new for the company.

IV   ORGANISATION

The company from 1975 to 1980 was organised in functional departments such as R & D, manufacturing, and marketing, with department heads reporting to the managing director. However, due to several large and rather different crane projects, this organisation has given problems in obtaining efficient cost control and motivation for profitability at various levels. The organisational problem was further complicated by the decision to embark on a diversification programme. Having considered various alternatives, a new organisation was put into operation in 1980 with basic structure as indicated below.

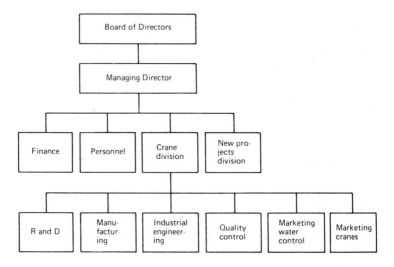

The major operations have been concentrated in two divisions, each managed by newly appointed division managers. Together with the managing director and the manager of finance they form a team which makes the major decisions.

The manager of the crane division is responsible for the traditional products. He has all necessary resources for R & D, manufacturing and marketing of these products.

The manager of the new projects division is responsible for the diversification effort; this division is also organised as a profit centre. The most important activities will be analysis of internal and external factors, formulation of evaluation criteria, development and implementation of a search methodology, selection of new product ideas, and planning and implementation of new product projects.

Through the delegation of operative responsibility it is expected that the managing director will be able to devote more time and effort to strategic planning and participation in the diversification process. It is also recognised that the management team, in addition to operative responsibilities, must participate actively in all major decisions regarding innovations.

V   PRODUCT DEVELOPMENT

Product development is an important part of current operations, and is also expected to play a major role in the later stages of the diversification process.

1.   Procedure

The current situation is characterised by a combination of standard products and geographical markets. This makes it possible with a higher degree of repeat orders for the main bulk of the production. The following procedure is used in managing the product development process:

employment of R & D resources is carefully evaluated by the management team in order to obtain a selection of products and projects which represent new members of the product family with long-range potential;
cost reduction through purposeful design is initiated and organised by a product committee which gives priority to standardisation and cost reduction activities. It has members from different fields in order to represent a qualified body for evaluation of results.

2.   Need assessment

In the last few years the strategy has been 'finding new customers for existing products'. This policy will be intensified in the coming years to ensure repeat production of standard products, which is of vital importance for making profit in the crane field. However, this should not blind the organisation for new needs which may create opportunities or threats to existing products. The following methods may be used for detecting and handling such problems:

application studies for determination of crane configurations (parametres) relevant to typical ship sizes and yard developments;
use of R & D staff together with marketing people in actual sales work in order to obtain information on needs and long-range thinking of customers;
good communication with national and foreign application consultants in yard development. They are important contacts for actual sales work as well as for getting information about trends and needs in shipbuilding methods and equipment;

a programme parallel to existing product sales where a system approach is used, e.g. instead of concentrating on the vertical lift operation, one takes a broader view and studies the complete handling problem of which the vertical lift is only a smaller part. This approach may lead to changes in existing products and to development of entirely new devices with great marketing possibilities;

the company has recently become aware of the concept of active need experience as a specific approach for systematical assessment of user needs. This method is attractive and the application of it is considered to play an important role in product development activities (Method 1.1, pp. 125-126).

VI   PRODUCT AND PROCESS TECHNOLOGY

1. Product lines and products

Presently the company has two principal product lines, large cranes and equipment for water control in hydro-electric power systems. In addition, one or several new products will be developed as a result of the diversification effort.

The crane line is dominated by heavy shipbuilding cranes of slewing type with lifting capacity up to 130 tons at an outreach of 25 m with maximum outreach of 50 m. The steel-weight of such a crane is 400–500 tons. The cranes are equipped with the most modern systems in electronic thyristor control for the large 100–300 HP motors and integrated electronic systems for load monitoring and overload protection. The steel design requires components with an optimal utilisation of the steel weight and the geometrical configuration. It is governed by complex international standards for steel and machinery design.

The skills needed comprise advanced level engineering in areas such as:

steel structure components subjected to complex forces, both dynamic and static load;

complex and modern machinery for lifting, slewing and translation with special emphasis on various kinds of gears, including design of large differential gearboxes;

complex design and installation of a large number of high power electric motors and control systems combined with extensive signal, operation and interlock systems. Electric motor controls and crane protective devices based on electronic capabilities are also required.

In order to be competitive both in design methods and design cost, modern computerised design is, to a large extent, employed.

The design capability represents the core of technological know-how and forms the basis for design of other crane products as well as products in the water control sector. For the diversification effort one tries to look for activities where this capability represents an asset. The crane line includes a spectrum of cranes for harbour application, mainly for handling of bulk such as coal, ore, etc. Specially designed goliath cranes and overhead travelling cranes are also in the programme.

Historically the company's main asset in the crane field was its design capability. This led to an approach of 'you name it, we design and deliver', resulting in a large variety of products. As already indicated, one now wants to concentrate the effort upon standard products. In the next five-year period this is hoped to be achieved together with development of a few new members in the crane family. The trend goes towards larger and more complex cranes, a development which Scansteel to some extent must follow.

The products in the water control sector are presently dominated by large installations of hatches for river regulation (high water volume and low pressure). Hatches for high pressure and low water volume is also part of the product range, although less frequently supplied. The hatches are hydraulically or electrically operated. The design know-how is the same as for cranes, a combination of machinery design and highly stressed steel structures. This requires know-how in design of sealing systems (gaskets) suitable for operation during frequent manoeuvring and at severe temperature changes and environmental conditions. The development of this product line is characterised by a steady increase in plant and unit sizes. Each order requires its own design process. The R & D department tries to develop basic concepts which can form the bases for computerised and repeated design processes. One expects the future tendency to include even larger units than the present typical equipment of 45 tons per unit. An increase in demand is expected, for equipment built in stainless steel as opposed to present ordinary steel designs (this to meet increasing requirements of withstanding pollution in lakes, rivers and waterways).

2. Plant, manufacturing processes and equipment

Production facilities are located in two different cities M and N. In addition, part of the production is performed at various sites belonging to customers in connection with assembly and final erection. This fact, to a large extent, is influencing the way of operations.

Of the production, 70% is high-quality steel components and assemblies. The remaining 30% is conventional machine-job and mechanical assembly of heavy engineering components.

The key manufacturing characteristics are:

lifting and handling capabilities of high unit weights;
automatic welding processes and semi-automatic processes for assembly prior to welding;
physical space for manufacturing operations and intermediate storage.

The *M plant* is divided in three parts:

machining and assembly (small inefficient buildings);
plate-shop (separate location with traffic communication to machining and assembly shop); it is relatively modern with conventional machine tools;
outside lifting capability and dockside transportation (moderate to poor condition).

The *N plant* is equipped to handle production of heavy components and to perform pre-erection processes. It is located at sea, has a dock and a 60 ton outreach crane for production, erection and loading on ships. Equipment for transportation of heavy components for intermediate storage is also available. Space for production and storage is very limited and frequently a bottle-neck in the production programme.

Both the M and N plants are equipped with modern automatic welding equipment. Some data are shown below:

	Site (m²)	Plateshop (m²)	Machine assembly (m²)	Office
M	4.000		1.500	1.200
M	21.000	2.500		
N	12.000	1.800	200	200
New area	200.000			

The administration of the company as well as R & D, sales, etc. is located in M in temporary, not suitable buildings and locations. It is the intention to correct this by:

bringing all administrative and manufacturing functions together in a suitable building being planned and designed for realisation in 1984;
developing a new industrial area in N having adequate space to grow and a suitable location for seaward transportation together with good facilities for attracting competent labour.

The new plant will be operated together with the present N plant which will receive some investments for correcting the most obvious deficiencies. It will be planned with great flexibility in order to combine present requirements with those presented by new products from the diversification process.

VII   MARKETING

1.   Annual sale

Data for traditional products are given below, comprising large cranes
and equipment for water control in hydro-electric power systems.

The export is currently about 65% of total sale. It comes mainly
from the crane product line as the water control equipment has been,
and is planned to be concentrated on the home market. The export
percentage of total sale is expected to decrease to about 40% in the
next five years due to the introduction of new products from the
diversification programme.

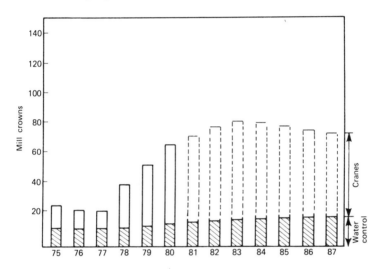

2.   The competitive situation

(a)   Water control equipment

Last year the sale of this product was about 10 million crowns. All
deliveries were to power companies in the home country. The competition is hard; six national companies are fighting for the home market.
Scansteel is market leader with 50%, number two has 25%, and number
three has 10%. The economic result has been rather stable in recent
years, but the profit margin is small. Therefore, Scansteel does not
expect to gain much by lowering prices. If a customer wants to change
to another firm, it can easily do so as all firms are able to offer first

class products and service. The future demand will be influenced by government authorities who give concessions for building power plants. A possible threat for the future market is increasing resistance from groups engaged in protection of the environment. All political parties are sensitive to this development; some of them are against the building of more hydro-electric power plants; others have a more balanced view. However, it is obvious that political decisions will influence future building of such plants.

(b) Cranes

For this product the sale last year was 62 million crowns; of these 50 million came from export. The cranes are mostly used at shipyards and at harbour installations. The market trend at home and in western Europe has been similar. After many years of expansion, one is now in a period with stagnation and increasing unemployment. Available building capacity for cranes is larger than market demand. Therefore, firms are reluctant to invest in new plants. The market is characterised by a large number of companies fighting to preserve or increase their market share. This creates a highly competitive situation with small profit margins. To a great extent the market is dependent on conditions outside the industry. One example is the oil crisis in 1973, which resulted in less demand for tankers, less orders for new ships, and less capital investment in shipyards.

At the *home market* several companies build cranes. They have no export, but are able to offer small cranes of the Scansteel product line. At times they give severe competition. Foreign companies increasingly threaten the position of Scansteel. However, so far the firm has been able to maintain a dominating share of the home market which has been rather stable.

At the *world market* for large cranes a few European companies dominate the picture. Three of them have about the same size and cover about 65% of the total market. Scansteel is among the remaining firms. It is expected that the number of firms will be reduced in the next years, in part through mergers, and in part through natural elimination caused by lack of competitive power. There are several indications that opportunities and fights between the crane builders will be in distant markets in developing countries.

Scansteel attempts to provide good service, but because of its geographic location it has a disadvantage compared with its competitors in central Europe. The management also feels that the firm is too small and that the staff do not have enough experience for competitive international marketing.

3. *Marketing of new products*

Based on the policy in recent years of consolidating the product range, the company has not gained much experience in marketing new products. However, one experience should be noted. One should be extremely cautious in this type of industry to adapt the tempting approach of 'introductory pricing' for new products. The process of later regaining the loss by starting with low prices is extremely difficult. No standard method should be looked for. One should rather recognise that each product and market must be analysed separately in order to find the optimal approach.

VIII   ECONOMY

1. *Results*

The economic result for 1979 and 1980, as well as the budget for 1981 is shown below. The zero result in 1981 is expected to be followed by a positive, but rather small profit in 1982. It is therefore obvious that the economic results are not yet satisfactory. Even with expected improvements in 1982, normal requirements on return on invested capital will not be reached. The strong effort presently being put into the diversification process is aimed at improving this situation.

Assets and liabilities	1979	1980	1981
Cash	1.200	1.552	2.000
Work in progress, raw materials, etc.	20.500	28.129	28.000
Machinery and equipment	4.100	5.477	5.000
Total assets	25.800	35.158	35.000
Current liabilities	4.050	5.087	5.000
Advance payments from customers and special credits	20.000	24.510	25.000
Funds	750	561	0
Share capital	1.000	5.000	5.000
Total liabilities	25.800	35.158	35.000

Profit and loss statement	1979	1980	1981
Annual sale	40.000	65.000	70.000
Change of work in progress	6.000	2.000	5.000
Total value of production	46.000	67.000	75.000
Material consumption and costs of subdeliveries	24.100	39.900	43.000
Added value	21.900	27.100	32.000
Salaries and wages	11.000	15.000	20.000
Other variable expenses	3.180	4.350	5.000
Other fixed expenses	2.520	2.830	3.500
Net operating profit	5.200	4.920	3.500
Interest charges	1.170	1.320	1.500
Depreciation	3.500	2.600	2.000
Net result	530	1.000	0

2.   Results from the product groups

With the project-oriented business of the company, the economic result
varies considerably from time to time, and with different products. The
'water control' field represents the most steady situation, although the
potential margin is small.

The crane sector varies considerably. The profitability in this sector
is, to a large extent, dependent on the sale of existing designs. If and
when a satisfactory volume is achieved, the profitability could become
more steady at an acceptable level.

The service sector including spare parts has, and is expected to continue to have, acceptable profitability.

IX   PERSONNEL RESOURCES

1.   Number of employees

Currently the firm has about 350 employees. Manual labour is about
2/3 of the total number.

2.   Top management

The top management group consists of the managing director, the
manager of the crane division, the manager of new projects, and the
manager of finance.

The managing director is 42 years and has the following background:

Education: Master of electrical engineering, University of Edinburgh (1965), Post graduate studies U.C.L.A. (1972), comprising feed-back theory/mathematics.

Experience: The Switchgear Company — design of electrical distribution systems, two years prior to Edinburgh; Bignor Electronics — research and development engineer, 11 years, the last four years as head of corporate R & D, in charge of approximately 200 engineers; five years as managing director of Scansteel.

Attitude: during his work at Bignor Electronics, which is a large, export-oriented and highly innovative firm in the electronical and electromechanical field, he developed a rather innovative attitude. This is reflected in the following statement:

'Looking at the competitive situation in the future, there is no indication that the Scansteel company should be behind the most important competitors with regard to technology. The threats that seem to be prevailing are in the following areas: (1) not creative enough, and therefore not good enough to be in the front line with regard to innovation, and (2) the wages may increase so much that the company will price itself out of the market.

'In order to be competitive, it is necessary to see that science and technology are used and lead to new or improved products. In order to be innovative, it is necessary to think in new ways and to be creative. Innovation cannot be left to chance. It must be guided with definite objectives in mind.

'Experience and tradition can be useful. Obsolescence, however, now comes quickly. It is therefore important to throw away things that can hamper innovative thinking. The traditional respect for authority is obsolete today. It is important to have people at all levels who can think in new ways. The human resources are the greatest asset. One must invest in the employees and develop a team spirit. It is innovation and creativity that will bring the company further ahead. However, one must not be so humanistic that one forgets the economic criteria.

'One problem hampering innovation is the customary practice of favouring those who follow the general 'office behaviour pattern'. The original person finds himself 'outside'. This is bad — these people are often very creative. It should not be important who has ideas for innovations. An idea should always be evaluated on its merits. Often a company is not positive towards innovations. In many cases it is the management that has to change — it is often there one finds most resistance. The managing director himself should take an active part in the work with innovation.

'Old fashioned managers have no success today — there is no use for them. It is impossible to solve problems with old tools or on the basis of old dogma. If a company is going to be innovative, this first of all depends on the managers. It is more necessary than ever for a manager to think in new ways. That is the base for progress and expansion of the company. Innovations and new ways of thinking must be given priority. The challenge to managers is enormous'.

The manager of the crane division is 43 years and has the following background:

Education: Technical college, three years, Department of Production engineering.
Experience: building of hydro-electric plants; Bignor Electronics — five years in the Department for manufacturing planning including M.T.M.; standard data implementation; Arnes Mek. Verksted — three years as head of the Industrial engineering department; development and implementation of standard data; Scansteel — four years as Production manager; from 1.1.1982 appointed manager of the crane division.

The manager of new projects is 35 years and has the following background:

Education: Master of shipbuilding engineering, Norwegian Institute of Technology.
Experience: Design engineer in Canadian Vickers Shipyard, Canada for three years; Bignor Electronics — sales engineer of electronic equipment in international markets, three years; Scansteel — head of sales function, four years; from 1.1.1982 appointed manager of new projects.

The manager of finance is 31 years and has the following background:

Education: Degree in business administration from the Norwegian School of Business Administration, Bergen.
Experience: two years in the Regional Investment Company; one year and a half in the Norwegian State Railroad system; one year in present position in Scansteel.

3. The staff in the R & D department

The head of R & D is 46 years and has the following background:

Education: Oslo Technical College.
Experience: Storviks Jernstøperi, 17 years; first as design engineer, later

as chief engineer for the crane sector; four years in Scansteel, two of which in marketing and two in present position.

The R & D staff consists of approximately 45 engineers. They develop system solutions for new projects and design products to customer orders, both electrical and mechanical. The group also does development work concerned with the application of numerical methods in crane design. The average age of the staff is quite low; the theoretical background is as follows:

university degree:	6
technical college (2-3 years):	30
lower technical education (assistants):	9

A limited number, less than 15, have broad experience from several companies. For the others the present position in Scansteel is the first or second employment after technical education. The level of experience in Scansteel is quite high, due to challenging design tasks.

4.   Marketing staff

Marketing is divided in departments for watercontrol equipment and cranes.

A manager with one assistant are responsible for watercontrol marketing. The manager was trained as a mechanical engineer at Oslo Technical College. His experience is 21 years with Norweld, first 15 years in design and then six years in sales.

The manager of crane marketing has two sales engineers and one installation and after-sales engineer at his disposal together with a secretary. The sales manager and the sales engineers all have a master degree in mechanical engineering. They have a varied background in sales from different companies, but no formal education in this area.

Appendix 2   Mentronics — Case Study

Perhaps the most important technological development in our time is the emergence of electronics. It has resulted in a number of pioneering innovations and the potential is overwhelming.

The electronics industry is one of the fastest growing and most innovative sectors. It will provide totally new products and radical changes in existing products. For good or bad, it will have a tremendous impact on human life both inside and outside industrial establishments.

It is difficult to classify the different types of products based on electronics. One rather common approach is to distinguish between the following:

Professional electronics: telecommunication, navigation, broadcasting, computers, automation and control equipment, measuring instruments, medical equipment, military products, etc.
Consumer electronics: radio, television, music equipment, video machines, musical instruments, etc.
Electronic components: active and passive electronic components as well as mechanical components.

In addition to the typical electronic products are a vast number of consumer and industrial products where mechanical functions are increasingly being replaced with electronically integrated components. As this development, called *mechatronics*, continues, the distinction between electronic and mechanical industries will be made and more blurred.

Recent developments have resulted in components and methods that make it possible, on one hand, to produce complex products in large quantities at low prices, and, on the other hand, to tailor-make products in small lots according to special customer requirements.

Both large and small firms have responded to the challenges and opportunities created by developments within electronics. Products such as telecommunication equipment, computers and electronic components are mostly made by large firms. In other areas, e.g. automation and instrumentation, small and medium-sized firms have been active and introduced a great number of highly innovative products. In many cases these firms have been established by entrepreneurial engineers

306

who are open for new ideas and willing to take the risk involved in the transformation of them into new products and processes. Many of them have previously worked in large firms. One example of such a situation is Mentronics.

I HISTORY OF MENTRONICS

The firm was founded in 1975 by a highly inventive electronics engineer who combined technological competence with a keen market awareness. At the start he was the only employee.

After graduation from a technical university, his first practical experience was in a research laboratory where he joined a group working on medical electronics. Four years later he was appointed development manager in a company which develops, manufactures and markets products in the same field. However, he gradually became more and more frustrated because of lack of support in developing his ideas. After six years he left to start his own firm.

Mentronics is a typical high-technology firm. It has grown with 30–50 per cent per year and has today about thirty employees. The annual turnover has grown from $20 000 to about $2 000 000. During its development, Mentronics has been hampered occasionally in utilisation of its ideas and inventions due to lack of capital — a situation that is not unknown for small innovative firms.

The firm uses a flexible pricing system. Most new projects are based on a cost plus principle; in some cases with an upper limit clause.

The profitability of the projects have varied considerably, a few have resulted in losses. Earnings have varied between 2 to 8% of annual sales. The financial situation is rather strained; the equity is only 18% of total capital employed.

In the first years most of the activity was development and manufacture of custom-made products based on individual orders, but there have gradually emerged two lines with standard products. The most important is a range of instruments for radioactive labelled blood cell harvesting, which accounts for 50% of annual sales. Mentronics is the largest manufacturer in the world of this instrument, which is used in tissue typing laboratories and in connection with cancer research. Currently it is used in 64 countries. The other product line is mobile reporting studios for radio broadcasting, which accounts for about 35%. In its homecountry, Mentronics is the only manufacturer of this type of product. The remaining 15% of sales is of custom-made products, most of them are invented and developed by the owner himself. In principle he is ready to solve any problem for which the firm has competence and resources.

II BUSINESS CONCEPT AND MAJOR OBJECTIVES

When the firm was founded, the owner had no definite product in mind, and Mentronics had no statement of its business concept. However, the following formulation covers the intention of the owner: the firm is basically an innovation company which actively searches for user problems and solves them by developing new technological solutions. When the firm was founded, the owner wanted to prove that his ideas on operating a firm would result in a profitable business. He intended to keep the firm small. The major reason is that he wants to stay in the entrepreneurial role of being both chief executive and innovator at the same time; with a growing number of employees more administration will be required and he does not like the idea of becoming primarily an administrator. Nor does he want to work as inventor in a firm owned by himself and run by professional managers. He is also much against the formalisation and bureaucratic procedures in larger firms.

With the small size and informal character of its operations, Mentronics has no written objective. However, it appears that the economic objective is to earn enough money to enable the owner to work on projects which he finds interesting and challenging. He is particularly motivated to continue within medical electronics in order to prove that some of his ideas, which had been rejected in the firm where he previously worked, are exploitable.

III STRATEGY

The major strategy appears to be one of product leadership by developing products that are quite new to the market. In addition, major improvements of current products are considered important. The firm is not interested in adopting or adapting products of other firms.

IV ORGANISATION

Mentronics has a very informal organisation centering around the owner. No organisation chart exists, but a simplified model of the structure is indicated below.

The development of medical products is handled by the owner himself. Broadcasting equipment is one of the major tasks of the development manager. Currently he is also involved in the development of a production control system.

```
                        ┌──────────┐
                        │  Owner   │
                        └──────────┘
              ┌──────────────┼──────────────┐
        ┌───────────┐ ┌───────────────┐ ┌──────────┐
        │Development│ │ Manufacturing │ │ Office   │
        │ manager   │ │ manager       │ │ manager  │
        └───────────┘ └───────────────┘ └──────────┘
        ┌──────┬──────────┼──────────┬──────────┐
  ┌──────────┐ ┌──────────────┐ ┌──────────┐ ┌────────────┐
  │ Medical  │ │ Broadcasting │ │Automation│ │ Mechanical │
  │ products │ │ products     │ │ systems  │ │ components │
  └──────────┘ └──────────────┘ └──────────┘ └────────────┘
```

The manufacturing manager is responsible for manufacturing of components, subcontracting, assembly of standard products, and manufacturing of models and prototypes in connection with development of new products. The office manager together with two employees handles accounting, correspondence, and other office services.

V PRODUCT PLANNING

Mentronics has no formal planning procedure. However, the owner is actively searching for new market opportunities through extensive contacts with present and potential customers. He considers it important to establish a reputation as a competent problem solver; those who have problems should know that they can go to him and discuss their problems in detail.

In order to implement such a policy, contacts are established and maintained through intensive travelling around the world. Actually, the owner spends more than 100 days per year travelling. He pays great attention to visiting exhibitions related to the medical field where he meets people from various countries, in part at the stands and in part at the social activities arranged in connection with the exhibition.

Both the owner and the development manager attend professional meetings in order to keep themselves informed about new developments. Valuable information is also received by means of subscription to a large number of professional journals.

VI PRODUCT DEVELOPMENT

The approach is flexible and depends on the problem that has to be solved. However, the attention that is given to early provision of information about user needs is typical for all projects.

A common method for need assessment in the industrial market is close contact with present or potential users. Normally this is done by sales representatives or by staff from the technical department. However, in Mentronics the chief executive does the contact himself as far as medical products are concerned. This gives him a big advantage as his position as head of the firm opens the door to chief decision makers in hospitals and gives him easy access to the medical staff.

Close contact is kept with a large hospital with a high reputation all over the world. This hospital co-operates actively with Mentronics in testing its prototypes. Such a form of co-operation is extremely important. If a product fails a test, the firm has a helpful and useful collaborator for improvements. On the other hand, if a product succeeds, the test results are presented in a scientific report by members of the medical staff.

In order to illustrate the approach to product development, two examples are given below.

1. The blood cell harvester

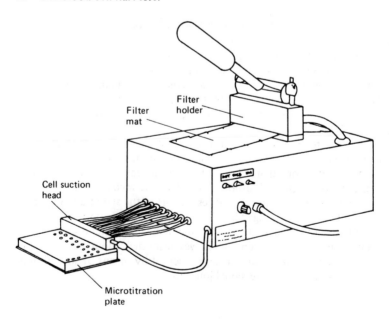

APPENDIX 2 311

This project, which is concerned with development of a semiautomatic instrument for harvesting blood cells (leucocytes) was handled by the owner himself. The principle design of the product is shown in figure 1. The cell suction head sucks the solution containing the radioactivated blood cells from a microtitration plate with 96 wells. The solution from each well is filtered, resulting in a filter mat with 96 spots containing the radioactive cells. The filter is dried and each spot is exposed to a scintillation counter for measuring of the radioactivity.

Initiation

At the time when the project was initiated the firm had existed for only half a year. During this period the major activity was development and manufacturing of equipment for automated painting of large surfaces. This equipment had been invented by the owner for a firm in the building industry.

During the spring of 1976, the owner was contacted about a laboratory problem by a medical doctor in a nearby hospital. The doctor knew about his background from the field of medical technology. He was convinced that the leader of Mentronics was the kind of person who would be able to help him with his problem, which was concerned with reducing the time-consuming and laborious work involved in measurement of the probability of success of transplantation operations.

In laboratory measurements cell division is carried out in a solution with radioactive labelled protein. When a cell divides, it absorbs a certain amount of the radioactive protein which thus results in radioactive labelled cells. By measuring the radioactivity of the cells in a test, one is able to calculate the number of divided cells.

As done traditionally, the preparatory work in connection with the measurements is a very time-consuming process. The number of measurements that can be carried out is limited by the capacity of the staff. A reduction of the manual work would therefore increase the capacity of the laboratory.

The development process

In an informal discussion with the medical doctor who initiated the project, the owner of Mentronics was introduced thoroughly to the problem which can be described as follows.

The hospital wants to minimise the human labour input in connection with preparation of leucocyte measurements. It was indicated that a possible solution might be automation of the process that was carried out manually. Such a solution seemed to be quite simple, but gradually the owner recognised that a better solution would be to use an entirely new technological concept. This idea was developed in close co-operation with chemists and medical staff at the hospital. During late winter, 1976, a prototype was made and tested. The results were satisfactory. Some medical researchers at another well-known hospital became aware of the instrument and expressed great interest in the project. For several months they took an active part in the testing of the prototype and its development. As a result of this co-operation, the concept was considerably simplified. This resulted in a second prototype which was tested with satisfactory results.

During the summer of 1977 two instruments were sold to well-known hospitals. They expressed satisfaction with the equipment. This was enough for the owner; as a problem solver he had done his job and had no intention of exploiting his invention further. He had experienced an interesting and stimulating inventing period, and he received a reasonable return on his investment. However, without any sales effort Mentronics received several orders and 30 instruments were sold during 1977.

Early in 1978 the owner learnt that a large health organisation in The Netherlands had started to develop an instrument based on a similar concept as the Mentronics harvester. This created an irresistible challenge. After a visit to the director of the organisation in The Netherlands, the owner persuaded the director to try the Mentronics harvester in his own laboratories. The results were so good that the director bought one instrument and terminated his own project. This director is known as a 'leader' in the medical field in Europe and his decision stimulated other hospitals to buy the instrument. This event caused Mentronics to manufacture and market the product on a regular basis.

Results

During the summer of 1978 the firm was contacted by one of the leading dealers in the world of microbiological equipment. After some discussion, a contract with exclusive rights to market the instrument world-wide was signed. The result of this was that one year later about 200 instruments had been sold.

2.   *The production control instrument*

This is a project which is not yet finished. It is handled by the development manager. The task is to develop an instrument for on-line production control.

Initiation

This project was initiated by the owner of a metal working firm who had severe delays in connection with his manufacturing operations. The reason is, in part, due to the rapid growth of the firm, and in part to an increasing volume of standard products in addition to a great variety of customer products. In order to improve the situation he feels that one should install a modern, automated system for production control. However, having investigated several systems available on the market, he has concluded that they are too expensive. Knowing the inventive owner of Mentronics, he has suggested that the firm should develop an instrument cheap enough to be used by small and medium sized firms. This suggestion has been positively received by the owner, who after a few weeks created a concept based on an entirely new principle. He recognises that the project is risky as one will have to break new ground.

As Mentronics is not able to provide the financial resources for development and marketing of the product, he has applied and got support from a research foundation that is willing to cover 50% of the expenses required to fully develop a prototype.

Organisation of the project

The experience gained over several years from the manufacturing operations of Mentronics provides a starting point for the project. However, it is recognised that this is not sufficient. The owner, therefore, has contacted a professor in production control at a neighbouring technical university. After some discussions of the project, he has been commissioned the task of specifying the requirements from a user point of view. The development of software, hardware and design of the prototype will be done by Mentronics.

For the planning and implementation of the project has been organised a project group headed by the production control professor. The other members of the group are two of his assistants, and the development manager and the manufacturing manager of Mentronics.

Problem definition

Based on the know-how within the project group with regard to production control systems and design of electronic instruments, the project has been defined by means of a preliminary specification. The instrument should be:

inexpensive and simple enough to be utilised by firms that cannot justify an expensive and complex system;
able to report simultaneously from at least 20 work stations the follow-

ing data: elapsed time, idle time, run time, set-up time, per cent of standard rate, idle per cent, set-up per cent, number of idle periods, number of set-ups, average idle period, count accumulation, gross rate, net rate, down time, premium time, and histograms of one or more of the preceding variables;

simple to install and operate, but powerful enough to provide satisfactory data collection and reporting capability;

a 'building block' for industrial firms to gain experience with automated data collection and reporting that could be integrated at a later date into a CAM system (Computer Aided Manufacturing);

directly usable by manufacturing engineers with no computer or software experience;

preprogrammed with algorithms, for presentation of input/output ratios usable for the manufacturing engineer, and allow, but not require, simple programming by the user;

capable of generating hard copy standard reports such as a status report indicating time log of any change in status of any or all machines, a notation of the change in status and the values of the associated machine data. A production summary report should be generated to provide the cumulative production statistics of each or of all work stations on a demand basis or at the end of a shift;

capable of printing reports on a data terminal or sending data over telephone lines to an inquiring remote terminal;

based on the Motorola M6809 pseudo 16-bit microprocessor chip with associated support chips (a microprocessor is a semiconductor consisting of an integrated electrical circuit on a thin silicon wafer).

Need assessment

In order to determine the needs of potential users, the project group has decided to use a two-stage questioning approach. The group first visited nine plants to discuss desirable attributes. Three of these plants were known to have modern monitoring systems in operation; the others were selected to offer a wide range of types and sizes. Based on the interviews the following conclusions were drawn:

the need for the contemplated instrument is most evident in plastic molding and metal press operations;

users prefer a supplier who is thoroughly familiar with such operations;

real time data are essential, but should be supplemented with periodic print-outs;

cost is a major determinant in any decision to install a monitoring system;

it is difficult for most firms to give even an order of magnitude estimate

of the price that might be attractive (in one place it was indicated that one might be interested at about $1.000 per channel); some way of highlighting areas that need attention is desirable. This can be done through the use of colour, but similar and superior results seem to be obtained at a much lower cost through the use of differing fonts and/or reverse imaging and flashing;
monitoring systems are particularly useful in multiple shift operations. They allow an incoming supervisor to see the status of all machines, allow him to determine the performance in the previous shift, and give the supervisor, and others, a comparison of the performance on various shifts;
many installations will require more than 20 channels; add-on monitoring devices that could use the intelligence of the main unit should be available. It might be well to contemplate the economies of offering an intelligent unit having ten channels with the capability of handling five to ten channel satellite units.

Based on the knowledge acquired by means of the first interviews, the group plans to visit a few more firms before making final recommendations on the precise specifications for the development of a prototype unit.

When the first unit has been built, tested and modified at Mentronics, three more prototypes will be built. They will be installed in three manufacturing companies for a 30-day performance and cost evaluation. The objective is to determine how well the system provides meaningful, real-time production information. Recommendations from the users will then be evaluated and implemented.

Commercialisation

Once the specifications of the production reporting instrument have been finalised, the exploitation will be undertaken by Mentronics. A difficult decision to make will be how to market it.

VII   CONCLUSION

The Mentronics case revolves around a technical entrepreneur, i.e. a person with technical background who has established his own business. It gives a good illustration of the contribution of small technology-based firms in technological innovation.

High technological competence is necessary but not sufficient for success. A profitable product represents a fusion between a need and a technology that fulfils the need. At Mentronic the entrepreneurial owner combines a high degree of innovativeness with a strong market orientation. He pays great attention to finding interesting problems by visiting existing and potential customers. Thereby he obtains first-hand knowledge about their difficulties and recognises where he can be of help. The advantage of having a direct coupling between user needs and technology can hardly be overestimated. However, in many situations one will have to use other approaches. This is also the situation with Mentronics.

Whether information is provided informally or systematically, great attention should be given to assess needs and reactions of users as early as possible in the product innovation process. This is clearly demonstrated at Mentronics.

The case also illustrates the great influence of the top man on the development of small entrepreneurial firms. First of all, due to his inventive capability, Mentronics is able to utilise modern technology for development of sophisticated products with superior performance. This should give the firm a good basis for rapid growth and thus make it a significant contributor to social development and economic growth. However, this potential is not utilised due to the owner who wants to keep the business small. This gives a dynamic and flexible organisation which is able to perceive and quickly respond to new market opportunities. By having a minimum of administration, he is able to devote a substantial part of his time to his real interest, i.e. to use his inventiveness and entrepreneurial skills to solve problems for other firms.

Finally, the case shows how easy it is for large organisations with bureaucratic procedures to hamper creative engineers in their innovative effort. In such situations some engineers give up their innovative behaviour and become 'organisation men'. They conform to established rules and procedures; they stick to 'good standard engineering practice', which usually results only in minor improvements in existing products and processes. Other engineers react to the pressure for conformist behaviour in a different way. If they do not get managerial support to realise their own ideas and inventions, they do as the innovative founder of Mentronics, they leave the job and start their own firm.

Recently the owner of Mentronics decided to retire. The firm was sold to a successful shipowner who intends to put his son in charge of the company. The son is a mechanical engineer with five years industrial experience from plastic moulding and one year's study of business administration.

The change of ownership is expected to have a significant impact on the future development of Mentronics.

Appendix 3
Norsk Data — Case Study

Within the rapidly developing electronics industry data and telecommunication is one of the fastest growing sectors. Actually, one is here faced with a new industry — the information industry — that is growing at an annual rate of 25–30%. A key element in this development is the computer.

Originally the market was dominated by large computers. Gradually minicomputers and microcomputers have become more powerful. They are now performing many tasks that only the big mainframe systems could do before. Being convenient and cheap to use, the distributed processing systems have conquered an increasing share of the market as indicated below.

Market share	Mainframe computers	Mini-computers	Micro-computers
1975	83%	10%	7%
1980	60%	17%	23%
1985	36%	21%	43%

This development is so profound that the structure of the industry is changing significantly.

In order to survive several of the large mainframe firms that previously dominated the business are now changing strategy. Instead of competing at all segments they concentrate their development and marketing effort on satisfying the needs of carefully selected niches. In addition to mainframes, they offer office automation equipment, small computers, and customised software and services. This requires new marketing skills and capacity to properly assess user needs.

Parallel with this trend entrepreneurial engineers have grasped the opportunities created by the new developments within distributed processing systems and established their own firms. American firms have dominated this development. Also in Europe many firms have been very clever in developing or using the most advanced technology. They

317

have made useful inventions, but often they have lacked the ability to bring the products to the market and make profit out of them. One exception is Norsk Data which, during the last 15 years, has grown annually by 40–50% to become one of the leading producers of mini-computers in Europe.

I HISTORY OF NORSK DATA

The firm was founded in 1967 by three electronics engineers working at a defence research institute. They had also had experience from M.I.T. (Massachusetts Institute of Technology), a leading technical university that, amongst other activities, is doing pioneering work in computer technology.

The entrepreneurial engineers saw that a big market was emerging for small computers and felt that they had the necessary background for making them just as easily as the existing companies. Together with friends and relatives they put up $25 000 (the majority provided by a shipowner and his family) and started Norsk Data. This turned out to be a wise decision. Over the years the firm has developed and intro-duced several minicomputers of a pioneering nature. Particular empha-sis has been given to the development of on-line operating systems.

The first product, Nord I, a 16-bit minicomputer, got off the ground in 1968. It was positively accepted and gave the firm a flying start. In 1972 was introduced Nord 5, the world's first 32-bit superminicom-puter. A big international breakthrough came in 1973, when CERN (Conseil Européen pour la Recherche Nucleaire) selected the Nord 10 as the best minicomputer on the market. In 1977 the firm got a con-tract from Singer Link to supply Nord computers for simulators for fighter pilot training. In the same year Norsk Data established its Nord-text division for provision of turnkey computer systems for the news-paper industry.

A system for word processing and administrative data processing, NOTIS, was released in 1980. In 1981 the firm introduced the third generation of its superminicomputer, the powerful Nord 500, based on a radically new technology. Current product lines are based on a flex-ible set of modules that can be supplemented and rearranged to meet the needs of individual customers. A network system COSMOS, permit-ting applications and databases to be shared through a data network came in 1982.

Important milestones were passed in 1981 and 1983 when the firm was listed at the London and the New York stock exchanges. In addi-tion to providing a strong international capital base, these events demonstrated that the firm has obtained a good reputation abroad for its advanced technology and competitive products. Norsk Data has grown annually by 40–45%. In 1982 the sale reached $83 millions; of this about 50% came from export. The firm has become the largest supplier of minicomputers in the Scandinavian market and is increasing its share outside Scandinavia. The number of employees has passed 1000, which gives about $85000 in sales per employee. Operating profit has, in recent years, been about 15% of annual sales. Currently it is about $10 000 per employee, one of the best results in the industry.

Norsk Data develops, manufactures and markets medium-sized, general-purpose minicomputer systems, including associated software products. Sales and customer support are undertaken by wholly owned subsidiaries operating out of 17 offices in Norway, Denmark, Sweden, England, France, Switzerland, West Germany and the USA. In addition, there are a further 12 offices providing customer support only. Four other overseas markets are served by agencies.

The computer systems, which are used both for technical and administrative applications, are sold to manufacturing enterprises, trading companies, public utilities, research institutes, educational institutions, defence agencies and newspaper and printing establishments. In addition, come original equipment manufacturers which represent around 15% of total sales.

II BUSINESS CONCEPT AND MANAGEMENT PHILOSOPHY

The basic *concept* underlying the operations of Norsk Data is to be a profitable computer company by using advanced technology to fulfil genuine user needs for integrated information systems. The systems must be developed in such a way as to give the highest possible difference between user value and production cost.

The management of the firm has a thoroughly considered *philosophy* focusing upon people, money, technology and marketing.

The principle asset is *people*. It is their know-how and energy that carry the firm forward. Motivation is obtained through extensive delegation of authority and responsibility and a consensus type of management.

Employees must have a real understanding of what the important considerations are rather than just following fixed rules and standard procedures. With the rapid rate of change, experience soon becomes obsolete. In developing a new computer, decisions cannot be taken from the top; they have to be made by those who have the best knowledge, i.e. those participating in the project. The managers and the employees involved must, therefore, discuss the important issues and make the necessary decisions based upon a consensus of what is the best in each case.

Another important source of motivation comes from the fact that not only managers, but most employees are share holders. Thus, if a wrong decision is made, it may reduce the value of the shares and thereby hurt their personal wealth.

Great attention is given to the development of an organisational climate that gives people enjoyment in their work. Privileges are avoided; all eat in the same place and use the same parking lots. In principle only wages should be different.

Those working on a project decide when and how they want to work. There are no time clocks in the company, and no over-time pay. However, most employees put in more hours than required by normal schedules, and employee turnover is very low compared with other firms.

The management of Norsk Data is extremely profit conscious. In order to grow, the firm must make *money*. Without a sufficient profit it will not survive, or the control of it will be taken over by people from outside. Such a situation is not wanted, the management wants to develop the firm itself without outside influence.

The successful establishment of Norsk Data was due to its high level of *technology*. And experience up to now has clearly demonstrated that in order to stay competitive, one must be able to utilise quickly the most advanced technology.

Perhaps the most important lesson from its rapid development is the importance of *marketing*. The company must offer products that satisfy the needs of the users at a price they are willing to pay. It is the customer value of the product that counts. This is primarily dependent upon the software that is delivered and the support that is given in terms of training, assistance and maintenance.

A good product is not enough in itself. Even the best product in the world has no chance if it is not brought to the users by means of a good and professional marketing organisation. This is a keystone in the operations of the firm.

III   MAJOR OBJECTIVES AND STRATEGIES

During its lifetime Norsk Data has changed from a small technology-oriented laboratory developing products for technical and scientific applications, to a modern market-oriented European computer company. During this period more than 3000 computers have been delivered.

Particularly in the last ten years the firm has experienced a rapid growth. On average the annual growth rate has been 44% for total sales, 59% for export sales, 55% for profit, and 48% for earnings per share. During the same period the number of employees has grown from 380 to 1047. The relatively low employee growth reflects a substantial increase in productivity.

The major objective of the firm is to maintain the high rate of growth in profit and earning that has been achieved in the last ten years. Particular emphasis is given to maximise earnings per share, in order that the shares may remain a profitable investment.

The major *strategy* is to develop, manufacture, sell and service general-purpose, medium-size minicomputers for integrated information systems in the price range of $40 000–$400 000.

With a fairly limited home market, great attention is given to the development and manufacturing of products that will sell on international markets.

As the firm has a relatively modest market share in the European countries with largest demand (France, West Germany and United Kingdom), there is considerable growth potential which can be actively explored. A great effort is also devoted to further penetration of the Scandinavian market.

In order to stay competitive, the strategy is to develop flexible, general-purpose computers based on modules that, to a large extent, are common to several computer systems. Each module is developed independently of others and utilises the latest technology.

The software products rest on a firm foundation of basic tools for systems development. These include one common operating system for all computer models and all types of applications, and compilers for all major programming languages.

With regard to technology the strategy is to control all essential elements through in-house research and development, while relying on specialised manufacturers for components and sub-assembly, which is not crucial for the future of the firm. Magnetic storage units, printers, video display terminals, semi-conductor components and production capacity for board processing and assembly are brought in. The critical technology which is maintained in-house includes that for central processing units, peripheral controllers, main memory subsystems, all final assembly and testing, operating system software including programming language compilers and data communication for system interconnection, and software tools for administrative data processing and office automation.

In addition to buying considerable amounts of components and sub-assemblies from outside, extensive use is made of subcontractors for parts developed by the company such as the central computer, its interfaces and the main memory. The main manufacturing activities, therefore, are final assembly, testing and quality control of the total system including software.

A large R & D staff is needed for continued development of competitive, profitable products with a high customer value. About 8% of annual sales are spent on R & D. The importance of this function is also reflected to the fact that of the employees more than 15% are engaged on R & D activities, 15% with manufacturing, 32% with sales, and 40% with customer support including repair, maintenance training and programme assistance.

As software will assume increasing importance in the usefulness of the computer system for the customer, about 75% of the R & D staff are working on development of general software.

In order to keep up with trends in the European minicomputer markets, a considerable amount of resources will be allocated to the areas of office automation and transaction processing. Here will be required more powerful general software and advanced programming tools which require larger systems.

The basic strategy of Norsk Data has always been to direct the resources towards high performance hardware and flexible general-purpose software that can serve a variety of customer requirements as opposed to a strategy of high-volume products for special market segments. The broad product base of Norsk Data provides an excellent foundation for satisfaction of new customer needs both home and abroad.

IV   ORGANISATION

The *basic structure* of Norsk Data is shown below.

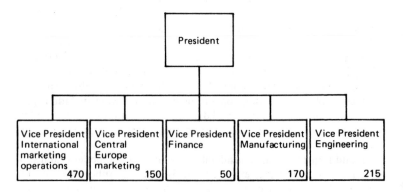

Under the Vice President, International marketing operations, are managers for defence systems, printing systems, marketing services, international sales, Sweden, Denmark, North America and Norway. Under Vice President Central European marketing are managers for CERN, France, Germany, Switzerland, United Kingdom, and marketing services in central Europe. Under Vice President Finance are managers for corporate budget control, personnel, internal data processing, facilities planning, and accounting. Under Vice President manufacturing are managers for production, purchasing, product co-ordination, system integration and orderoffice/transport. Under Vice President engineering are managers for development, quality assurance, and customer support.

A high degree of *delegation* is used with regard to authority and responsibility. This is due, in part, to the management philosophy of employee motivation, and, in part, to the rapid change of technology in the computer field. Technological knowledge is not located according to place in the organisation hierarchy. On the contrary, those best fitted for solving the highly complex technological problems are well-educated young engineers with rather limited practical experience. Most modern computers are designed by teams where the experience of the typical team member is between two and four years. In one of the most successful products of Norsk Data the leader of the project team had only 18 months' experience when the work started. In such a situation the manager cannot tell the group what to do. He has to discuss the important issues with the members and make a decision based on a consensus of what is best. This implies that one must have managers who are able to work in an environment where it is not the formal position but the natural authority that counts.

Delegation is a key concept not only in R & D, but throughout the whole company. Thus, market decisions are made by the people in the various markets — only they have first-hand knowledge about the situation in their areas. The situation may be very different in Sweden from that in England or Norway.

The growth of the firm has been followed by a high degree of specialisation. Necessary *co-ordination* of the various experts is obtained by means of product committees, project groups, and rotation of employees.

The firm has five *product committees* for decision making on products and marketing. One is for basic computer hardware, one for office automation, one for newspaper and publishing systems, one for the scientific market, and one for the commercial market. These committees are composed of managers from R & D, sales and marketing; in addition, specialists from R & D and marketing participate when products related to their field are treated.

For development of new major products special *project groups* are organised. Most members participate on a part-time basis. The size of the group varies according to the size of the project; 10–15 members being typical. The groups are mostly composed of R & D staff, but at the end of the process they are supplemented by engineers from manufacturing and customer support. In most cases the majority of the R & D members participate throughout the whole process.

Due to the importance of introducing new products at the right time, the members must assume responsibility for the project. No members of the team will wish to be a 'bottleneck' and reduce the value of the team effort. As a result, team members will occasionally work long hours when difficulties appear.

In addition to formal devices, co-operation between marketers and technologists is greatly facilitated by creating mutual understanding and respect. This is obtained by employee rotation, giving managers and key staff experience from practical work both on the marketing and the technological side.

V PRODUCT PLANNING

The major activities related to product planning are done by five product committees. The committee for basic general hardware has the longest time perspective. In addition to new products and improvements within existing lines, a considerable amount of time is devoted to planning of new generations. With the rapid change within the computer industry, the life cycle of each generation is now down to three years.

The various projects are listed in a product calendar covering a period of 18 months. This shows when the various products will be released, and how the various products tie together. Normally is not changed more than one element of a system at any time. This means that most projects are modifications of existing products and not radically new solutions.

In addition to the formal planning procedure, the management group devotes a considerable amount of time thinking further ahead, to what the situation will be in a more distant future. Considerations about the future architecture of computers, the integration of various systems into large information systems by means of net works, etc. are taken into account. The solutions have to be oriented towards the needs of end users, which will require systems that can be used without programmers.

The time perspective is getting increasingly longer. In the 1970s one could look three years ahead and feel quite safe. Now the horizon has increased to five years or even more.

VI   PRODUCT DEVELOPMENT

An important consideration in connection with the product innovation process is to find out what the needs of the market are at time of introduction. With rapid change in need patterns, the chances of a failure are rather high if one develops a product that is right at the time when the decision to start the project is made. This means that one is faced with the difficult task of assessing future needs, the situation two or three years ahead. New products are the result of a combination of 'technology push' and 'market pull'. Therefore, one has to obtain information both regarding technological developments and future needs. As far as technology is concerned, developments abroad are closely followed by having people within R & D visit leading institutions in Europe and USA, but the primary source of new knowledge is professional publications.

In order to assess future user needs, people from the marketing department spend much time in the field discussing problems and future requirements of customers. This is done through formal and informal meetings.

Future needs are also assessed by means of brainstorming groups. Five to seven people participate in a typical session, but on a few occasions groups have been organised with 15–30 people. All who participate are from the company, but several have been given the task to talk to customers before the session.

Information about the user environment is also obtained by recruiting R & D staff who have previously worked with computers and information technology in other organisations and institutions. With their practical experience and knowledge about problems and difficulties facing users, they can make important contributions in assessing future needs and requirements.

Direct information about user needs is also obtained by having R & D staff participate in sales teams. Most customers appreciate to be able to talk directly with R & D people. However, one is careful in not over-using this approach. The R & D staff is one of the most critical resources, and they have to spend most of their time in the company developing new products. They therefore are used in the field only on very important problems or when direct user feedback is of special value.

The needs that have been assessed are formulated in a specification indicating key parameters such as speed, flexibility, physical dimensions, etc. The effort that is put into formulation of the specification depends on the type of project. A highly innovative project may start with a discussion of needs and solution concepts among key people from various areas. One example is the development of a new product generation. Here experience from bottlenecks and limitations of current products gave an indication in which direction the market was going. After numerous discussions during half a year, one concluded that it was not enough to radically improve current products. One therefore decided to start over again by forgetting what one had and ask what the real needs were. Important input to these discussions came from staff who had been employed with developing user-oriented software, first of all people in charge of commercial software, operating systems, and compilers. Based on the requirements thus formulated, the hardware experts indicated that one would have to do a pioneering job by developing a new technology that would break entirely with previous traditions. Based on the discussions that had taken place, the software people formulated a specification in the form of a draft reference manual for the hardware. This provided the basis for development of the new computer.

On large projects one in addition to the main project group often appoints subgroups for special areas such as hardware, basic software, user-oriented software, product manual, etc.

When the development work has resulted in one or several prototypes, tests are undertaken in-house. In some cases one of the largest customers get prototypes and participate in the testing and debugging of them.

In developing a new product, technologists have a tendency to strive after the perfect solution without realising that proper timing of the introduction is essential. It is more important to make a compromise by leaving out some features and keep the time schedule. In order to make profit, it is of no help to have the best product in the world in the laboratory — it must be brought out to the market at the right time without being perfect. One, therefore, is using a sequence of introductions, for example every six months, by specifying what features should be involved in the first step. Then the product is developed as specified and released, then improved, and so on. Such an approach is possible due to the fact that most of the development work is in the software field.

VII FINANCE

The development and introduction of high technology products require a substantial amount of capital. In some cases this can be done through internal financing, i.e. by retaining part of the earnings for further development of the company.

Often it is necessary to provide capital from outside by issuing new shares. This is difficult for small, innovative, but unknown firms.

However, if the company has been able to demonstrate profitable growth over several years, the access to the capital market is much easier. Norsk Data has experienced this to a high degree.

In the early years, when the earnings were much less impressive than today, the firm had to rely upon money borrowed from outside. This gave the firm very high financial costs. After several years of rapid growth in sales and profit, the firm has increasingly improved its equity capital by issuing shares. The first increase in share capital came in 1968. The next two followed in 1974 and 1978, and from then on the share capital has been increased every year. A certain amount of the share issued has been reserved for the employees which have about 12% of the share capital. They have been able to buy these shares at very reasonable prices.

The first public sales of shares were done in Norway. However, as the capital market here is not large enough to cover the rapidly increasing needs of Norsk Data, the firm has been granted a concession from the Norwegian Government to cover up to 70% of its share capital by selling shares to foreign investors.

Today the shares are quoted at stock exchanges in Oslo, Stockholm, London and New York. Norsk Data was the first Norwegian company to raise capital in these markets by public placing of shares. Of the share capital, 60% is in foreign ownership. The firm has close to 5000 share holders. About 50% are foreign investors with non-voting b-shares; the controlling majority is therefore still in Norway.

The access to foreign capital markets has resulted in a steady improvement of the financial situation and provided good opportunities for further expansion of the firm. The equity ratio improved drastically in 1982 and 1983 due to sale of new shares in London and New York at market prices. It is now more than 60%, which is considerably higher than in most firms. Thus, the solidity of Norsk Data is very healthy.

VIII   CONCLUSION

The development of Norsk Data from a small Norwegian laboratory to an internationally known 'high technology flyer' is remarkable. The outstanding achievements must first of all be credited to a dynamic and foresighted management with a great capability to learn both from others' and from one's own mistakes.

Perhaps the most important development is the change from a research-oriented technology environment towards a modern market and profit oriented company. The basic proprietary technology is still considered to be the key to future success. One does not want to become dependent upon the technology of somebody else. However, increasingly the technological orientation has been combined with the marketing point of view. This has not been an easy process — 'we have made enormous mistakes in this company in the early years by focusing too little upon marketing. However, we have learnt the hard way the necessity of having a very good marketing organisation'.

The company still appears to be relatively too strong on the technology side or too weak on the marketing side to have a properly balanced company. This is recognised by management who are willing to give higher priority and spend more resources on marketing. Here the potential is very promising. Compared with mainframe computers the market for minicomputers is growing rapidly, and it is less dependent on large-scale production than the even more rapidly growing microcomputer markets. With this situation prevailing, and with a capable and highly motivated staff, the odds for reaching the ambitious objectives of the firm should be rather high.

Appendix 4 Acquisition of Knowledge — Checklist

1. *Indicate what you have learned* from this event (lecture, case discussion, book, article, etc.) with regard to: organisation culture, management philosophy, attitudes, business concept, major objectives, formulation of strategy, diversification planning, selection of products, assessment of user needs, creation of solution concepts, formulation of proposals, formulation of R & D projects, organisation structure, organisation of product innovation activities, marketing, ...
   ....
2. *Make a critical analysis* of the information you have received:
   How reliable is the source?
   What is missing?
   What is not satisfactory?
   What can be improved?
   What is positive and useful?
3. *Indicate how the knowledge acquired*:
   Expands previous knowledge (what is new?)
   Reinforces previous knowledge (strengthens your belief)
   Weakens previous knowledge (makes you more sceptical)
   Can be of practical usefulness (what action should be taken?
   What obstacles will be met?
   How should they be overcome?)
4. *Indicate what you have learned about influence factors (parameters)* such as culture, attitudes, type of industry, type of market, type of product, product technology, process technology, size of firm, product life cycle, etc.
5. *Compare material from various sources*:
   What is equal?
   What is different?
   Why?

Appendix 5 Organisation Theories/Management Schools

It is a striking contrast between the technological and the managerial aspects of innovations. Technology is advancing rapidly based on a scientific foundation going more than 2000 years back. From the fundamental work of men like Pythagoras, Aristotle, Euclid and Archimedes, through the discoveries of Copernicus, Galileo, Kepler, Descartes and Newton up to Plank and Einstein, there has been a rapidly expanding body of knowledge supporting technological advances.

In the management field, the scientific foundation is rather limited. It is not necessary to spend much time in industry to find out that managers largely base their work on experience, and that they meet a rather confusing picture if they turn towards science for theoretical support. (Koontz, J., 'The management theory jungle', *J. of the Academy of Management*, 4, No. 3, 171–188, (December 1961), and Alton, J.A., 'Co-operative management today — how useful to the practitioner?', *Management International Rev.*, 9, No. 1, 3–9, (1969).) This situation is due to the fact that there exists no unified theory of organisations. On the contary, the word organisation theory stands for a great number of schools and directions developed by people with highly different backgrounds. Important contributions have come from practitioners such as managers, technologists, marketers, etc., and academics with a background in psychology, social psychology, sociology, cultural anthropology, political science, economics, mathematics, etc. In common for most schools is that they describe how organisations function — some also try to provide a basis for determining how organisations should be in order to survive and develop.

Several attempts have been made to classify the various schools. In the article referred to above, Koontz makes a distinction between the operational (management process) school, the empirical (case) school, the human behaviour school, the social system school, the decision theory school, and the mathematical school. In a recent paper, The management theory jungle revisited', (referred to in *International Management Development*, No. 4, (1982)), he identifies 11 different schools. This reflects the development in recent years, where a number of new directions have emerged.

In a paper, 'Management of technological innovation', (*Management International Review*, No. 4–5, 21–37, (1970)), Holt classifies the various schools in four groups as indicated below.

The *traditional schools* (classical, conventional, empirical, operational schools) – from around 1900 – are largely developed by practitioners, to some extent by scholars by means of empirical studies. They are characterised by being highly structured, emphasis on the formal organisation, autocratic leadership, and control by superior.

The traditional schools have, to a considerable extent, been influenced by military and church organisations. The more important directions are Taylor's 'Scientific Management' (Taylorism, Shop management, Machine theory), Fayol's 'Administrative management' (General management), and Weber's 'Bureaucratic management'. Other well-known names are Barth, Bedaux, Ford, Gannt, Gilbreht, Gulick, Kosiol, Nordsieck, Tippet, Ulrich and Urwick.

Common for most of them is the presumption that the human resources, by economical motivation, can be programmed and utilised in the same way as the physical resources ('the economical man'). Most of the 'principles' are generalisation and unverified hypothesis. Although much criticised, they work —— at least up to a certain point. They have given good results, particularly under stable conditions, but appear not to be flexible enough when the company has to adapt to changes in the environment. These schools still have a rather important place in both management practice and theory.

The *human factors schools* (motivation-oriented schools) —— from around 1930 —— are based on research by behavioural scientists; they are characterised by a low degree of structure, emphasis on the informal organisation, participative leadership, and self control. These schools take into account human needs as determinants for behaviour. Focus is upon individual motivation, group behaviour and interpersonal relationships. The organisation is viewed as a social system with interactions, communications, conflicts and alliances, where perceptions and feelings are important aspects. Among the more important directions are the 'Human relations' schools, with emphasis on creating satisfaction among employees, the 'Participative management' schools, largely concerned with employee participation in planning and decision making, and 'Group dynamics' schools, which stress co-operation in small groups.

The human factor schools put the human being in focus ('the social man'). An important concept is the *informal organisation*, which is formed to satisfy human needs. It may, however, also facilitate the operation of the *formal organisation* through development of informal relationships and procedures. Most of these schools accept by and large the principles and rules advocated by the traditional schools, but show how they may be modified by human behaviour. Among the pioneers can be mentioned Dickson, Emery, Hertzberg, Maslow, Mayo, McGregor, Roethlisberger, Thorsrud and Trist.

The *decision theory schools* (economical factors schools) — from around 1950 — are based on research from scholars in fields like economics, mathematics, statistics and engineering. The organisation is viewed as a decision-making system, where the objective is the efficient utilisation of the resources. Emphasis is on the development of models for planning and decision making. Among the more important directions are the 'Classical economical' schools (profit maximation), the 'Utility maximation' schools, and the 'Mathematical' schools (operations research, management science, industrial dynamics). These schools represent a more sophisticated approach than the scientific management schools. At present there is a considerable gap between theory and practice. However, this gap will be narrowed and the decision theory schools are expected to get a considerable impact on management in the future. Well-known names here are Barnard, Cyert, Forrester, Heinen, Kirsch, March, Marschak, von Neumann and Simon.

The *system oriented schools* — from around 1960 — are based on research from scholars with different backgrounds, most of them are behavioural scientists and engineers. These schools can be considered to be an expansion of the human factor schools, also taking into account the technological factors and the external environment. They focus upon change adaptation. The aim is to find an optimal solution of the total system. Technology, the formal and the informal organisation are considered as integrated parts; the organisation is considered to be an open *socio-technical system* under constant influence of internal and external forces.

By analysis of the total system, the relationship between the organisation and the external environment are important. Changes of technological, marketing, economical, social and political nature may have considerable consequences for the design and function of the organisation.

The system-oriented schools seem to be well fitted for the analysis of industrial organisations. They are new and not much tested, but offer a great potential. Of particular value is the way they take the technological factors into the analysis, and thus make it possible to get a better balance between the technical, economical, marketing and social requirements. Important contributions have been made by Ashby, Burns, Bertalanffy, Boulding, Checkland, Lawrence, Lorsch, Luhmann, Parsons, Stalker, Thompson, Wiener, etc.

In three articles, 'Die Organisations-Theorie', (*Management Zeitschrift* **50**, No. 9, 442–6, (1981); No. 11, 565–9, and No. 12, 609–613), Dyllick uses a similar classification: task-oriented theories (Aufgabenorientierte Ansätze), motivation-oriented theories (Motivations-orientierte Ansätze), decision-oriented theories (Entscheidungs-orientierte Ansätze), and system-oriented theories (System-orientierte Ansätze). Each of the main groups are subdivided in several sub-groups. Several *new directions* — from 1970 — have appeared in recent years. It is difficult to classify them, as they reflect a development that is going on. Common for most of them is the emphasis they give to problems related to change and renewal — problems about which most firms feel strongly. Depending on the degree of emphasis, one may distinguish between directions focusing upon innovation, creativity, market problems and needs, and total productivity (the latter covers both renewal and efficiency of current activities). Of increasing importance are organisation theories reflecting behaviour in Japanese firms (often called *Japanese management*); they have created great interest in the West, and they are also to some extent used in Western firms. To a large extent Japanese management has been influenced by Western schools ('Japanese and American management is 95% the same, but differ in all important respects'). Perhaps one of the most characteristic features of this direction is the emphasis that is given to organisation culture and management philosophy. Among the names attatched to the new schools can be mentioned Abernathy, Ackoff, Ansoff, Athos, Drucker, Marquis, Myers, Ouchi, Pascale and Utterbach.

In addition to the schools referred to above should be mentioned the so-called *Contingency theory*. The underlying assumption is that there is a causal relationship between function and structure of the organisation, and factors such as external environment, company size, strategy, technology, tasks, people, etc.

Our knowledge is limited both with regard to relevant factors, their importance, and to what degree they are interrelated. Many of them have not been defined operationally, and others have not been measured in a satisfactory way. At present it is therefore not possible to quantify the factors and their relationships. By and large one has to rely on 'educated guesses' supported by whatever knowledge is available, be it of a theoretical or practical nature. An attempt in this direction, supported by research in American and Norwegian firms, is made by Holt (*Management International Rev.*, No. 4–5, 21–37, (1970)). The major results are indicated below.

Looking at the company on an overall basis, it appears that increasing company size, number of products and number of projects tend towards a mechanistic highly structured system based on a rather autocratic type of leadership and control by superiors. On the other hand, both

Factors influencing the design of a management system

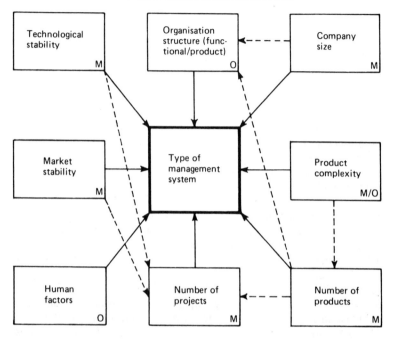

changes in technology and markets, and human factors are strong forces pointing towards an organic system with a low degree of structure, emphasis on informal relationships and participative leadership. An organisation structure based on autonomous product divisions gives a more organic system than a structure based on functions.

When developing the management system it is important to take into account that each department has different needs. In general, research and development need a more organic system, whereas manufacturing can operate under a rather mechanistic system. Marketing usually falls in between. In research and development product complexity is a factor pointing towards an organic system — the opposite effect seems likely in manufacturing.

The overall conclusion is that there is no patent solution. Different situations require different solutions. Each firm is unique, and each department has special requirements.

In developing a management system, the challenge is to find what the real problem is, and to utilise what is relevant in the various schools with the aim of arriving at a solution that satisfies the needs in the best possible way of those involved.

References

Aaker, D. A., *Marketing Research*, 698, John Wiley, New York (1986)

Ayres, R. U., 'Envelope Forecasting' in Bright, J. R. (ed.), *Technological Forecasting for Industry and Government*, 236, New Jersey (1968)

Ayres, R. U., *Technological Forecasting and Long Range Planning*, 236, New York (1969)

Bailey, R., *Disciplined Creativity for Engineers*, 614, Ann Arbor Science, Ann Arbor (1978)

Baruch, J., 'Demanufacturing — Threat and Opportunity for Manufacturers', *Innovation*, 29, 2–10 (1972)

Battelle, *Vademecum der Ideenfindung*, 81, Battelle, Frankfurt (1979)

Beenhakker, H. L., *Replacement and Expansion Investments*, 119, Rotterdam (1975)

Berridge, T., *Product Innovation and Development*, 236, Business Books, London (1977)

Bierman, H. and Smidt, S., *The Capital Budgeting Decision*, 420, New York (1966)

Bishop, R. E. D. and Johnson, D. C., *The Mechanism of Vibration*, 592, Cambridge (1960)

Blanchard, B. S., *Engineering Organization and Management*, 526, Prentice-Hall, Englewood Cliffs (1976)

Bright, J. B., *Research, Development and Technological Innovation*, 783, Irwin, Homewood (1964)

Bruce Merrifield, D., 'How to Select Successful R&D Projects', *Management Review*, 25–28, 37–89, December (1978)

Buffa, E. S., *Modern Production Management*, 743, Wiley, New York (1977)

Burns, R. O., *Innovation, the Management Connection*, 157, Lexington Books, Lexington (1975)

Burns, T. and Stalker, G. M., *The Management of Innovation*, 269, Tavistock, London (1961)

Buzzel, R. D. *et al.*, 'Market Share – a Key to Profitability', *Harvard Business Review*, 97–106, January–February (1975)

Calabro, S. R., *Reliability Principles and Practices*, 371, McGraw-Hill, New York (1962)

Capey, J. D., Carr, N. C., *People and Work Organizations*, 255, Holt, Rinehart and Winston, London (1982)

Cetron, M. J., *Technological Forecasting: a Practical Approach*, 345, Technological Forecasting Institute, New York (1969)

Cetron, M. J. and Bertocha, N. (eds), *Technology Assessment in a Dynamic Environment*, 358, Gordon and Breach, New York (1973)

Cheaney, E. S., *Technical Forecasting as a Basis for Planning*, 12, ASME, New York (1966)

Child, J., *Organization – a Guide to Problems and Practice*, 243, Harper & Row, London (1977)

Chisnall, P. M., *Strategic Industrial Marketing*, 352, Prentice Hall, London (1985)

Clark, F. D. and Lorenzoni, A. B., *Applied Engineering*, 297, Marcel Dekker, New York (1978)

Claude, J. C. and Morize, F., 'Delphi in the Assessment of R&D Projects', *Futures*, 5, 467–483 (1972)

Colinvaux, P., *Ecology*, 724, John Wiley, New York (1986)

Cronstedt, V., *Engineering Management and Administration*, 345, McGraw-Hill, New York (1961)

Cross, N. (ed.), *Design Participation*, 124, Academy Editions, London (1972)

David, F. R., *Fundamentals of Strategic Management*, 894, Merrill Publishing, Columbus (1986)

Davis, G. A. and Scott, J. A., *Training in Creative Thinking*, 302, Krieger, New York (1978)

De Bono, E., *Lateral Thinking for Management*, 225, Penguin Books, Harmondsworth (1983)

Den Hartog, J. P., *Mechanical Vibration*, 436, McGraw-Hill, New York (1956)

Dervinitois, E. S., *System Dynamics I–II*, DTH Copenhagen (1973)

Design Council, *Management of Innovation*, 36, London (1975)

Durand, U., 'A New Method for Consulting Scenarios', *Futures*, 5, 325–330 (1972)

Eisner, R. L., *Fault Tree Analysis to Anticipated Potential Failure*, New York (1972)

Ekvall, G., *Creativity at the Work Place*, 219, Reklamlito, Malmö (1971)

Elmaghraby, E. S., *Some Network Models in Management Science*, 176, Springer, New York (1970)

Encarnacao, J. and Schlechtendahl, E. G., *Computer Aided Design*, 346, Springer, Berlin (1983)

Enzer, S., *A Case Study Using Forecasting as a Decision-Making Aid*, 42, Middletown, Connecticut (1969)

Esch, M. E., 'Planning Assistance Through Technical Evaluation of Relevance Numbers', 346–360, IEEE (1965)

Forrester, J. W., *Industrial Dynamics*, 464, MIT Press (1961)

Fraser, R., *Design in the Built Environment*, 142, London (1972)

Gee, E. A. and Tylor, C., *Managing Innovation*, 267, Wiley, New York (1976)

General Electric, 'The Effects of Organizational Climate on Performance', *Project Report*, 2, 12, New York (1969)

Gerstenfeld, A., *Effective Management of Research and Development*, 150, Addison-Wesley, Reading (1970)

Geschka, H., 'Modern Techniques for Solving Problems', *Chemical Engineering*, 91–97, August 6 (1973)

Geschka, H., *Idea Generation Methods in Industry*, Paper presented at International Seminar on Creativity Development, Helsinki, October 10–11 (1975)

Geschka, H., Hamilton, H. R., Starkloff, B. and Storvik, K., *Using Scenarios in Corporate Planning*, Battelle Memorial Institute, Columbus (1980)

Geschka, H. and Pausewang, V., 'Systematic Diversification', *Battelle Information*, 15–22, April (1974)

Geschka, H. and Pausewang, V., 'Diversification' in *Marketing-Handbuch*, Luchterhand-Verlag, Neuwied (1978)

Gibson, J. E., *Managing Research and Development*, 367, John Wiley, New York (1981)

Girogosian, N. H. (ed.), *Successful Product and Business Development*, 320, Marcel Dekker, Basel (1979)

Glie, R., *Speaking of Standards*, Cahnvis Publishing Company (1972)

Gordon, W. J. J., *Synectics*, 180, Harper & Row, New York (1961)

Gorle, P. and Long, J., *Essentials of Product Planning*, 100, McGraw-Hill, London (1973)

Gregory, S. A. (ed.), *Creativity and Innovation in Engineering*, 313, Butterworths, London (1972)

Hake, B., *New Product Strategy*, 116, Wiesbaden (1971)

Hamilton, P., *Espionage and Subversion in an Industrial Society*, 230, Hutchinson, London (1967)

Hammer, W., *Handbook of Systems and Product Safety*, 351, Prentice Hall, New York (1972)

Harlem Brundtland, G., *Our Common Future*, 400, Oxford University Press, Oxford (1987)

Hayes, R. H. and Wheelwright, S. C., *Restoring Our Competitive Edge – Competing Through Manufacturing*, 427, John Wiley, New York (1984)

Helmer, O., *Social Technology*, 122, Basic Books (1966)

Hertz, D. P., 'Risk Analysis in Capital Investment', *Harvard Business Review*, 95–106, Jan.–Feb. (1964)

Hetman, F., *Society and the Assessment of Technology*, 420, OECD, Paris (1973)

Higson, C. J., *Business Finance*, 490, Butterworths, London (1986)

Hinterhuber, H. H., *Strategische Unternehmungsfiirung*, 280, de Gruyter, Berlin (1977)

Hirschmann, R. G. and Kramar, S., 'Ein Mittelbetrieb findet neue Produktfamilien', *Plus*, 38–41, No. 7 (1974)

Hisrich, R. D. and Peters, M. P., *Marketing a New Product*, 358, Benjamin/ Cummings, Menlo Park (1978)

Holt, K., 'Creativity and Organizational Climate', *Work Study and Management Services*, 576–583, Sept. (1971)

Holt, K. (a), *The Scanship Case. A Program for Promotion of Innovation*, 69, The International Institute for the Management of Technology, Milan (1972)

Holt, K. (ed.), *Innovation*, 396, The International Institute for the Management of Technology, Milan (1973)

Holt, K. (a), *Notes on Innovation and Creativity*, 131, University of Trondheim, Norwegian Institute of Technology, Division of Organization and Work Science, Trondheim (1973)

Holt, K., 'Generating Creativity, Ideas and Inventions — Information and Needs Analysis in Idea Generation', *Research Management*, 24–27, May (1975)

Holt, K., *Organization for Product Innovation*, 211, University of Trondheim, Norwegian Institute of Technology, Division of Organization and Work Science, Trondheim (1977)

Holt, K. (a), *Innovasjon — markedsföring*, 67, Aschehoug, Oslo (1977)

Holt, K., 'Information Inputs to New Product Planning and Development', *Research Policy*, 342–360, No. 7 (1978)

Holt, K., *Innovation – a Challenge to the Engineer*, 452, Elsevier, Amsterdam (1987)

Holt, K., Geschka, H. and Peterlongo, G., *Need Assessment – a Key to User-Oriented Product Innovation*, 187, John Wiley, Chichester (1984)

Hübner, H. (ed.), *The Art and Science of Innovation Management*, 452, Elsevier, Amsterdam (1986)

Hussey, D. E., *Inflation and Business Policy*, 150, Longham, London (1976)

Imdieke, L. F., *Financial Accounting*, 820, John Wiley, New York (1987)

Ireson, W. G., *Reliability Handbook*, McGraw-Hill, New York (1966)

Jantsch, E., *Technological Forecasting in Perspective*, 401, OECD, Paris (1967)

Jones, J. C., *Design Methods*, 407, Wiley, London (1970)

Juran, J. M., *Quality Control Handbook*, 1850, McGraw-Hill, New York (1974)

Kahn, H., *On Alternative World Futures: Some Basic Techniques, Issues, Themes and Variables*, 44, Chicago (1966)

Kaufmann, G., *Problemløsning og kreativitet. Organisasjonspsykologiske perspektiver*, 275, Cappelen, Oslo (1980)

Kawlath, A., *Theoretische Grundlagen der Qualitätspolitik*, 161, Gabler, Wiesbaden (1969)

Kelly, W. T., *Marketing Intelligence*, 248, London (1968)

Kerzner, H., *Project Management*, 487, Van Nostrand Reinhold, New York (1979)

Khanwalla, P. N., *The Design of Organizations*, 713, Harcourt, New York (1977)

Kieser, A. and Kubicek, H., *Organization*, 438, de Gruyter, Berlin (1977)

Kilmann, R. H., Pondy, L. R. and Slevin, D. P., *The Management of Organization. Design, Strategies and Implementation*, Vol. I, 296, North-Holland, New York (1976)

Kinnear, T. C. and Taylor, J. R., *Marketing Research*, 718, McGraw-Hill, New York (1987)

Kleine, M., *Die neuen Techniken der Kreativität und Problemlösung*, 160, Moderne Industrie, Munich (1975)

Kleine, S. J., *Similitude and Approximation Theory*, 229, McGraw-Hill, New York (1965)

Koller, R., *Konstruktionslehre für den Maschienenbau*, 327, Springer, Berlin (1985)

Kotler, P., *Marketing Management*, 792, Prentice-Hall, New Jersey (1984)

Kotter, J. P., *Organizational Dynamics: Diagnosis and Intervention*, 99, Addison-Wesley, Reading (1978)

Kramer, F. and Appelt, H. G., *Die neuen Techniken der Produktinnovationen*, 272, Moderne Industrie, Munich (1974)

Langhaar, H. L., *Dimensional Analysis and Theory of Models*, 166, John Wiley, New York (1951)

Lewis, E. E. and Steen, H., *Design of Hydraulic Control Systems*, 360, McGraw-Hill, New York (1962)

Libesny, F., *Mainly on Patents*, 210, London (1972)

Lombares, H. J. M., *Project Planning and Network Analysis*, 456, Amsterdam (1969)

Luch, D. J., *Product Policy and Strategy*, 118, New Jersey (1972)

Martino, J. P., *Technological Forecasting for Decision Making*, 750, New York (1972)

Maynard, H. B. (ed.), *Industrial Engineering Handbook*, 1856, McGraw-Hill, New York (1963)

McAdams, *Heat Transmission*, 532, New York (1954)

McCormick, E. J., *Human Factors Engineering*, 639, McGraw-Hill, New York (1970)

Medcalf, G., *Marketing and the Brand Manager*, 268, Pergamon Press (1967)

Medford, D., *Environmental Harrassment of Technology Assessment*, 358, Elsevier, Amsterdam (1973)

Merlino, M., 'Innovazione Technologica e Strategia aziendale', *Mondo Economico*, 42–45, 8 July (1978)

Michael, M., *Produktideen und Ideenproduktion*, 177, Gabler, Wiesbaden (1973)

Midgley, D. F., *Innovation and New Product Marketing*, 296, Croom Helm, London (1977)

Miles, L. D., *Techniques of Value Analysis and Engineering*, 267, McGraw-Hill, New York (1972)

Moose, S. O., 'Divestment — Cleaning up Your Corporate Portfolio', *European Business*, 19–26, Autumn (1971)

Morton, J. A., *Organization for Innovation, a System Approach to Technical Management*, 171, McGraw-Hill, New York (1971)

Newman, W. M. and Sproull, R. F., *Principles of Interactive Computer Graphics*, 540, McGraw-Hill, New York (1979)

Nichols-Manning, C., 'Sales to Marketing: The Critical Transition', *Management Review*, 56–61, July (1978)

Nicholson, E. G., The Advantages of Making Corporate Goals Public, *AMA International Forum*, 32–33, January (1979)

Normann, R., *Management of Growth*, 210, Wiley, London (1977)

Olson, R. M., *Essentials of Engineering Fluid Mechanics*, 583, Harper & Row, New York (1980)

O'Shaugnessy, J., *Competitive Marketing – a Strategic Approach*, 372, George Allen & Unwin, London (1984)

Pahl, G. and Beitz, W., *Engineering Design*, 450, Springer, London (1984)

Papanek, V., *Design for the Real World*, 339, Pantheon, New York (1972)

Parker, R. H., *Understanding Company Financial Statements*, 176, Penguin Books, Harmondsworth (1983)

Parnes, S. J., *Creative Behaviour Guidebook*, 312, Scribner, New York (1967)

Parnes, S. J. and Harding, H. F., *A Source Book for Creative Thinking*, 393, Scribner, New York (1972)

Pessemier, E. A., *Product Management – Strategy and Organization*, 668, John Wiley, New York (1982)

Peterson, R. B., *Professional, Technical and Managerial Perception of Organizational Climate in Eighteen Norwegian Firms*, 57, Bergen (1972)

Prince, G. M., *The Practice of Creativity*, 197, Harper & Row, New York (1970)

Prosjektplan, *Project Management Tools and Visions*, Proceedings of the 7th Internet World Congress, 1980, Teknisk Forlag, Copenhagen (1982)

Ramo, S., *The Management of Innovative Technological Corporations*, 476, John Wiley, New York (1980)

Raudsepp, E., 'Testing for Creativity', *Machine Design*, 106–113, 123–128, 137–141 (1965)

Rhenman, E., *Organization Theory for Long-range Planning*, 226, Wiley, London (1973)

Rhyne, R., 'Technological Forecasting within Alternative Futures Projections', *Technological Forecasting and Social Change*, 133–162 (1974)

Riggs, J. L., *Production Systems*, 649, John Wiley, New York (1981)

RKW-Handbuch Forschung, Entwicklung, Konstruktion, Erich Schmidt, Berlin (1976)

Rossiter, J. R. and Percey, L., *Advertising and Promotion Management*, 649, McGraw-Hill, New York (1987)

Roth, K., *Konstruieren mit Konstruktionskatalogen*, 475, Springer, Berlin (1982)

Sanders, T. R. B., *The Aims and Principles of Standardization*, International Organization for Standardization (1972)

Scheuing, E. E., *Das Marketing neuer Produkte*, 238, Gabler, Wiesbaden (1972)

Schlicksupp, H., *Kreative Ideenfindung in der Unternehmung*, 255, de Gruyter, Berlin (1977)

Schmidt, E., *Einführung in die technische Thermodynamik*, 559, Springer-Verlag, Berlin (1963)

Schmidt, H., *Kontrolle der Lizenzvertragen*, 58, Weinheim (1969)

Schmitt-Grohé, J., *Produktinnovation*, 172, Gabler, Wiesbaden (1972)

Shackel, B., *Applied Ergonomics Handbook*, 122, IPC Science and Technology, Surrey (1974)

Shillinglaw, G., 'Profit Analysis for Abandonment Decisions', *Journal of Business*, XXX, 17–29 (1957)

Shinners, S. M., *Modern Control Systems Theory and Application*, 544, Addison-Wesley, Reading, Mass. (1979)

Siemens, *Systematik und Einsatz der Wertanalyse*, 128, Siemens AG, Berlin (1971)

Siemens, *Organisationsplanung, Planung durch Kooperation*, 376, Siemens AG, Berlin (1977)

Spitz, A. E. (ed.), *Product Planning*, 412, Petrocelli, New York (1977)

Sonntag, R. E. and van Wylen, G. J., *Introduction to Thermodynamics*, 810, John Wiley, New York (1982)

Steele, L. V., *Innovation in Big Business*, 245, Elsevier, New York (1975)

Stone, M., *Product Planning*, 142, Macmillan, London (1976)

Strassmann, P. N., *Risk and Technological Innovation*, 249, Cornell University Press, New York (1959)

Strutz, H., *Wandel industriebetrieblicher Organisationsformen*, 170, Enke, Stuttgart (1976)

Sveriges Mekanförbund, *Värdering och val av produktutveklingsprosjekt*, 60, Stockholm (1973)

Sveriges Mekanförbund, *Produktplanläggning*, 52, Stockholm (1974)

Tagiuri, R. and Litwin, G., *Organizational Climate*, 246, Boston (1968)

Taylor, C. and Barron, F. (eds), *Scientific Creativity, its Recognition and Development*, 419, Wiley, New York (1963)

Thackray, J., 'GE's Planned Prognosis', *Management Today*, 66–69, August (1978)

Thomason, R., *An Introduction to Reliability and Quality*, 150, London (1969)

Timoshenko, S. and Goodier, J. N., *Theory of Elasticity*, 567, McGraw-Hill, New York (1970)

Toffler, A., *The Third Wave*, 543, Pan Books, London (1980)

Tushman, M. L. and Moore, W. L., *Readings in the Management of Innovation*, 652, Pitman, Boston (1982)

Twiss, B., *Managing Technological Innovation*, 237, Longman, London (1974)

Twiss, B. C. and Weinshall, T., *Managing Industrial Organizations*, Pitman, London (1980)

Ulrich, W., *Kreativitätsförderung der Unternehmung*, 218, Haupt, Bern (1975)

Vaitos, C. V., 'Technology Licensing', *Industrial Research and Development News*, United Nations Development Organization, VI, 4, 3–8 (1973)

Van Cott, H. P. and Kinkade, R. E. (eds), *Human Engineering Guide to Equipment Design*, 752, New York (1972)

Van Doren, H., *Industrial Design*, 379, McGraw-Hill, New York (1954)

Varble, D. L., 'Social and Environmental Considerations in New Product Development', *Journal of Marketing*, I, 36, 4, 11–15 (1972)

Villars, R., *Research and Development: Planning and Control*, 185, New York (1964)

Wade, W., *Industrial Espionage and Misuse of Trade Secrets*, Advance House Publisher, Pennsylvania (1966)

Watt, K. E., *Ecology and Resource Management*, 450, McGraw-Hill, New York (1968)

Webster, F. E., *Industrial Marketing Strategy*, 279, John Wiley, New York (1979)

Wilson, A., *The Assessment of Industrial Markets*, 406, Cassel/Associated Business Programmes, London (1973)

Wilson, B., Berg, C. C. and French, D. (ed.), *Efficiency of Manufacturing Systems*, Plenum Press, New York (1983)

Wonnacott, R. and Wonnacott, T., *Econometrics*, 445, Wiley, New York (1970)

Zallen, J., 'Product Protection', in Putt, W. D. (ed.), *How to Start Your Own Business*, 259, Cambridge, Mass. (1974)

Zemanik, P. D., *Failure Mode Analysis to Predict Product Reliability*, New York (1972)

Zienkiewicz, O., *The Finite Element Method*, 448, McGraw-Hill, New York (1987)

Zwicky, F., *Discovery, Invention, Research through the Morphological Approach*, 276, New York (1969)

Index

Acquisition
  knowledge, 329
  licenses, 175
  technology, 28, 30, 73, 175
Active need experience, 125
Administrative innovation, 14
Adoption of innovations, 15, 19
Advertising, 43, 45, 225
Air pollution analysis, 167
Alternative design approaches, 197
Analysis, preliminary, 179–181
Appearance, 32
Applied research, 14, 31, 32, 37, 193
Approaches to product planning, 67–76
Assets, 284

Balance sheet, 284, 301
Basic organisation, 86
Bottom-up planning, 67
Brainstorming, 157
  fault analysis, 210
  negative, 210
Brainwriting, 158
Business concept, 52, 54, 292, 319

Capability analysis, 245
Capital
  development, 96
  expansion, 98
  first stage, 96
  fixed, 94
  public funds, 103
  requirements, 94
  seed, 95
  sources, 98
  working, 94

Cases, Appendix, 289
Catalogue-aided design, 196
Centralisation, 69, 84, 85
Checklist
  factor, 271
  idea generation, 279
  idea realisation, 281
  integration, 275
  preparation, 269
  problem definition, 273
  structure, 277
Climate, measurements, 153
Commercial risk, 93
Company information, 116
Competition, 76
Competitive strengths – market
  attractiveness matrix, 247
Competitor surveillance, 129
Complaints procedure, 235
Computer-aided design, 198
Consumer market, 64, 75
Control processes, 5
Cost
  estimates, 37, 189
  recording and analysis, 47
Corporate objectives, 55, 58, 117, 292, 320
Creativity
  brainstorming, 157
  brainwriting, 158
  climate measurements, 153
  definition, 16
  development, 152
  eclectic approach, 161
  forced relationship techniques, 158
  morphological technique, 155
  need for, 17, 23

suggestion system, 162
synectics, 159
tests, 152
work simplification,
Criteria, performance, 254
Cross-impact analysis, 149
Culture, organisational, 53–54
Current market studies, 186
Cybernetic calculation, 215

Dealer questioning, 69
Decentralisation, 67, 82, 85
Delphi technique, 141
Demanufacturing (recycling), 202
Design
    alternative approaches, 197
    applied research, 193
    calculation, 214
    catalogue-aided, 196
    computer-aided, 198
    cybernetic calculation, 215
    engineering, 31
    ergonomic analysis, 206
    evaluation, 38, 204
    fault analysis
        by brainstorming, 210
        by logical methods, 211
    flow calculation, 214
    for demanufacturing (recycling),
        202
    for disposability, 202
    for manufacturing, 220
    industrial, 32, 195
    maintenance analysis, 209
    mechanical vibration calculation,
        214
    methods, 37
    models, 199
    reliability analysis, 205
    review, 212
    standardisation, 201
    stress calculation, 214
    styling (shape and colour), 194
    testing of models, 199
    thermal calculation, 215
    useful life analysis, 208
    value analysis, 204
Develop/buy analysis, 174

Development
    capital, 96
    exploratory, 31
    of creativity, 152
    of technological competence,
        134
    order, 265
    specifications, 265
Diffusion, 17
    definition, 18
    process, 19
Discovery, 14, 17
Distinctive competence, 52
Distribution, 42, 222
    planning, 222
Diversification, 59
    area, 62
    area-capability matrix, 258
    continuous, 60
    conference, 62
    horizontal, 59
    lateral, 59
    methods, 62
    need-technology – customer
        matrix, 256
    portfolio analysis, 59, 247–252
    screening procedures, 259
    strategy, 5
    studies, 59, 256
    vertical, 59

Eclectic approach for creative
    thinking, 161
Ecological analysis, 167
Elimination analysis, 48, 238
Employment of users, 128
Engineering design, 31
Equipment planning, 219
Equity, 284
Ergonomic analysis, 206
Espionage, industrial, 136
Evaluation
    of ideas, 259
    of design, 204–213
    of products and processes, 235
Expansion capital, 98
Expert system, 119
External market statistics, 184

Factor checklist, 271
Fault analysis by brainstorming, 210
Fault analysis by logical methods, 211
Feasibility study, 32, 62, 163
Field reports, 235
Financial
  evaluation, 48
  function, 90
  information, 112, 118
  innovation, 14
  planning, 90
  proposal, 105
  ratios, 287
  resources, 4, 90
  risk, 93
  tools, 284
Financing
  examples, 326
  of innovations, 90
  internal, 99
  public funds, 103
  traditional sources, 100
  venture capital, 94, 102
Fixed capital, 94
Flow
  calculation, 214
  model, 24
Forced relationship technique, 158
Forecasting, 139
  cross-impact analysis, 149
  Delphi technique, 141
  difficulties, 59
  relevance-tree technique, 144
  scenario technique, 116, 139
  structural models, 148
  system dynamics, 146
  tools for, 26
  trend extrapolation technique, 142
Formal approach, 69, 84
Functional
  requirements, 35, 65
  specifications, 33
Fusion model, 22

Gantt charts, 182

Gap analysis, 244
Generation of ideas, 6, 21-29
Government
  regulations, 130
  surveillance of market, 65

High-tech companies
Human risk, 93

Idea generation
  checklist, 279
  methods, 25-29
  models, 21-25
Idea realisation, 281
Idea utilisation, 6, 30-39
  methods, 33-39
  models, 31
Illegal research
Implementation, preparation for, 40-43
Income statement, 285
Industrial
  design, 32, 195
  espionage, 136
Information
  company, 116
  financial, 112, 118
  market, 109, 117
  provisions, 7
  technical, 111
  tools, 7
Innovation, 13-16
  adopted, 15
  basic, 15
  classification, 15
  definition, 13
  diffusion, 17
  improvement, 15, 46
  incremental, 15, 46
  process, 14
  projects, 91
  promotion of, 16
  social, 14
Intelligence, 25-26, 125-131
  need related, 25, 125-132
  technology-related, 26, 133-137
Integration, 81, 239, 275

Internal
  financing, 99
  market statistics, 183
  rate of return, 113
Institutional market, 64, 76
Introduction of product, 46-47,
    231-232
Invention, 14
Investment cost, 191

Japanese organisation theory,
    54, 333
J-curve, 50

Laboratory testing, 216
Leadership, 27
Legal
  analysis, 170
  protection, 176
Legislation, surveillance of, 130
Liabilities, 284
Licence
  acquisition, 30, 175
  sale of, 224
Life
  cycle, 66, 239
  analysis, 202, 208
  style, 76
Liquidity, 288
Logistical growth curve, 19

Maintenance analysis, 209
Major objectives, 55, 58, 118, 292,
    320
Make/buy analysis, 219
Management
  philosophy, 54, 319
  schools, 330
Manufacturing, 7, 44-49, 117
  data, 47, 233-234
  design for, 220
  equipment and tooling, 219
  make and buy analysis, 219
  material planning, 220
  methods, 46
  model, 45
  operation planning, 219
  preparation, 42, 219
  process evaluation, 47

quality, 34, 220
Market
  concept, 73
  consumer, 64
  government, 65
  information, 109, 117
  institutional, 64
  introduction, 231, 98
  oriented approach, 73
  share-market growth matrix, 250
  research, 36, 183
  sectors, surveillance, 131
  statistics
    external, 184
    internal, 183
  studies
    current, 186
    special, 187
  type, 64
Marketing, 7, 42-49, 299
  data, 47
  registration, 196
  innovation, 14
  methods, 46
  model, 48
  preparation, 42, 222
  research, 36
  test, 43, 227-228
Material planning, 220
Matrix organisation, 86
Mechanical vibration calculation,
    214
Mechanistic management system,
    84-85
Models
  design, 199-200
  flow, 24
  fusion, 22
  limitations, 7
  of product innovation process, 3
  perception, 21
  testing, 199-200
Morphological technique, 155
Multi-interest concept, 77

Need
  assessment, 25, 36, 64, 69, 71
    73, 295

Need (*cont'd*)
confrontation (active need experience), 125
related intelligence, 125-132
satisfaction, 30
simulation, 127
specifications, 31, 33, 75
technology — customer matrix, 256
weighting, 77
Network models, 34, 180
Niche strategy, 5, 57

Objectives, major, 55, 292, 320
Operation planning, 219
Organisation, 79
climate, 27, 72, 81, 153
culture, 53, 82
degree of centralisation, 82
degree of formalisation, 84
factor checklist, 271
idea generation, 80, 85, 279
idea realisation, 80, 86, 281
innovation, 14
integration, 81, 275
integration checklist, 239
mechanistic, 84
models, 79
modules, 80
organic, 84
problem definition checklist, 273
product innovation, 269
structural alternatives, 81
structure, 277, 322
theories, 330
Overadopt, 20

Packaging, 32
Patent search, 166
Pay-back, 114
Perception model, 21
Performance criteria, 58, 254
Policies, 5
Pollution analysis, 167
Portfolio analysis, 59
competitive strengths — market attractiveness matrix, 247

market share — market growth matrix, 250
Preliminary analysis
quality level planning, 179
scheduling, gantt charts, 182
scheduling, network models, 180
Preliminary study, 163
ecological analysis, 167
feasibility study, 163
legal analysis, 170
patent search, 166
resource analysis, 169
technology assessment, 164
Preparation
for implementation, 7, 10, 40-40-43
checklist, 269
Price/earning, 288
Pricing, 42, 191
Problem solving
definition, 273
iterative, 57
knowledge development, 57
traditional, 57
Process
evaluation, 198
planning, 219
specifications, 41, 45
Product
calender, 267
cost, 97, 191
council, 263
development, 117, 295, 310, 325
elimination analysis, 48
evaluation, 47, 49, 235
innovation
classification, 15
process models, 46
organisation, 269
introduction, 231
proposal, 262
market matrix, 238
market — strategic option matrix, 252
Product planning, 64, 309, 324
'bottom up' approach, 67
formal approach, 69

informal approaches, 67
key criteria, 77
market-orientated approaches, 73
methods, 77
tools, 262
'top-down' approach, 69
Product specifications, 9, 32, 40, 45, 65, 265
Production capital, 94
Profit data, 242
Profit and loss statement, 285
Profitability, 191
  internal rate of return, 113
  pay-back, 114
  return on investment, 113
Project
  cost, 191
  description, 108
  evaluation, 172, 236
  formulation, 28, 172
    development/buy analysis, 174
    legal protection, 176
    licence acquisition, 175
    selection technique, 172
  portfolio, 62
  proposal form, 262
  staff, 107
  type, 91–92
Proposal
  financial, 105
  form, 262
  product, 262
Psychotronics, 21

Quality
  control planning, 220
  intended level, 33
  laboratory testing, 216
  of design, 33
  of manufacturing, 47
  planning, 33, 179
  parameters, registration, 47, 233
  user testing, 217
  verification, 41, 216
Quantity recording, 234

Questioning of
  dealers, 128
  users, 128

R and D, 69
  expenditures, 97, 98
Recycling, 202
Registration
  costs, 234
  sales, 234
  quality parameters, 233
  quantity, 234
Regulation, surveillance of, 130
Relevance-tree technique, 144
Reliability analysis, 205
Research
  applied, 14, 31, 37, 193
  basic, 14
  illegal, 72
  marketing, 63
  smuggled, 72
Resource
  analysis, 169
  surveillance, 135
Resources
  financial, 4, 90
  human, 4
  physical, 4
Requirements,
  aesthetic, 34
  functional, 34
  manufacturing, 34
  technical, 34
Return on investment, 113
Review
  of design, 212
  of products, 49
Risk, 92
  analysis, 189
  assessment, 114
  commercial, 93
  financial, 93
  human, 93
  technical, 93
  timing, 93

Sales
  recording of, 47, 232
  licenses, 43, 224

Sales (cont'd)
    planning, 225
    promotion, 43, 45, 225
    recording, 232
    trends, 240
Scenario technique, 116, 139
Scheduling, 35, 180
    gantt charts, 182
    network models, 180
Screening procedures, 259
Seed capital, 95
Segmentation strategy, 5, 56, 75
Selection of project, 172
Selling, 42
Sensitivity analysis, 115
Service, 42
Simulation, 127
Smuggled research, 72
Social innovation, 14
Solidity, 288
Special market studies, 187
Specifications
    development, 9, 33, 265
    functional, 33
    need, 31, 33, 75
    product, 9, 32, 34, 40, 45, 65,
        265
    process, 41, 45
Spread sheet, 119
Stakeholders, 76
Standardisation, 37, 201
Strategy, 5, 50, 56, 69, 72, 293,
        308, 320
    diversification, 5
    follow-the-leader, 92
    formulation, 52, 56, 58, 244
    leadership, 91
    me-too, 92
    for market introduction, 231
    methods, 58
    product, 56
    R and D, 69
    segmentation, 5, 56, 75
Stress calculation, 214
Structural models, 148
Styling (shape and colour), 37, 194
Suggestion system, 162

Surveillance
    competitors, 129
    government regulations, 130
    market sectors, 131
    resources, 135
    technology, 133
Synectics, 159
System
    approach, 34
    dynamics, 146
    suggestion, 162

Target group, 75
Technical risk, 93
    information, 111
Technical competence
    development, 134
    innovation, 14
Technology,
    assessment, 28, 164
    orientation, 73
    related intelligence, 133
    surveillance, 133
Terminology, 13–20
Test
    area, 227
    creativity, 152
    laboratory, 216
    marketing, 227
    models, 199
    production, 46
    prototype, 32
    user, 217
Thermal calculation, 215
Timing risk, 93
Tooling, 219
Tools, 1, 2, 7
Top-down approach, 69
Trade
    fairs for test marketing, 228
    marks, 43, 226
Transformation processes, 5
Trend extrapolation, 142

Useful life analysis, 208
User
    contacts, 127

cooperation (projects), 128
need, *see* Need
observation, 126
panels, 128
testing, 217
questioning, 128
Utilisation of ideas, 6, 9, 31–39

Value
    analysis, 204

concept, 77
Venture capital, 94, 102
Vision, 57

Water pollution analysis, 168
Weighting of needs, 77
Work simplification, 162
Working capital, 94